THE SOUTH
AND THE SECTIONAL IMAGE

INTERPRETATIONS OF AMERICAN HISTORY

★ ★ ★ JOHN HIGHAM AND BRADFORD PERKINS, EDITORS

THE SOUTH AND THE SECTIONAL IMAGE

The Sectional Theme
Since Reconstruction

EDITED BY

DEWEY W. GRANTHAM, Jr.
Vanderbilt University

HARPER & ROW, PUBLISHERS
NEW YORK, EVANSTON, AND LONDON

THE SOUTH AND THE SECTIONAL IMAGE: The Sectional Theme
Since Reconstruction

Library of Congress Catalog Card Number: 67-10793

For
LOUELLA THOMPSON BURLESON
and
FRANK E. BURLESON

CONTENTS

EDITORS' INTRODUCTION

This volume—and companions in the series, "Interpretations of American History"—makes a special effort to cope with one of the basic dilemmas confronting every student of history. On the one hand, historical knowledge shares a characteristic common to all appraisals of human affairs. It is partial and selective. It picks out some features and facts of a situation while ignoring others that may be equally pertinent. The more selective an interpretation is, the more memorable and widely applicable it can be. On the other hand, history has to provide what nothing else does: a total estimate, a multifaceted synthesis, of man's experience in particular times and places. To study history, therefore, is to strive simultaneously for a clear, selective focus and for an integrated, over-all view.

In that spirit, each volume of the series aims to resolve the varied literature on a major topic or event into a meaningful whole. One interpretation, we believe, does not deserve as much of a student's attention as another simply because they are in conflict. Instead of contriving a balance between opposing views, or choosing polemical material simply to create an appearance of controversy, Professor Grantham has exercised his own judgment on the relative importance of different aspects or interpretations of a problem. We have asked him to select some of what he considers the best, most persuasive writings bearing on The South and the sectional image, indicating in the introductory essay and headnotes his reasons for considering these accounts convincing or significant. When appropriate, he has also brought out the relation between older and more recent approaches to the subject. The editor's own competence and experience in the field enable him to provide a sense of order and to indicate the evolution and complexity of interpretations. He is, then, like other editors in this series, an informed participant rather than a mere observer, a student sharing with other students the results of his own investigations of the literature on a crucial phase of American development.

JOHN HIGHAM
BRADFORD PERKINS

THE SOUTH
AND THE SECTIONAL IMAGE

INTRODUCTION

Southernism is an old concept in America, rich in historical significance and charged with meaning in our own day. During the course of American history other areas have also developed clear-cut sectional identities, but in modern times the South has usually been the region most sharply at odds with the rest of the nation. In surveying the southern scene during the late nineteenth and early twentieth centuries, Wilbur J. Cash emphasized, in 1941, "how essentially superficial and unrevolutionary remain the obvious changes; how certainly do these obvious changes take place within the ancient framework, and even sometimes contribute to the positive strengthening of the ancient pattern!"[1] Even as Southerners gave new demonstrations of their faith in progress and their growing commitment to ideas and techniques dominant in other regions, they held on to their regional identity and viewed the world against the background of their regional heritage. From the First Reconstruction that followed the war of the 1860s to the Second Reconstruction of the 1960s, the South has continually projected a sectional image.

The sources that nourish the sectional image of the South are numer-

[1] Cash, *The Mind of the South* (New York, 1941), p. 219.

ous and elusive. The region has been and continues to be measurably different from any other section. Sectional conflicts involving important questions of national policy have occurred during the years since Reconstruction. There is, moreover, an exotic quality about the South, and its mystery and mystique make it, in David M. Potter's phrase, an enigma, "a kind of Sphinx on the American land."[2] At a more profound level, the sectional theme may owe some of its vitality to the fact that many Americans have been able to externalize inner conflicts by focusing on the South as a deviating section. Non-Southerners have long been accustomed to thinking of the southern region as separate from the rest of the country, as aberrant in attitude and defiant in mood, and as differentiated in some mysterious and irrational way from the national experience and the national ideals.

Despite the regional bonds that united great numbers of white Southerners from Reconstruction onward, the mind of the modern South has been, characteristically, a divided mind. Forces of change and continuity have frequently collided in the post-Civil War South, and in no other part of the country have such conflicts been more intense and poignant. Significantly, these conflicts have almost always been defined by reference to the "North." The North as military victor and source of political interference might serve as a rallying point for white unity below the Potomac, but the North as a symbol of economic affluence, success, and innovation exerted a continuous and subtle influence upon southern thought. As Louis D. Rubin has remarked about the young southern writers who went to the Northeast during the second and third decades of this century, "All their lives they had been feeling its impact."[3] It is true that when the white South contended against itself both sides appealed to presumed regional traditions and values, but it is also true that one of the contending elements frequently related its position to that of the North and cited the northern experience to prove its point.

A remarkable convergence in the thinking and behavior of Southerners and non-Southerners has occurred during the last hundred years. Changes in the South's economic, social, and political habits have done much to nationalize the region. In some respects, of course, this nationalization is simply a part of the homogenizing process long under way in all parts of the country. The South has shared a common culture with other Americans and has responded to the cumulative effects of a national business system, powerful new transportation and communications media,

[2] Potter, "The Enigma of the South," *Yale Review,* LI (October, 1961), 142.

[3] Rubin, "Southern Literature: The Historical Image," in Louis D. Rubin, Jr., and Robert D. Jacobs (eds.), *South: Modern Southern Literature in Its Cultural Setting* (Garden City, 1961), p. 46.

migration into and out of the region, and the emergence of the modern welfare state centered in Washington. The result is that Southerners have become increasingly less distinguishable from other Americans, even though their historical experience has woven its own pattern in the fabric of the nation's past. It is difficult to measure the relative weights of the various forces that have pulled the South toward more complete national integration or to mark out very clearly the stages in the erosion of southern sectionalism. Many factors were involved in the gradual diminution of southern particularism and they have sometimes been ambivalent in their effect.

The first stage in the nationalization of the South after Reconstruction was the era dominated by the so-called Redeemers—the champions of a "New South." The Redeemers were ardent advocates of northern investments below the Potomac, of southern industrialization, and of sectional reconciliation. Paul M. Gaston has reminded us that the national reconciliation they promoted did not mean "a surrender of southern will to northern superiority. It signified, rather, a recognition in the South that the road to affluence and power led to the adoption of those national patterns which had accounted for American greatness."[4] Indeed, the nationalism of the New South leaders rested in considerable part on the triumph of the southern will, as reflected in northern concessions in the Compromise of 1876–1877 and in the modus vivendi on the race issue that emerged during later years. This triumph was also evident in the concessions made by northern philanthropists during the southern education movement early in the twentieth century and in the manner in which the southern region kept its sectional politics and fundamental creed intact while being pulled into the orbit of national affairs during the Wilson administration.

World War I broadened southern horizons and in numerous ways brought the South more fully into the mainstream of American life. But by the end of that war a more coercive quality was apparent in the outside forces impinging upon the region. It was less and less possible for the South to assert its will in confrontations with the North and more and more difficult for it to ignore critical voices from the outside. During the Populist upheaval of the 1890s, the region suffered what C. Vann Woodward has described as "a second alienation from the dominant national spirit."[5] In the 1920s the South suffered a third alienation from the national spirit. This was largely the result of the cultural

---

[4] Gaston, "The 'New South,'" in Arthur S. Link and Rembert W. Patrick (eds.), *Writing Southern History: Essays in Historiography in Honor of Fletcher M. Green* (Baton Rouge, 1965), p. 322.

[5] Woodward, *The Burden of Southern History* (Baton Rouge, 1960), p. 141.

conflict that identified the South with such things as religious fundamentalism, the Ku Klux Klan, and Prohibition sentiment. The interne-
cine struggle for control of the Democratic party was one manifestation
of the sectional ·conflict in the 1920s, while the agrarian manifesto,
I'll Take My Stand (1930), was another. In the 1950s another resurgence of sectionalism threatened to interrupt the South's steady drift
toward national conformity. It grew out of the Negro rights movement
and the establishment of momentous national policies in response to the
movement. This Second Reconstruction, while primarily aimed at conditions in the southern states, pointed beyond sectionalism and promised
far more durable social changes than had taken place during the First
Reconstruction.

In examining the stages by which the South has become more closely
linked with the rest of the nation, one should not make the mistake of
assuming that various periods and movements were monolithic in their
regional implications. They seldom pointed in only one direction. Thus
the New South champions favored national reconciliation but were nevertheless largely responsible for many of the ideas and institutions that set
the South apart and perpetuated its sectionalism. Populism, to take
another example, contributed to the South's political solidarity, but it
also encouraged many Southerners to respond favorably to Woodrow
Wilson's New Freedom and to Franklin D. Roosevelt's New Deal. The
New Deal itself tended to nationalize southern politics but the Roosevelt
administration was forced to make concessions to powerful Southerners
in Congress who skillfully defended the southern position. The Second
Reconstruction of the South in the 1950s and 1960s exacerbated the
sectional feelings of many white Southerners but it also fostered a mighty
protest movement by southern Negroes (and some white liberals) which
in turn did much to bring the South closer to national patterns.

The South has been subjected to intensive scrutiny during the twentieth
century, making it perhaps the most thoroughly interpreted part of the
United States. Travelers and journalists have long found fascinating
materials in the region, and since the turn of the century a host of
memoirs and personal interpretations of a regional and subregional character has been published by native sons and daughters. The Southern
Renascence in fiction—the most celebrated part of the literature emanating
from the South—was itself an expression of regionalism. Nor have
scholars neglected the South. Sparked by Howard W. Odum's work at
the University of North Carolina during the second quarter of the century and stimulated by the Great Depression and the New Deal, as well
as by the growing professionalization of their disciplines, southern social
scientists produced a stream of articles and books on the region's eco-

nomics, race relations, mill villages, tenancy, and prisons. Indeed, as a sort of academic laboratory the South received increasing attention from scholars and investigators in other regions. The process of change in such areas as race relations, politics, and economic institutions has encouraged historians and other writers to probe the region's past. During the past generation interest in southern history has been encouraged by a robust historical organization, an excellent regional journal of history, new state historical societies and magazines, the assembling of records in archives and libraries, the establishment of southern university presses, the introduction of college and university courses on the South, the approaching completion of a ten-volume history of the South by leading historians, and an outpouring of monographs on almost every aspect of southern history.

In many respects southern historiography may be said to have followed the main twentieth-century trends in the writing of American history. In recent years, for example, the appeal to homogeneity, continuity, and American culture by historians whose interpretations stress the fundamental "consensus" in American history has found support in southern historical writing.[6] But it is nevertheless true that the South and its historians provide one of the best examples of conflict and differentiation in the modern nation. Many factors are doubtless involved in the continuing approach to the South as a distinct entity. In addition to a deep attachment to the land of their birth, most Southerners are keenly aware of regional tradition and history—of defeat, poverty, frustration, and social evil in the southern experience. These experiences and the mythology that grew up around them do much to perpetuate regional attitudes and images, in the North as well as in the South. Far upstream in the course of southern sectionalism, at that juncture in our history represented by the Civil War, the South was given a psychological heritage which Robert Penn Warren has labeled "the Great Alibi," by which the region "explains, condones, and transmutes everything." The war also provided the North with a powerful myth, "the Treasury of Virtue," by which Northerners ever since have felt "redeemed by history, automatically redeemed . . . for all sins past, present, and future. . . ."[7] There are other myths that strengthen the image of the sectional South. In a perspective discussion of this mythology, George B. Tindall has asked

[6] For a perceptive essay on the consensus theme in recent American historiography, see John Higham, "The Cult of the 'American Consensus': Homogenizing Our History," *Commentary,* XXVII (February, 1959), 93–100. On the South see Burl Noggle, "Variety and Ambiguity: The Recent Approach to Southern History," *Mississippi Quarterly,* XVII (Winter, 1963–1964), 21–35.

[7] Warren, *The Legacy of the Civil War: Meditations on the Centennial* (New York, Vintage ed., 1964), pp. 54–55, 59–60.

if many of these myths about the South have not served "the function of national catharsis," creating for many Americans "a convenient scapegoat upon which the sins of all may be symbolically laid and thereby expiated."[8]

Another historian has argued that the South is in reality a mirror in which the national character is reflected. Far from being utterly different from the rest of the country, he writes, the South is really the essence of the nation; for it contains, "in concentrated and dangerous form, a set of characteristics which mark the country as a whole."[9] The richness and vitality of Southernism as a concept in American thinking make this interpretation seem plausible. In any case, since antebellum days the South and the rest of the country have carried on a kind of dialogue and even, one suspects, a kind of dialectic involving profoundly significant problems and attitudes. The most obvious of these relate to the Negro's place in American life, but there have been others of great importance: imperialism and foreign policy, sectional politics and the conduct of the national government, the colonial economy, industrialism versus the agrarian tradition, and cultural conflict along sectional lines.

What, then, is one to say about the role of the region in recent America? What does the South's separateness tell us about the character of the nation's politics, its economic development, its attitudes toward ethnic problems, the extent of its cultural homogeneity, its commitment to democracy? Is the South, as Professor Zinn argues, really the essence of America? If sectionalism seeks to protect special interests of particular regions, does it have other uses that transcend narrow parochial bounds? Has the southern region served as the nation's scapegoat, as Professor Tindall suggests? How does one explain the outside interest in the South as a social laboratory? Is this interest related to the tendency in other regions to define the nation in terms of what the South is popularly assumed *not* to represent? Does it reflect an awareness of the failure to assimilate the South into the national pattern? And what of the potential value to the nation of the South's unique heritage, so brilliantly illuminated by C. Vann Woodward?

One must begin with the reality of sectional conflict in America. The periods of sharpest sectional antagonism between the South and other parts of the country since the Civil War do reveal a great deal about the differences that have divided Americans at particular times in the past. In virtually all of these periods of intense sectional hostility, the contours

[8] Tindall, "Southern Mythology: A New Frontier in Southern History," in Frank E. Vandiver (ed.), *The Idea of the South: Pursuit of a Central Theme* (Chicago, 1964), p. 14.

[9] Howard Zinn, *The Southern Mystique* (New York, 1964), p. 218.

of American politics, both at the national and at the state and local levels, were significantly affected. In the 1890s, economic issues were at the heart of sectional struggle; in the 1920s, cultural conflict was dominant; and in Reconstruction in the nineteenth century and the last decade of our own generation the Negro and civil rights have loomed largest. But if such encounters as these disclose regional differences, they also reveal, upon closer examination, important differences and disagreements of an intraregional character which have frequently pitted Southerner against Southerner and Northerner against Northerner. Furthermore, periods of heightened animosity tend to obscure other periods of intersectional harmony, as well as the basic cultural and ideological values that most Americans have always shared. There is a special irony in the fact that the Negro, whose treatment in the South was so long a major source of sectional conflict, should emerge in the middle of the twentieth century as a powerful nationalizing force in all parts of the country.

This book examines some of the more conspicuous points in the interaction between the South and the larger nation since Reconstruction. Although the Negro Southerner is frequently mentioned in the pages that follow, the focus in this book is on the white South, which, until recently, determined the "place" of the Negro in southern life and regarded him as only a shadowy object and not an actor or doer. Southern history, in a broad sense, has little meaning when looked at as an isolated and exotic phenomenon half-hidden by regional walls that set it apart from other areas and other people. This history of the South, no less than the history of other American sections, has meaning chiefly within the context of the nation's development. On the other hand, we cannot really understand the meaning of our national history since the Civil War without coming to grips with the essence of the New South. In focusing upon the South's historic encounters with the nation at large, we may be able to understand the conflict between change and continuity within the region and to appreciate more fully the significance of sectional differences in modern America and the remarkable way in which these differences epitomize the continuing struggle for the realization of the nation's fundamental values and aspirations.

1. Southern Mythology

GEORGE B. TINDALL

A native South Carolinian, George B. Tindall was educated at Furman University and at the University of North Carolina, where he is now Professor of History. Editor of *A Populist Reader* (1966) and author of *South Carolina Negroes, 1877–1900* (1952), his history of the South from 1913 to 1946 will be the final volume in the ten-volume "History of the South" series.

Professor Tindall believes that one of the best ways to get at the meaning

Originally published as "Mythology: A New Frontier in Southern History," in Frank E. Vandiver (ed.), *The Idea of the South: Pursuit of a Central Theme*, Rice University's Semicentennial Series (Chicago, 1964), pp. 1–15. Reprinted by permission of Rice University and The University of Chicago Press. The footnotes in the original essay have been omitted.

of the South is to study the mythology that has grown up about it. In the provocative essay that follows he examines several of the "mythical images of the South that have so significantly affected American history." He not only makes a case for mythology as a source of historical insight but also throws light on many nineteenth- and twentieth-century ideas about the South—ideas that show how Southerners viewed themselves and how their region was seen by other Americans. It is less important that these mental pictures often exaggerated and distorted reality than that they were widely believed to be true. Thus they became part of the reality of history.

The more durable southern myths, rooted in nineteenth-century sectional conflict or in more modern regional differences, have served many polemical uses and in a vicarious way have satisfied certain regional expectations. But southern mythology, as Professor Tindall suggests, may explain not only the South's identity but also some of the nuances of our national character.

THE IDEA OF THE SOUTH—OR MORE APPROPRIATELY, THE IDEAS OF the South—belong in large part to the order of social myth. There are few areas of the modern world that have bred a regional mythology so potent, so profuse and diverse, even so paradoxical, as the American South. But the various mythical images of the South that have so significantly affected American history have yet to be subjected to the kind of broad and imaginative historical analysis that has been applied to the idea of the American West, particularly in Henry Nash Smith's *Virgin Land: The American West as Symbol and Myth.* The idea of the South has yet to be fully examined in the context of mythology, as essentially a problem of intellectual history.

To place the ideas of the South in the context of mythology, of course, is not necessarily to pass judgment upon them as illusions. The game of debunking myths, Harry Levin has warned us, starts "in the denunciation of myth as falsehood from the vantage-point of a rival myth." Mythology has other meanings, not all of them pejorative, and myths have a life of their own which to some degree renders irrelevant the question of their correlation to empirical fact. Setting aside for the moment the multiple connotations of the term, we may say that social myths in general, including those of the South, are simply mental pictures that portray the pattern of what a people think they are (or ought to be) or what somebody else thinks they are. They tend to develop abstract ideas in more or less concrete and dramatic terms. In the words of Henry Nash Smith, they fuse "concept and emotion into an image."

They may serve a variety of functions. "A myth," Mark Schorer has observed, "is a large, controlling image that gives philosophical meaning to the facts of ordinary life; that is, which has organizing value for experience." It may offer useful generalizations by which data may be tested. But being also "charged with values, aspirations, ideals and meanings," myths may become the ground for belief, for either loyalty and defense on the one hand or hostility and opposition on the other. In such circumstances a myth itself becomes one of the realities of history, significantly influencing the course of human action, for good or ill. There is, of course, always a danger of illusion, a danger that in ordering one's vision of reality, the myth may predetermine the categories of perception, rendering one blind to things that do not fit into the mental image.

Since the Southern mind is reputed to be peculiarly resistant to pure abstraction and more receptive to the concrete and dramatic image, it may be unusually susceptible to mythology. Perhaps for the same reason our subject can best be approached through reference to the contrasting experiences of two Southerners—one recent, the other about forty-five years ago.

The first is the experience of a contemporary Louisiana writer, John T. Westbrook.

During the thirties and early forties [Westbrook has written] when I was an English instructor at the University of Missouri, I was often mildly irritated by the average northerner's Jeeter-Lester-and-potlikker idea of the South. Even today the northern visitor inertia-headedly maintains his misconception: he hankers to see eroded hills and rednecks, scrub cotton and sharecropper shacks.

It little profits me to drive him through Baton Rouge, show him the oil-ethyl-rubber-aluminum-chemical miles of industry along the Mississippi River, and say, "This . . . is the fastest-growing city of over 100,000 in America. We can amply substantiate our claim that we are atomic target number one, that in the next war the Russians will obliterate us first. . . ."

Our northerner is suspicious of all this crass evidence presented to his senses. It bewilders and befuddles him. He is too deeply steeped in William Faulkner and Robert Penn Warren. The fumes of progress are in his nose and the bright steel of industry towers before his eyes, but his heart is away in Yoknapatawpha County with razorback hogs and night riders. On this trip to the South he wants, above all else, to sniff the effluvium of backwoods-and-sand-hill subhumanity and to see at least one barn burn at midnight. So he looks at me with crafty misgiving, as if to say, "Well, you *do* drive a Cadillac, talk rather glibly about Kierkegaard and Sartre . . . but, after all, you *are* only fooling, aren't you? You do, don't you, sometimes, go out secretly by owl-light to drink swamp water and feed on sowbelly and collard greens?

The other story was the experience of a Southern historian, Frank L. Owsley, who traveled during World War I from Chicago via Cincinnati to Montgomery with a group of young ladies on the way to visit their menfolk at an army camp. He wrote later that, "despite everything which had ever been said to the contrary," the young ladies had a romantic conception of the "Sunny South" and looked forward to the journey with considerable excitement. "They expected to enter a pleasant land of white columned mansions, green pastures, expansive cotton and tobacco fields where negroes sang spirituals all the day through." Except in the bluegrass basins of central Kentucky and Tennessee, what they actually found "were gutted hill-sides; scrub oak and pine; bramble and blackberry thickets, bottom lands once fertile now senile and exhausted, with spindling tobacco, corn, or cotton stalks . . . ; unpainted houses which were hardly more than shacks or here and there the crumbling ruins of old mansions covered with briars, the homes of snakes and lizards." The disappointment of Dr. Owsley's ladies was, no doubt, even greater than that of Mr. Westbrook's friend in Baton Rouge.

There is a striking contrast between these two episodes, both in the picture of Southern reality and in the differing popular images that they present. The fact that they are four decades apart helps to account for the discrepancies, but what is not apparent at first is the common ancestry of the two images. They are not very distant cousins, collateral decendants from the standard image of the Old South, the plantation myth. The version of Owsley's lady friends is closer to the original primogenitor, which despite its advancing age and debility, still lives amid a flourishing progeny of legendary Southern gentility. According to Francis Pendleton Gaines, author of *The Southern Plantation,* the pattern appeared full-blown at least as early as 1832 in John Pendleton Kennedy's romance, *Swallow Barn.* It has had a long career in story and novel and song, in the drama and motion picture. The corrosions of age seem to have ended its Hollywood career, although the old films still turn up on the late late. It may still be found in the tourist bait of shapely beauties in hoop skirts posed against the backdrop of white columns at Natchez, Orton, or a hundred other places.

These pictures are enough to trigger in the mind the whole euphoric pattern of kindly old marster with his mint julep; happy darkies singing in fields perpetually white to the harvest or, as the case may be, sadly recalling the long lost days of old; coquettish belles wooed by slender gallants in gray underneath the moonlight and magnolias. It is a pattern that yields all too easily to caricature and ridicule, for in its more sophisticated versions the figure of the planter carries a heavy freight of the aristocratic virtues: courtliness, grace, hospitality, honor, *noblesse oblige,* as well as many no less charming aristocratic vices: a lordly indifference to the balance sheet, hot temper, profanity, overindulgence, a certain stubborn obstinacy. The old-time Negro, when not a figure of comedy, is the very embodiment of loyalty. And the Southern belle: "Beautiful, graceful, accomplished in social charm, bewitching in coquetry, yet strangely steadfast in soul," Gaines has written, "she is perhaps the most winsome figure in the whole field of our fancy." "The plantation romance," Gaines says, "remains our chief social idyl of the past; of an Arcadian scheme of existence, less material, less hurried, less prosaically equalitarian, less futile, richer in picturesqueness, festivity, in realized pleasure that recked not of hope or fear or unrejoicing labor."

But there is still more to the traditional pattern. Somewhere off in the piney woods and erosion-gutted clay hills, away from the white columns and gentility, there existed Po' White Trash: the crackers; hillbillies; sand-hillers; rag, tag, and bobtail; squatters; "po' buckra" to the Negroes; the Ransy Sniffle of A. B. Longstreet's *Georgia Scenes* and his literary descendants like Jeeter Lester and Ab Snopes, abandoned to poverty and degeneracy—the victims, it was later discovered, of hookworm, malaria, and pellagra. Somewhere in the pattern the respectable small farmer was lost from sight. He seemed to be neither romantic nor outrageous enough to fit in. His neglect provides the classic example in Southern history of the blind spots engendered by the power of mythology. It was not until the 1930's that Frank L. Owsley and his students at Vanderbilt rediscovered the Southern yeoman farmer as the characteristic, or at least the most numerous, ante bellum white Southerner. More about the yeoman presently; neglected in the plantation myth, he was in the foreground of another.

In contrast to the legitimate heirs of the plantation myth, the image of John T. Westbrook's Yankee visitor in Baton Rouge seems to be descended from what might be called the illegitimate line of the plantation myth, out of abolition. It is one of the ironies of our history that, as Gaines put it, the "two opposing sides of the fiercest controversy that ever shook national thought agreed concerning certain picturesque elements of plantation life and joined hands to set the conception unforgettably in public consciousness." The abolitionists found it difficult, or even undesirable, to escape the standard image. It was pretty fully developed even in *Uncle Tom's Cabin*. Harriet Beecher Stowe made her villain a Yankee overseer, and has been accused by at least one latter-day abolitionist of implanting deeply in the American mind the stereotype of the faithful darkey. For others the plantation myth simply appeared in reverse, as a pattern of corrupt opulence resting upon human exploitation. Gentle old marster became the arrogant, haughty, imperious potentate, the very embodiment of sin, the central target of the antislavery attack. He maintained a seraglio in the slave quarters; he bred Negroes like cattle and sold them down the river to certain death in the sugar mills, separating families if that served his purpose, while Southern women suffered in silence the guilty knowledge of their men's infidelity. The happy darkies in this picture became white men in black skins, an oppressed people longing for freedom, the victims of countless atrocities so ghastly as to be unbelievable except for undeniable evidence, forever seeking an opportunity to follow the North Star to freedom. The masses of the white folks were simply poor whites, relegated to ignorance and degeneracy by the slavocracy.

Both lines of the plantation myth have been remarkably prolific, but the more adaptable one has been that of the abolitionists. It has repeatedly readjusted to new conditions while the more legitimate line has courted extinction, running out finally into the decadence perpetrated by Tennessee Williams. Meanwhile, the abolitionist image of brutality persisted through and beyond Reconstruction in the Republican outrage mills and bloody shirt political campaigns. For several decades it was more than overbalanced by the Southern image of Reconstruction horrors, disarmed by prophets of a New South created in the image of the North, and almost completely submerged under the popularity of plantation romances in the generation before Owsley's trainload of ladies ventured into their "Sunny South" of the teens. At about that time, however, the undercurrents began to emerge once again into the mainstream of American thought. In the clever decade of the twenties a kind of neoabolitionist myth of the Savage South was compounded. It seemed that the benighted South, after a period of relative neglect, suddenly became an object of concern to every publicist in the country. One Southern abomination after another was ground through their mills: child labor, peonage, lynching, hookworm, pellagra, the Scopes trial, the Fundamentalist crusade against Al Smith. The guiding genius was Henry L. Mencken, the hatchet man from Baltimore who developed the game of South-baiting into a national pastime, a fine art at which he had no peer. In 1917, when he started constructing his image of "Baptist and Methodist barbarism" below the Potomac, he began with the sterility of Southern literature and went on from there. With characteristic glee he anointed one J. Gordon Coogler of South Carolina "the last bard of Dixie" and quoted his immortal couplet:

> Alas, for the South! Her books have grown fewer—
> She never was much given to literature.

"Down there," Mencken wrote, "a poet is now almost as rare as an oboe-player, a dry-point etcher or a metaphysician." As for "critics, musical composers, painters, sculptors, architects . . . there is not even a bad one between the Potomac mud-flats and the Gulf. Nor an historian. Nor a sociologist. Nor a philosopher. Nor a theologian. Nor a scientist. In all these fields the south is an awe-inspiring blank. . . ." It was as complete a vacuity as the interstellar spaces, the "Sahara of the Bozart," "The Bible Belt." He summed it all up in one basic catalogue of Southern grotesqueries: "Fundamentalism, Ku Kluxry, revivals, lynchings, hog wallow politics—these are the things that always occur to a northerner when he thinks of the south." The South, in short, had fallen prey to its poor whites, who would soon achieve apotheosis in the Snopes family.

It did not end with the twenties. The image was reinforced by a variety of episodes: the Scottsboro trials, chain gang exposés, Bilbo and Rankin, Senate filibusters, labor wars; much later by Central High and Orval Faubus, Emmett Till and Autherine Lucy and James Meredith, bus boycotts and Freedom Riders; and not least of all by the lush growth of literature that covered Mencken's Sahara, with Caldwell's *Tobacco Road* and Faulkner's *Sanctuary* and various other products of what Ellen Glasgow labeled the Southern Gothic and a less elegant Mississippi editor called the "privy school" of literature. In the words of Faulkner's character, Gavin Stevens, the North suffered from a curious "gullibility: a volitionless, almost helpless capacity and eagerness to believe anything about the South not even provided it be derogatory but merely bizarre enough and strange enough." And Faulkner, to be sure, did not altogether neglect that market. Not surprisingly, he was taken in some quarters for a realist, and the image of Southern savagery long obscured the critics' recognition of his manifold merits.

The family line of the plantation myth can be traced only so far in the legendary gentility and savagery of the South. Other family lines seem to be entirely independent—if sometimes on friendly terms. In an excellent study, "The New South Creed, 1865–1900," . . . Paul M. Gaston has traced the evolution of the creed into a genuine myth. In the aftermath of the Civil War, apostles of a "New South," led by Henry W. Grady, preached with almost evangelical fervor the gospel of industry. Their dream, Gaston writes, "was essentially a promise of American life for the South. It proffered all the glitter and glory and freedom from guilt that inhered in the American ideal." From advocacy, from this vision of the future, the prophets soon advanced to the belief that "their promised land [was] at hand, no longer merely a gleaming goal." "By the twentieth century . . . there was established for many in the South a pattern of belief within which they could see themselves and their section as rich, success-oriented, and just . . . opulence and power were at hand . . . the Negro lived in the best of all possible worlds."

As the twentieth century advanced, and wealth did in fact increase, the creed of the New South took on an additional burden of crusades for good roads and education, blending them into what Francis B. Simkins has called the "trinity of Southern progress": industrial growth, good roads, and schools. When the American Historical Association went to Durham in 1929 for its annual meeting, Robert D. W. Connor of the University of North Carolina presented the picture of a rehabilitated South that had "shaken itself free from its heritage of war and Reconstruction. Its self-confidence restored, its political stability assured, its prosperity regained, its social problems on the way to solution. . . :" Two months before Connor spoke, the New York Stock Exchange had broken badly, and in the aftermath the image he described was seriously blurred, but before the end of the thirties it was being brought back into focus by renewed industrial expansion that received increased momentum from World War II and postwar prosperity.

Two new and disparate images emerged in the depression years, both with the altogether novel feature of academic trappings and affiliations. One was the burgeoning school of sociological regionalism led by Howard W. Odum and Rupert B. Vance at the University of North Carolina. It was neither altogether the image of the Savage South nor that of industrial progress, although both entered into the compound. It was rather a concept of the "Problem South," which Franklin D. Roosevelt labeled "the Nation's Economic Problem No. 1," a region with indisputable shortcomings but with potentialities that needed constructive attention and the application of rational social planning. Through the disciples of Odum as well as the agencies of the New Deal, the vision issued in a flood of social science monographs and programs for reform and development. To one undergraduate in Chapel Hill at the time, it seemed in retrospect that "we had more of an attitude of service to the South as the South than was true later. . . ."

The regionalists were challenged by the Vanderbilt Agrarians, who developed a myth of the traditional South. Their manifesto, *I'll Take My Stand*, by Twelve Southerners, appeared by fortuitous circumstance in 1930 when industrial capitalism seemed on the verge of collapse. In reaction against both the progressive New South and Mencken's image of savagery they championed, in Donald Davidson's words, a "traditional society . . . that is stable, religious, more rural than urban, and politically conservative," in which human needs were supplied by "Family, bloodkinship, clanship, folkways, custom, community. . . ." The ideal of the traditional virtues took on the texture of myth in their image of the agrarian South. Of course, in the end, their agrarianism proved less important as a social-economic force than as a context for creative literature. The central figures in the movement were the Fugitive poets John Crowe Ransom, Donald Davidson, Allen Tate, and Robert Penn Warren. But, as Professor Louis Rubin has emphasized, "Through their vision of an agrarian community, the authors of *I'll Take My Stand* presented a critique of the modern world. In contrast to the hurried, nervous life of cities, the image of the agrarian South was of a life in which human beings existed serenely and harmoniously." Their critique of the modern frenzy "has since been echoed by commentator after commentator."

While it never became altogether clear whether the Agrarians were celebrating the aristocratic graces or following the old Jeffersonian dictum that "Those who labor in the earth are the chosen people of God . . . ," most of them seemed to come down eventually on the side of the farmer rather than the planter. Frank L. Owsley, who rediscovered the ante bellum yeoman farmer, was one of them. Insofar as they extolled the yeoman farmer, the Agrarians laid hold upon an image older than any of the others—the Jeffersonian South. David M. Potter, a Southerner in exile at Stanford University, has remarked how difficult it is for many people to realize that the benighted South "was, until recently, regarded by many liberals as the birthplace and the natural bulwark of the Jeffersonian ideal. . . ." The theme has long had an appeal for historians as well as others. Frederick Jackson Turner developed it for the West and William E. Dodd for the South. According to Dodd the democratic, equalitarian South of the Jeffersonian image was the norm; the plantation slavocracy was the great aberration. Dodd's theme has been reflected in the writing of other historians, largely in terms of a region subjected to economic colonialism by an imperial Northeast: Charles A. Beard, for example, who saw the sectional conflict as a struggle between agrarianism and industrialism; Howard K. Beale, who interpreted Reconstruction in similar terms; C. Vann Woodward, defender of Populism; Arthur S. Link, who first rediscovered the Southern progressives; and Walter Prescott Webb, who found the nation divided between an exploited South and West on the one hand, and a predatory Northeast on the other. Jefferson, like the South, it sometimes seems, can mean all things to all men, and the Jefferson image of agrarian democracy has been a favorite recourse of Southern liberals, just as his state-rights doctrines have nourished conservatism.

In stark contrast to radical agrarianism there stands the concept of monolithic conservatism in Southern politics. It seems to be a proposition generally taken for granted now that the South is, by definition, conservative—and always has been. Yet the South in the late nineteenth century produced some of the most radical Populists and in the twentieth was a bulwark of Wilsonian progressivism and Roosevelt's New

Deal, at least up to a point. A good case has been made out by Arthur S. Link that Southern agrarian radicals pushed Wilson further into progressivism than he intended to go. During the twenties Southern minority leadership in Congress kept up such a running battle against the conservative tax policies of Andrew Mellon that, believe it or not, there was real fear among some Northern businessmen during the 1932 campaign that Franklin D. Roosevelt might be succeeded by that radical Southern income-taxer, John Nance Garner! The conservative image of course has considerable validity, but it obscures understanding of such phenomena as Albert Gore, Russell Long, Lister Hill, John Sparkman, Olin D. Johnston, William Fulbright, the Yarboroughs of Texas, or the late Estes Kefauver. In the 1960 campaign the conservative image seriously victimized Lyndon B. Johnson, who started in politics as a vigorous New Dealer and later maneuvered through the Senate the first civil rights legislation since Reconstruction.

The infinite variety of Southern mythology could be catalogued and analyzed endlessly. A suggestive list would include the Proslavery South; the Confederate South; the Demagogic South; the State Rights South; the Fighting South; the Lazy South; the Folklore South; the South of jazz and the blues; the Booster South; the Rapacious South running away with Northern industries; the Liberal South of the interracial movement; the White Supremacy South of racial segregation, which seems to be for some the all-encompassing "Southern way of life"; the Anglo-Saxon (or was it the Scotch-Irish?) South, the most American of all regions because of its native population; or the Internationalist South, a mainstay of the Wilson, Roosevelt, and Truman foreign policies.

The South, then, has been the seedbed for a proliferation of paradoxical myths, all of which have some basis in empirical fact and all of which doubtlessly have, or have had, their true believers. The result has been, in David Potter's words, that the South has become an enigma, "a kind of Sphinx on the American land." What is really the answer to the riddle, what is at bottom the foundation of Southern distinctiveness has never been established with finality, but the quest for a central theme of Southern history has repeatedly engaged the region's historians. Like Frederick Jackson Turner, who extracted the essential West in his frontier thesis, Southern historians have sought to distill the quintessence of the South into some kind of central theme.

In a recent survey of these efforts David L. Smiley of Wake Forest College has concluded that they turn upon two basic lines of thought: "the causal effects of environment, and the development of certain acquired characteristics of the people called Southern." The distinctive climate and weather of the South, it has been argued, slowed the pace of life, tempered the speech of the South, dictated the system of staple crops and Negro slavery—in short, predetermined the plantation economy. The more persuasive suggestions have resulted from concentration upon human factors and causation. The best known is that set forth by U. B. Phillips. The quintessence of Southernism, he wrote in 1928, was "a common resolve indomitably maintained" that the South "shall be and remain a white man's country." Whether "expressed with the frenzy of a demagogue or maintained with a patrician's quietude," this was "the cardinal test of a Southerner and the central theme of Southern history." Other historians have pointed to the rural nature of Southern society as the basic conditioning factor, to the prevalence of the country gentleman ideal imported from England, to the experience of the South as a conscious minority unified by criticism and attack from outside, to the fundamental piety of the Bible Belt, and to various other factors. It has even been suggested by one writer that a chart of the mule population would determine the boundaries of the South.

More recently, two historians have attempted new explanations. In his search for a Southern identity, C. Vann Woodward advances several crucial factors: the experience of poverty in a land of plenty; failure and defeat in a land that glorifies success; sin and guilt amid the legend of American innocence; and a sense of place and belonging among a people given to abstraction. David M. Potter, probing the enigma of the South, has found the key to the riddle in the prevalence of a folk society. "This folk culture, we know, was far from being ideal or utopian," he writes, "and was in fact full of inequality and wrong, but if the nostalgia persists was it because even the inequality and wrong were parts of a life that still had a relatedness and meaning which our more bountiful life in the mass culture seems to lack?"

It is significant that both explanations are expressed largely in the past tense, Potter's explicitly in terms of nostalgia. They recognize, by implication at least, still another image—that of the Dynamic or the Changing South. The image may be rather nebulous and the ultimate ends unclear, but the fact of change is written inescapably across the Southern scene. The consciousness of change has been present so long as to become in itself one of the abiding facts of Southern life. . . . As far back as the twenties it was the consciousness of change that quickened the imaginations of a cultivated and sensitive minority, giving us the Southern renaissance in literature. The peculiar historical consciousness of the Southern writer, Allen Tate has suggested, "made possible the curious burst of intelligence that we get at a crossing of the ways, not unlike, on an infinitesimal scale, the outburst of poetic genius at the end of the sixteenth century when commercial England had already begun to crush feudal England." Trace it through modern Southern writing, and at the center—in Ellen Glasgow, in Faulkner, Wolfe, Caldwell, the Fugitive-Agrarian poets, and all the others—there is the consciousness of change, of suspension between two worlds, a double focus looking both backward and forward.

The Southerner of the present generation has seen the old landmarks crumble with great rapidity: the one-crop agriculture and the very predominance of agriculture itself, the one-party system, the white primary, the poll tax, racial segregation, the poor white (at least in his classic connotations), the provincial isolation—virtually all the foundations of the established order. Yet, sometimes, the old traditions endure in surprising new forms. Southern folkways have been carried even into the factory, and the Bible Belt has revealed resources undreamed of in Mencken's philosophy—but who, in the twenties, could have anticipated Martin Luther King?

One wonders what new images, what new myths, might be nurtured by the emerging South. Some, like Harry Ashmore, have merely written *An Epitaph for Dixie*. It is the conclusion of two Southern sociologists, John M. Maclachlan and Joe S. Floyd, Jr., that present trends "might well hasten the day when the South, once perhaps the most distinctively 'different' American region, will have become . . . virtually indistinguishable from the other urban-industrial areas of the nation." U. B. Phillips long ago suggested that the disappearance of race as a major issue would end Southern distinctiveness. One may wonder if Southern distinctiveness might even be preserved in new conditions entirely antithetic to his image. Charles L. Black, Jr., another *émigré* Southerner (at Yale Law School) has confessed to a fantastic dream that Southern whites and Negroes, bound in a special bond of common tragedy, may come to recognize their kinship. There is not the slightest warrant for it, he admits, in history, sociology, or common sense. But if it should come to pass, he suggests, "The South, which has always felt itself reserved for a high destiny, would have found it, and would have come to flower at last. And the fragrance of it would spread, beyond calculation, over the world."

Despite the consciousness of change, perhaps even more because of it, Southerners still feel a persistent pull toward identification with their native region as a ground for belief and loyalty. Is there not yet something more than nostalgia to the idea of the South? Is there not some living heritage with which the modern Southerner can identify? Is there not, in short, a viable myth of the South? The quest for myth has been a powerful factor in recent Southern literature, and the suspicion is strong that it will irresistibly affect any historian's quest for the central theme of Southern history. It has all too clearly happened before—in the climatic theory, for example, which operated through its geographical determinism to justify the social order of the plantation, or the Phillips thesis of white supremacy, which has become almost a touchstone of the historian's attitude toward the whole contemporary issue of race. "To elaborate a central theme," David L. Smiley has asserted, is "but to reduce a multi-faceted story to a single aspect, and its result . . . but to find new footnotes to confirm revealed truths and prescribed views." The trouble is that the quest for the central theme, like Turner's frontier thesis, becomes absorbed willy-nilly into the process of myth making.

To pursue the Turner analogy a little further; the conviction grows that the frontier thesis, with all its elaborations and critiques, has been exhausted (and in part exploded) as a source of new historical insight. It is no derogation of insights already gained to suggest that the same thing has happened to the quest for the central theme, and that the historian, *as historian,* may be better able to illuminate our understanding of the South now by turning to a new focus upon the regional mythology.

To undertake the analysis of mythology will no longer require him to venture into uncharted wilderness. A substantial conceptual framework of mythology has already been developed by anthropologists, philosophers, psychologists, theologians, and literary critics. The historian, while his field has always been closely related to mythology, has come only lately to the critique of it. But there now exists a considerable body of historical literature on the American national mythology and the related subject of the national character, and Smith's stimulating *Virgin Land* suggests the trails that may be followed into the idea of the South.

Several trails, in fact, have already been blazed. Nearly forty years ago, Francis Pendleton Gaines successfully traced the rise and progress of the plantation myth, and two recent authors have belatedly taken to the same trail. Howard R. Floan has considerably increased our knowledge of the abolitionist version in his study of Northern writers, *The South in Northern Eyes,* while William R. Taylor has approached the subject from an entirely new perspective in his *Cavalier and Yankee.* Shields McIlwaine has traced the literary image of the poor white, while Stanley Elkins' *Slavery* has broken sharply from established concepts on both sides of that controversial question. One foray into the New South has been made in Paul Gaston's "The New South Creed, 1865–1900." Yet many important areas—the Confederate and Reconstruction myths, for example—still remain almost untouched.

Some of the basic questions that need to be answered have been attacked in these studies; some have not. It is significant that students of literature have led the way and have pointed up the value of even third-rate creative literature in the critique of myth. The historian, however, should be able to contribute other perspectives. With his peculiar time perspective he can seek to unravel the tangled genealogy of myth that runs back from the modern Changing South to Jefferson's yeoman and Kennedy's plantation. Along the way he should investigate the possibility that some obscure dialectic may be at work in the pairing of obverse images: the two versions of the plantation, New South and Old, Cavalier and Yankee, genteel and savage, regionalist and agrarian, nativist and internationalist.

What, the historian may ask, have been the historical origins and functions of the myths? The plantation myth, according to Gaines and Floan, was born in the controversy and emotion of the struggle over slavery. It had polemical uses for both sides. Taylor, on the other hand, finds its origin in the psychological need, both North and South, to find a corrective for the grasping, materialistic, rootless society symbolized by the image of the Yankee. Vann Woodward and Gaston have noted its later psychological uses in bolstering the morale of the New South. The image of the Savage South has obvious polemical uses, but has it not others? Has it not served the function of national catharsis? Has it not created for many Americans a convenient scapegoat upon which the sins of all may be symbolically laid and thereby expiated—a most convenient escape from problem solving? To what extent, indeed, has the mythology of the South in general welled up from the subconscious depths? Taylor, especially, has emphasized this question, but the skeptical historian will also be concerned with the degree to which it has been the product or the device of deliberate manipulation by propagandists and vested interests seeking identification with the "real" South.

Certainly any effort to delineate the unique character of a people must take into account its mythology. "Poets," James G. Randall suggested, "have done better in expressing this oneness of the South than historians in explaining it." Can it be that the historians have been looking in the wrong places, that they have failed to seek the key to the enigma where the poets have so readily found it—in the mythology that has had so much to do with shaping character, unifying society, developing a sense of community, of common ideals and shared goals, making the region conscious of its distinctiveness?[1] Perhaps by turning to differ-

---

[1] Josiah Royce's definition of a "province" is pertinent here: ". . . any one part of a national domain which is geographically and socially sufficiently unified to have a true consciousness of its own ideals and customs and to possess a sense of its distinction from other parts of the country." Quoted in Frederick Jackson Turner, *The Significance of Sections in American History* (New York, 1932), p. 45.

ent and untrodden paths we shall encounter the central theme of Southern history at last on the new frontier of mythology.

2. The "New South"

PAUL M. GASTON

The most distinctive institutions and habits of thought associated with the recent South originated in the last quarter of the nineteenth century. In the post-Reconstruction years the Solid South emerged in politics, Jim Crow was institutionalized, tenant farming and the crop-lien system became typical of southern agriculture, and the new ideology of industrialization, sectional reconciliation, and regional progress was popularized by prophets like Henry W. Grady.

In the historiographical essay that follows, Professor Paul M. Gaston of the University of Virginia analyzes the "New South" creed and the era in which it flourished. His discussion not only evokes the *zeitgeist* of the period but, by tracing the historiographical trends in treating the New South, also throws light on the durability of southern traditions, the extent of southern unity, and the way in which the region reflected, imitated, and differed from national patterns. It is important to note that the whole complex of ideas associated with the New South crusade, like the opposition to the movement within the region, was based on an acute awareness of the South's position within the nation. In fact, the situation of the South vis-à-vis the rest of the country was at the very heart of New South ideology.

IN 1893, IN A PIONEER ATTEMPT TO PROBE THE MEANING OF THE "New South," Amory Dwight Mayo, a northern exponent of new developments below the Potomac, found that there was "a good deal of unnecessary friction in the heated discussion of the question

From Arthur S. Link and Rembert W. Patrick (eds.), *Writing Southern History: Essays in Historiography in Honor of Fletcher M. Green* (Baton Rouge, 1965), pp. 316–336. Reprinted by permission of the Louisiana State University Press. A portion of the original essay and the footnotes have been omitted.

whether there really is a new South." Doubting his own ability to produce a definitive picture, Mayo offered little encouragement to the historians of the future. "Probably the time will never come," he predicted,
"when the journalist, or even the average statesman, will be able to take
an all-around view of a theme so large that it may be compassed only
by many observations of many minds." Since Mayo's time a good many
historians, though not so many as one might wish, have set out to "com-
pass" the "New South," but we today are likely to agree that they have
yet to produce the "all-around view" with which our guild can be
permanently satisfied.

Part of the difficulty—and it is a problem that grows with the passage
of time—lies in the extraordinary ambiguity of the term itself. C. Vann
Woodward, for example, feels that it has caused so much "mischief"
that, if possible, it ought to be abandoned entirely. Most of the confusion
stems from the fact that "New South" has customarily implied at least
two quite different things. On the one hand, it denotes a particular
ideology—thus the "New South School," referring to the Henry Gradys
who were prophets of a "New South." On the other hand, it is used with
equal, if not greater, frequency to mark off various, and vaguely defined,
periods of southern history. It may signify the South since 1865; since
1877; from 1877 to 1913; since 1900, or simply the South of the present.
Moreover, many writers who use the term to denote a particular period
are not careful to state that "New South" has no connotative meaning. Or,
conversely, the term may be implicitly invested with a vague meaning, stemming from the Grady ideology, and the progress of the region measured
against achievement of those ideals. In this case one finds, in almost any
post-Civil War period one investigates, that the "New South" is emerging,
or must be resisted, or has triumphed, or, as Harry S. Ashmore put it a
few years ago, is now "coming to reluctant maturity." Finally, diverse
groups have taken the term to describe themselves and their particular
periodicals. Among these we find nineteenth-century journals devoted to
industrialization and reconciliation, the familiar theme; a twentieth-century
communist periodical; and the monthly publication of the Southern
Regional Council, advocating a South free of racial discrimination.

Clearly, then, before one can discuss the historiography of the "New
South," some definitions and limitations must be established. As for
the term itself, the position taken here is that it should be used almost
exclusively as an adjective and seldom as a noun; and in its adjectival
form it will be restricted largely to modification of the men of the post-
Reconstruction years who first worked out in detail an ideology which
was enthusiastically preached throughout the region. In addition, it will
be used to describe the point of view of historians of a later period
whose interpretations reflected the ideas of the original New South

crusaders. As for periodization, the discussion will be restricted largely to the period from the end of Reconstruction to the Populist Revolt, the era in which the New South movement had its largest following and made its greatest impact.

There is only one genuinely historiographical essay on this period, a recent paper published by Professor Jacob E. Cooke. Actually, his "New South" extends from 1877 to 1914, and he finds that this period "does not readily lend itself to historiographical discussion" because, he explains, "few historians have presented a monistic interpretation which gives unity and meaning to the varied facts of Southern experience." Historians, he declares, have tended to emphasize different aspects of the region's history—economic development, political practices, race relations—and "few have argued that any single interpretive key would unlock the door of this vast storehouse of historical material." Perhaps, as a comment on recent studies, this judgment has merit. But there was a time when, under the spell of the New South magic, historians found a central theme for most of the period and developed it with great enthusiasm, conviction, and oftentimes elaborate documentation. If, by a "school" of historians we mean a group of scholars all writing more or less toward the same end, there was in the years between 1900 and the Great Depression a group, composed mostly of Southerners, deserving to be called the New South school of historians.

Albert Bushnell Hart, the Harvard historian, confronted one of the principal characteristics of this group when he wrote, in 1910, that the southern tendency toward exaggeration had to be understood before one could properly evaluate southern writings. In the hands of southern writers, he declared, "the clever but no-wise distinguished professor of Latin is 'Probably the greatest classical scholar in the United States,' the siege of Vicksburg was 'the most terrific contest in the annals of warfare'; the material progress of the South is 'the most marvelous thing in human history.'" Later in the same volume, Hart exposed a critical truth when he explained that the exaggerated statements of southern material growth were widely believed in the region. "In every discussion of Southern affairs," he declared, "an important thing to reckon with is a fixed belief that the South is the most prosperous part of the country, which fits in with the conviction that it has long surpassed all other parts of the world in civilization, in military ardor, and in the power to rise out of the sufferings of a conquered people."

The themes of prosperity and power which Hart noted were rapidly becoming the stock-in-trade of writers on the South's recent history. Guy Carleton Lee, in the preface to Philip Alexander Bruce's *The Rise of the New South*, found the "subject of the South since the Civil War" to be an "inspiring one." Actually, he continued, the years since the war offered "such examples of heroic effort, such persistent struggle, such triumphant results, that the historian finds himself tending to an exaltation of the mind." Bruce's volume, praised by Lee as an authentic and comprehensive study of recent southern history, was "a vital narration of the progress of a mighty people, who, from adversity such as no other section of North America has ever experienced," had brilliantly "won the race with adverse fate and become the pride of the Union."

Bruce's history stands as the capstone of the New South crusade itself; in fact, the New South school of historians, of which Bruce was the first major representative, had its origins in the promotional literature of the New South editors and publicists of the 1880's and 1890's. During these years the New South propagandists flooded the nation with an insistent literature in which historians of our generation find an astonishing mixture of fact and fancy, wish and reality. Few observers from the North were unimpressed by what they read. To cite a typical example, Charles Dudley Warner, writing in 1886, was persuaded that the South was in the throes of a mighty "economical and political revolution" whose story "will be one of the most marvellous the historian has to deal with."

The marvel lies not so much in the history with which one must deal as in the descriptions that appeared in the eighties and nineties from the pens of the New South promoters. A New South creed, born in the seventies, nurtured in the early eighties, and brought to maturity with Grady's address before the New England Society of New York in 1886, was compounded of two distinct parts, the blending of which by the New South spokesmen accounts for numerous historiographical difficulties. On the one hand was the doctrine that the South was poor, frustrated, and despised because it had, by decree of history, become entangled in wrong policies; the road to the future lay in abandoning one-crop agriculture, militant sectionalism, and outright repression of the Negro, and adopting instead a diversified industrial economy, a spirit of reconciliation, and a program of education providing separate independence for the Negro. The dream which they created was essentially a promise of American life for the South. It proffered all the glitter and glory and freedom from guilt that inhered in the American ideal. Sloughing off those characteristics which had marked him as poor, quarrelsome, unprogressive, guilt-ridden, and unsuccessful, the Southerner would —if he heeded the New South prophets—become a true heir of his heritage: prosperous, successful, confident of the future.

Before long, however, the promotional literature of the New South spokesmen included wondrous descriptions of a people who had already achieved, or were on the verge of achieving, all that had been promised as fruits of long toil. Testimony to the achievements of the new order was produced in copious quantity. From his headquarters in Baltimore, Richard Hathaway Edmonds, editor of the *Manufacturers' Record,* ground out statistics to substantiate his claim that the region was "throbbing" with industrial activity and that capitalists of the North and Europe were "looking to the South as the field for investment." Henry Watterson thanked God that, at last, one could say of the South, "it is simply a geographic expression." And, finally, a Vanderbilt professor [Wilbur Tillett] declared that the "New South, which had first showed itself in 1880," had by 1886 "proved its name by evidences so powerful and convincing that only the blindest can fail to see them."

Proclaiming the reality of an affluent and triumphant South, these spokesmen were equally fervent in depicting a South innocent of racial injustice. "Each has his own place," [Henry] Grady declared of white and black "and fills it, and is satisfied." The program of paternalism, education, regulated franchise, and increasing segregation was advanced as the final solution to the conundrum presented by the demands of Negro freedom and the American tradition of equality. The New South image thus underwent in a short period a metamorphosis. Emerging from a program of action to save a despondent region from ruin, it evolved into a declaration of triumph. Uncritically it could be assumed that, because "facts" proved it, affluence and power were at hand and that the Negro lived in the best of all possible worlds, righteously separated from, but nurtured by, his white brethren. This was the intellectual tradition which historians of the twentieth century inherited; and with certain exceptions, it was this tradition which dominated southern historical writing until the 1930's when the revisionist erosion set in.

Before that era of devasting reappraisal, however, a pattern of history was established which was comprehensive in scope and appealing in tone. The New South school of historians developed, as the central theme of their works, the concept of triumph over adversity, of steel will and impeccable character overcoming staggering problems, often against what seemed impossible odds. The South that was depicted in most of these early histories rose from the extraordinary devastation of the Reconstruction to a glorious plateau of achievement. Viewed from the plateau, the story was one of hope and inspiration. Holland Thompson, the first academic historian to write a general history of the period, opened his work with the declaration that "somehow, somewhere, sometime, a new hopefulness was born and this spirit—evidence of new life—became embodied in 'the New South.' " To optimism and cheerfulness was added the element of daring and romance. Broadus Mitchell, in *The Rise of the Cotton*

Mills in the South, enticed his readers with the assurance that his story, properly understood, was "not only an industrial chronicle, but a romance, a drama as well." Here, then, were powerful romantic elements to compete with the more popular and more numerous histories of the gallant South that had fallen at Appomattox. And the histories of the new regime had the one virtue denied chronicles of the Old South: they were success stories.

An essential ingredient was the element of strong moral fiber. While the New South historians agreed that the new order differed from the old in innumerable ways, few were willing to concede that the peculiar moral superiority of the Southerner had perished with the Lost Cause. As Bruce put it, the war and Reconstruction had shattered the South's economic structure and visited economic ruin on the region; but they had not destroyed the extraordinary "moral qualities of the people." These, in fact, were strengthened in adversity and were the principal weapons available to Southerners to meet new challenges. Ironically coupled with this sense of moral superiority was the common belief that the war and Reconstruction had emancipated the white South from the shackles of an old order that had barred material progress and prosperity. "The Civil War," Mitchell wrote, "brought into glaring view the absence of Southern economic self-sufficiency," and its outcome freed "not just the slaves, but the South as a whole." The "emancipated" whites, no longer fettered by the economic chains of the past but still endowed with the ancient traits of their forebears, were required to rebuild on new foundations. Driven by "moral incitement" and "civic piety," Southerners undertook the task of creating a prosperous industrial society. In response to a "moral stimulus," their leaders built cotton mills that provided work for impoverished poor whites and, one is almost led to believe, gave little thought to self-enrichment.

It is important to remember that, almost without exception, New South historians wrote as confirmed nationalists and interpreted southern development within the context of national trends. Reconciliation and conversion to national ways and values were central to their histories. To Paul Herman Buck, the historian of reconcilation and, in many ways, a characteristic representative of the New South school, "the central theme of American life after the war . . . is not to be found in . . . sectional divergence. It was national integration which marked every important development in the years that followed." This theme of national reconciliation is likely to be deceptive, and one should observe that it was never meant to imply a surrender of southern will to northern superiority. It signified, rather, a recognition in the South that the road to affluence and power led to the adoption of those national patterns which had accounted for American greatness. This is what Edwin Mims meant when he wrote, in his biography

of Sidney Lanier that southern progress had been made possible by the
"adoption of the national point of view"; it is what Burton J. Hendrick,
the biographer of Walter H. Page, had in mind when he declared that the
new nationalism was the essential force underlying the South's resurgence,
that "above all," the period of Page's crusading "was an era that wit-
nessed the transformation of the backward Civil War South into a progressive part of a united country." A generation of New South historians
was vindicated in 1937 when Buck concluded that, by 1900, "a union of
sentiment based upon integrated interests had become a fact."

New South historians, in stressing the theme of nationalism, were particularly careful to emphasize two complementary aspects. In the first place,
they argued that the primary force binding the sections was the adoption
by the South of what E. L. Godkin once called "the industrial stage of
social progress." To Buck, the South's new departure had brought about an
"interlocking of economic dependence" which promoted similarity and
destroyed particularism. Broadus and George Mitchell, in *The Industrial
Revolution in the South,* argued that the industrialization of the South
destroyed "separatism" and invited "national consciousness." In 1908,
their historian father, Samuel C. Mitchell, attempted to place the movement toward American nationalism in a universal context, concluding of
the South, "We have simply found out God's plan in our generation, and
have fallen in line. . . . Whatever tends to equalize economic conditions in
different sections of our country," he explained, "promotes similarity of
view and identity of purpose." Bruce also concluded that the industrial
revolution in the South was the major factor in producing a republic
"united in all its parts," free of debilitating antagonisms.

In the second place, these historians were convinced that the resurgent
southern economy had brought into existence a South of affluence, power,
and independence which fully vindicated the New South spokesmen who
had called the movement into being. As early as 1885, according to Mims,
"factories were prospering, farm products were becoming more diversified,
more farmers owned their own places, . . . the national spirit was growing,
and . . . [a] day of hope, of freedom, of progress, had dawned." By the
end of the century, Mims believed, the South was assured of a "brilliant
future." To other historians brilliance did not have to await future developments. Bruce was struck by a "recuperative power in the Southern
people" which was "perhaps unsurpassed in history." The Mitchells believed that there "arrived nearly overnight an Industrial Revolution as
swift and as vigorous as that in England." Buck pronounced the "economic revolution" to have been both "remarkable" and "sensationally
rapid." Reenforcing this sense of material greatness was the common
belief that the South had been master of its own destiny, achieving its

eminence virtually unaided. Moreover, nothing is so striking to the historian of today as the common absence of suggestions that the region was in any sense a colony of the North. Bruce, for example, noted the prominence of northern financiers in southern railroad development, but his analysis did not lead him to attach any special significance to the fact. Buck, summing up the matter, could declare: "Thirty years after Appomattox there remained no fundamental conflict between the aspirations of North and South. The people of the United States constituted at last a nation integrated and united in sentiment."

It would have been paradoxical in the extreme had these historians coupled their accounts of a pioneering, progressive, and energetic industrial leadership with an interpretation of political development which conceded the truth of the occasional northern charge that "Bourbon" politicians in the South stubbornly held to the past, refusing to adapt to the changing conditions of a new order. The truth is, such concessions were seldom made. The New South historians agreed with the editor of the Memphis *Appeal* who declared as early as 1875, "We do not know what a Bourbon Democrat means . . . unless it implies there is a class of politicians, who, . . . forgetting nothing and learning nothing, do not recognize any issues as settled by the war and are ready to inaugurate another rebellion. We know of no such Democrats." On the contrary the early historians believed that the role played by the political leaders of the South was essentially the same as that played by the industrial leaders. Just as the latter had redeemed the South from economic error, so the former had redeemed the region from political error and, in addition, had assured conditions which facilitated sectional reconciliation and material progress.

To understand this favorable interpretation of the "Redeemers," one must recapture something of the perspective from which the New South historians wrote. To them the experience of Reconstruction was a horror unique in American history and for this reason doubly noxious and degrading. Against this background, the Redeemers appeared virtually as knights in shining armor. Their primary task—indeed, their knightly duty —was to cut away the "poisonous growth," as Bruce put it, planted by a band of alien bandits and desecrators.

Thus the image of the Redeemers is a relatively uncomplicated one. They began their careers in glory, especially those who participated in the noble act of securing definitive home rule as a result of the "Wormley House Bargain." They were, in contrast to the "aliens" who had ruled the South before redemption, the "natural" leaders of the region, men who had distinguished themselves during the Civil War. This is not to say that they were the old plantation aristocracy. Several New South historians recognized that many of the leaders came from the new commercial-industrial urban class rather than from the older planter class. In either case, however, they were *natural* leaders, men born to the region.

Their achievement, in the view of the New South historians, amply justified the trust that the masses confided in them. Responsible men, they reversed the corrupt and fraudulent practices of Reconstruction. Holland Thompson pronounced their administrations free from scandal of any kind. "No governments in American history," he wrote, "have been conducted with more economy and more fidelity." Impeccable honesty was coupled with a high sense of fiscal responsibility. The ruinous taxes and extravagant appropriations of the carpetbag regimes were abolished as the Redeemers faced up realistically to the demands of recovery. Expenses were diminished by scaling down dishonest debts, eliminating unnecessary governmental positions, and lowering salaries. A new tax structure released capital for investment. In brief, an atmosphere was created in which business could thrive and men could exercise their initiative without fear of retaliation by a capricious government.

Moreover, none of these achievements would have been secured had the Redeemers not guaranteed freedom from political instability and resumption of Negro-Republican rule. It is in this sense that the New South historians generally applauded the Redeemer creation of a one-party, solid South. Taking the explanations of the political leaders more or less at face value, the historians gave credence to the simple formula that the South's suffering had come as a consequence of Republican domination resulting in "Negro rule." Bruce was convinced that, even after home rule, "an enormous number of black voters" continued to threaten "the stability of Southern institutions." The threat could have become a reality, however, only if the Republican party had found support among native whites, and this could have occurred only if the whites had divided. Patriotism, loyalty to race and region, demanded, then, unswerving support of the Democratic party. The permanence of a "redeemed" South, in short, depended upon the maintenance of a "solid" South.

Thus it was that one-partyism, white supremacy, patriotism, morality in government, and the industrial revolution were all part of one pattern. Finding this connection, the historians of the early part of the century discovered much of which to be proud in the "New South": Reconstruction had been successfully undone, and a superior southern will had charted a prosperous, successful course for the once defeated and occupied land.

Reaction to this felicitous interpretation of the Redeemer era was bound to occur, and signs of dissent began to appear in the 1920's. But it was not until the Depression that full scale revision began to take shape. The glowing picture of a prosperous and triumphant South made little sense to a region soon to be accurately, if somewhat undiplomatically, labeled the nation's "economic problem no. 1." The excruciating plight of the South provided new perspectives that helped to provide new interpretations of the Redeemer era.

The most eloquent and heated, if not the most thoroughly researched, interpretation emanated primarily from Nashville and is associated with the Vanderbilt Agrarian movement. The Nashville Crusaders, in their manifesto, *I'll Take My Stand,* wrote charmingly of an ordered, conservative, soil-oriented style of life, presumably characteristic of the Old South, which had been betrayed by the New South promoters. Lamenting the seduction of younger Southerners by the industrial gospel, the Agrarians called for a critical examination of the "advantages of becoming a 'new South' which," they insisted, would "be only an undistinguished replica of the usual industrial community." Concerned with the present, wishing to launch the counterrevolution which they believed still had chances of success, they charged the New South historians with perpetuating original errors by failing to write genuinely critical history. What should be written, declared Donald Davidson in *The Attack on Leviathan,* was that America's need in 1900 was "to set off the tendencies that were leading the country straight into overindustrialization and social degeneracy." This could have been accomplished most effectively, he concluded, by "strengthening the conservative culture of the South, to the virtues of which [Walter Hines] Page and his followers were blind."

Despite their appeal to traditional values rooted deeply in southern history, the Agrarians produced no historical studies of the Redeemer era, apart from occasional essays such as those by John Donald Wade on Henry Grady and Joel Chandler Harris. Frank Lawrence Owsley, the most distinguished historian in the group, rediscovered the plain people of the Old South, but he did not investigate the social and economic history of this class after the Civil War. The significance of the Agrarians, then, lies primarily in the fact that they heightened awareness of an anti-New South tradition in the region and suggested to historians the profitability of exploring the patterns of conflict and antagonism in modern southern history.

The theme of conflict soon appeared in several works. Benjamin B. Kendrick and Alex M. Arnett, in *The South Looks at Its Past* (1935), found that "the quarter-century that followed the restoration of native white rule in the South was marked by a conflict between those who looked to the past and those who looked to the future." The Redeemer era could be described as a conflict between an Old South party of agrarianism and a New South party of industrialism, with the former fighting a rear-guard action. A similar interpretation was included in William B. Hesseltine's general history of the South, first published in 1936.[1] To him, the South was beset by a conflict between the values of the Old South, embodied in Jefferson Davis, and the New South, embodied in Robert E. Lee, which left a lasting mark on the South. Hesseltine's conflict was developed in more detail in his *Confederate Leaders in the New South* (1950).

However, the new views of conflict between an agrarian and an industrial tradition—a conflict that presumably reached its point of greatest intensity during the Redeemer era—resulted in relatively few serious monographic studies of that period. Commenting on the paucity of such studies, Judson C. Ward suggests that "the slower evolutionary processes of economic and social reconstruction carried on under one-party domination have not possessed for historians the dramatic appeal of the more spectacular period of the Civil War and Reconstruction which preceded this period or the Populist revolt which followed it." Here Ward raises a point that is crucial in understanding the nature of the revisionism of the 1930's and 1940's. To many scholars of the Depression era, the Populist period held very special attraction. As C. Vann Woodward has pointed out, the two periods had much in common. There was, first of all, the common setting of depression and economic dislocation, coupled with a common antagonism toward the dominant business interests of the country. In addition, a sense of urgency and desperation infected large elements of the population. And, for Southerners, agricultural problems were among the most pressing and agrarian reform was at the center of much political and economic discussion.

Southern scholars began asking themselves why the New South historians had almost uniformly passed over the Populist revolt, as though it were some form of temporary aberration, best neglected and forgotten. Could it be that, in minimizing the significance of southern populism, previous historians had missed a key element in post-Reconstruction history? More important, could it be true that the harmonious structure of New South historiography, based on a general concept of unity, absence of conflict, and progress and reconciliation, might be dismantled by studies that exposed the proportions of the revolt against the New South regimes? Was the seething discontent of the nineties a reflection of agrarians struggling to maintain an old order, or did it represent a much more fundamental and comprehensive indictment of the power structure of the South? These and other questions were raised with

[1] The most recent edition of this textbook is William B. Hesseltine and David L. Smiley, *The South in American History* (Englewood Cliffs, N.J., 1960).

increasing frequency in a decade in which thoughtful men found much to condemn in their own generation.

The point here is that the most searching revisionist studies of the Redeemer era—the ones upon which our present view of the period has been built—were primarily studies of Populism and not of the Redeemer era itself. It is true, of course, that some important studies of Populism were written before the Depression. Alex M. Arnett's *The Populist Movement in Georgia* (New York, 1922) is a good example. And John D. Hicks's standard work, *The Populist Revolt,* was published in 1931 at the very beginning of the Depression. But the most important works, which fundamentally challenged the New South view of the Redeemers, appeared after the onset of the Depression. A selective listing of these studies would include Roscoe C. Martin, *The People's Party in Texas* (Austin, 1933); Daniel M. Robison, *Bob Taylor and the Agrarian Revolt in Tennessee* (Chapel Hill, 1935); William D. Sheldon, *Populism in the Old Dominion* (Princeton, 1935); articles by James A. Sharp on Populism in Tennessee, published in 1937 and 1938;[2] and articles by Kathryn T. Abbey on Florida, published in 1938;[3] Woodward, *Tom Watson* (1938); Francis B. Simkins, *Pitchfork Ben Tillman* (Baton Rouge, 1944); and Stuart Noblin, *Leonidas LaFayette Polk* (Chapel Hill, 1949).

The full impact of the revisionist departure was not apparent until 1951 when Professor Woodward, building on the new monographs and his own extensive research, published his *Origins of the New South.* It was the first general history of the post-Reconstruction South since Holland Thompson's brief volume of 1919 and the first detailed study since Bruce's work of 1905. Resemblances between the new and older works were difficult to find. Not only, of course, had Woodward written from a different perspective, but his skeptical, ironic approach to the materials was in direct contrast to the relatively uncomplicated and uncritical studies of the New South school. The results were generally devastating to the old tradition.

A significant clue to Woodward's approach was offered in a shorter book published earlier in the same year, *Reunion and Reaction,* a study of the Compromise of 1877 and the inauguration of the Redeemer regime. Its Beardian interpretation attacked the "Wormley House Bargain" legend

---

[2] "The Entrance of the Farmers' Alliance into Tennessee Politics," East Tennessee Historical Society *Publications,* No. 9 (1937), 77–92, and "The Farmers' Alliance and the People's Party in Tennessee," East Tennessee Historical Society *Publications.* No. 10 (1938), 91–113.

[3] Abbey, "Florida Versus the Principles of Populism, 1896–1911," *Journal of Southern History, IV* (November, 1948), 462–75.

and suggested that reunion was built, in large part, on a community of economic interests, with the Redeemers pledging support of nationalistic economic policies in return for economic aid to the South. Implicit in the settlement was an alliance of capitalists of the South and Northeast to preserve the status quo. Ironically agreeing with the New South historians that reunion was premised on the marriage of southern and northern capitalists, Woodward's revisionism lay in his assertion of the opportunistic and shortsighted motives that underlay the union.

Incorporating this interpretation in *Origins of the New South,* Woodward analyzed in detail the character of the Redeemer leadership, concluding that a high percentage of the new leaders were prewar Whigs, forced into the Democratic party because of the exigencies of white supremacy politics. Few, he found, came from the old planter class; nearly all, including most of those with agrarian connections, were oriented toward the commercial and industrial interests of the region. Redemption, then, was not a restoration of the old order but, rather, "a new phase of the revolutionary process begun in 1865. Only in a limited sense can it be properly called a 'counter-revolution.' "

In describing the policies of the Redeemers, Woodward differed in almost every respect from the New South historians. Retrenchment, hailed by the earlier scholars as an indication of realism, was regarded by Woodward as an abdication of social responsibility. But perhaps a more permanent injury, he wrote, "was the set of values imposed upon the Southern mind by the rationalization of this neglect." Equally devastating to the Redeemer reputation was the lengthy documentation of thievery in official places that marked the careers of many state administrations. Although finding that the stealing was less extensive than during the Reconstruction era, Woodward's history nonetheless tarnished another of the major claims made for the service of the Redeemers to their region.

In dissecting the anatomy of the "Solid South," Woodward cut away the shibboleths of white supremacy to reveal a politics of class and interest that cleverly exploited race and tradition to perpetuate its hold over the region. Detailing the mounting grievances of various anti-Redeemer elements within the South, he attributes the success of the one-party machines to Machiavellian techniques that had been perfected in the fight against the carpetbaggers. The result, at least until the Populist revolt, was political apathy and despair, "a period of political torpor more stultifying, perhaps, than any in . . . [the South's] long history."

But the New South promoters and the historians who followed in their tradition had not built their image of a triumphant South on a basis of political achievement alone. Political leaders, honest and loyal though they might have been, were regarded as benefactors of the region chiefly because they created the order and the atmosphere in which an industrial revolution could take place. Here Woodward does not equivocate in challenging completely the New South point of view. While conceding that the South, in many respects, did hold its own in rates of relative growth, he finds that, in absolute terms, the economic disparity between North and South increased, rather than decreased, during the period 1880–1900. Moreover—and here was the unkindest cut of all—the economy of the South became increasingly controlled by northern and other outside capitalists. The South, Woodward concluded, "was limited largely to the role of a producer of raw materials, a tributary of industrial powers, and an economy dominated by absentee owners." The unhappy result was "low wages, lack of opportunity, and poverty."[4]

• • •

Tracing the shifting interpretations of the Redeemer era, as attempted in this essay, raises a number of intriguing questions. Studying the original New South idea leads one to wonder why it had such appeal and persistence, what gave its spokesmen their persuasiveness and ability to deceive others as well as themselves, and why it aroused such enduring partisanship and antagonisms in contemporaries as well as in their descendants.

In trying to understand the New South historians, one feels almost as though they were looking through a powerful telescope. The background against which their histories were written heightened the contrasts and exaggerated the images they saw. They saw southern economic achievements against a scene of grinding poverty, increasing political power and self-determination against an experience of galling powerlessness, attempts at reconciliation against the legacy of hatred and mistrust, and concessions to the Negro against a backdrop of slavery and black codes. It is not surprising that in describing their region's attempt to don the mantle of the American heritage they were lured into admiring the emperor's new clothes. Today, the South's more cosmopolitan historians see the region's history silhouetted against American and world experience; and bitter southern memories are no longer so potent. The most thoroughgoing of the revisionists reveal New South claims in all their factitiousness and find the era that gave birth to them barren and stultifying. Like the child in Andersen's fairy tale, they look at the emperor and exclaim, "But he has got nothing on!"

It is thus clear that New South historians and revisionists alike have

---

[4] A discussion of recent writings at this point in the original essay has been omitted.—Ed.

shared a fundamental moral concern, a sense of the responsibility to judge, not simply describe, the past. In large measure, the "facts" upon which the changing interpretations have rested have not changed, but values have undergone a revolution. Thus, within the framework of their own value judgments, the earlier historians created an image of inspiration; later historians replaced it with a picture of near degradation. The trend of the future is uncertain. Increasing demand for detailed and impartial testing of current generalizations suggests that the next stage may involve less attention to ultimate meaning. On the other hand, the potent paradoxes and contrasts of the period itself will continue to confront historians with the perennial task of explaining the mentality of the era and the inheritance that it bequeathed.

3. The South and the Politics of Sectionalism

DEWEY W. GRANTHAM, JR.

In no area has southern sectionalism been more conspicuous than it has been in politics. The next essay, written by the editor of this volume and published here for the first time, sketches the dimensions of the South's political sectionalism during the last ninety years. It describes the ingredients of the Solid South, outlines the role of one-party politics both in the region and in its response to national issues, and examines the continuing clash between forces for southern unity and those moving in the opposite direction. The major thesis is that, despite internal conflicts and nationalizing pressures in southern politics, sectionalism has been and remains a major factor in political affairs below the Potomac. Once it became institutionalized, the one-party system was supported by the most powerful economic and social interests in the region. It was skillfully defended by politicians who ceaselessly identified the Democratic South with regional traditions, and who were able to perpetuate the system by taking advantage both of local prejudices and national pressures. Since the New Deal the nationalization of southern politics has proceeded rapidly, but the writer is cautious in speculating about any final erosion of the South's sectionalism.

T HE SOUTHERNER, WE ARE FREQUENTLY REMINDED, IS A PECULIAR man in a peculiar land. The extent of his peculiarity as an American has doubtless been exaggerated, but few people would deny that for well over a century now the South has provided the most striking example of particularism in our national experience. It was inevitable, of course, that sectional rivalries would develop in a country as large and diversified as the United States, and sectionalism has been a major theme of the nation's political history. "In domestic politics," wrote the late V. O. Key, "sectionalism represents a sort of sublimated foreign war in which one part of the country acts as a unit against the rest of the nation."[1] New England, the Middle Atlantic States, the South, the Old Northwest, the Great Plains, and other broad provinces west of the Mississippi River at one time or another have assumed a conspicuous character in the sectional typology of American politics. But the South is the great exemplar of modern sectionalism.

Certain aspects of the South's political solidarity need to be noted at the outset. In the first place, southern sectionalism has seldom been incompatible with American nationalism. It is significant that the sectional rivalry engendered by economic and cultural differences was conducted, except for the great controversy of the 1850s and the resort to war in the 1860s, within the framework of a common nationalism. Southerners have always shared with other Americans the essential features of the national culture, and the seeming paradox of continuing sectionalism in a republic steadily growing in homogeneity is to be explained by the fact that acute conflicts of interest may be generated within an integrated culture.[2]

A second consideration is that historically southern sectionalism has been greatly influenced by the nature of the federal system on the one hand, and by chronic threats of internal division on the other. If undesirable federal policies adopted at the behest of nonsouthern regions encouraged the political unification of the South, the federal structure of government and party politics also tempered sectional recalcitrance and promoted a degree of national involvement. It was the federal

[1] V. O. Key, Jr., with the assistance of Alexander Heard, *Southern Politics in State and Nation* (New York, 1949), p. 15.
[2] David M. Potter, "The Historian's Use of Nationalism and Vice Versa," *American Historical Review, LXVII* (July, 1962), 924–950.

system that made possible alliances of southern spokesmen with conservatives from other regions, as well as the South's great influence in the Democratic party and its administrations in Washington. Moreover, the changing character of federalism has inevitably affected the politics of sectionalism. Whether the federal government represented intervention at the state and local levels or whether it became the source of appropriations and welfare legislation which state and local governments could not or would not provide, the growing authority of the central government relentlessly nationalized the politics of all regions, even though it frequently generated new waves of sectional dissent in the process.

At the same time, the South's political response has depended upon internal requirements for solidarity. These have not always been easily satisfied. Indeed, the contending groups spawned by the South's social structure and geography have been a continuing obstacle to the region's political unity. Recurrent social and economic cleavages have been present in virtually all southern political crises—in the interparty competition of the Old South, in the struggle over secession and southern independence, in the agrarian upheaval of the eighties and nineties, and in the factionalism of southern politics in the twentieth century.[3] No matter how assiduously they played upon the themes of race and tradition, the advocates of sectional solidarity were never able to impose sufficient unity on the white majority to override its internal divisions for very long.

This suggests a third point that should be emphasized in an interpretation of modern southern sectionalism: the forging of the Solid South took much pulling and hauling and its completion required the better part of a generation after the Redemption of the seventies. For one thing, Republicanism did not disappear from the scene in 1877. Nor was Republicanism the only threat to the Bourbon Democrats and southern unity. Almost from the beginning Democratic leaders were faced with intraparty dissension and the emergence of independent movements that held out the dreaded possibility of a merger with the Republicans and a transfer of political control. The greatest challenge of all came in the agrarian revolt of the 1890s. This crisis was not unlike the secession crisis in that the black belts and their allies overcame their opponents and used the specter of insurgency as a means of suppressing future nonconformity. But the situation in the 1890s differed in several respects from that of the 1860s, and the outcome of the later crisis revealed the possibility of greater sectional cohesion. For one thing, most men of Whiggish persuasion had joined the Democratic party by the 1880s,

[3] For an analysis of this factor and other "democratic" components of southern politics, see Dewey W. Grantham, Jr., *The Democratic South* (Athens, Ga., 1963).

giving that party overwhelming ascendancy among the most affluent and influential people of the region. In addition to their control of the black belts, the historic centers of southern wealth and power, Bourbon leaders found support in river towns and piedmont industrial centers, whose spokesmen represented the commercial and bourgeois elements associated with the "New South" movement. Moreover, the black-belt politicians strengthened their position through disproportionate representation in legislatures and party conventions, and through astute use of Negro votes and alliances. Yeoman farmers and ordinary workingmen, usually supporters of the Democratic party, were unable to exert much political influence.

Furthermore, the economic privation and cultural neglect of the southern masses fostered a mood of hopelessness and political apathy. Writing in 1889, a critical and informed Virginian described the South as a backward land—a land of wretched poverty for "the six millions of Negroes who are in the depths of indigence," as well as 90 percent of the whites who had "nothing beyond the commonest necessaries of life," if that.[4] The commanding influence of the plantation element and the rising commercial interests in an environment of minimum government and niggardly appropriations rendered the small farmers and lower classes generally almost impotent. In such an atmosphere political independence and experimentation were not likely to flourish.

Meanwhile, the shining vision of the Old South, the romantic cult of the Lost Cause, and the mythology growing up around Radical Reconstruction were infusing the folklore of the southern whites and erecting another support for the Solid South in politics. "We may say," observes Robert Penn Warren, "that only at the moment when Lee handed Grant his sword was the Confederacy born; or to state matters another way, in the moment of death the Confederacy entered upon its immortality."[5] Southern white unity was also enormously strengthened by the Redeemers' version of Reconstruction, a grim story of human suffering and of the southern battle for civilization. The folklore that helped sustain the Solid South was filled with mystic overtones of white unity and heroic sacrifice in that earlier time of trial and tribulation. The emotional attachment to the idea of "the South," constantly reinforced by vague memories, family tales, and endless rhetoric in public places, produced

[4] Lewis H. Blair, *A Southern Prophecy: The Prosperity of the South Dependent Upon the Elevation of the Negro (1889)*, ed. C. Vann Woodward (Boston and Toronto, 1964), p. xxix.

[5] Warren, *The Legacy of the Civil War: Meditations on the Centennial* (New York, 1961), p. 15.

what was surely one of the most remarkable loyalties in American history. Its rationale that was to explain and justify "southern" politics was itself transmuted into a set of trusted political principles: state rights, economy in government, southern unity, and distrust of active government, especially in Washington.

Finally, there was the Negro. With the abolition of the Negro as property, Cash has noted, "the road stood all but wide open to the ignoble hate and cruel itch to take him in hand which for so long had been festering impotently in the poor whites."[6] The temptation to draw the color line and to make the Negro the scapegoat grew with every challenge to the precarious white solidarity of the post-Reconstruction years. Ironically, even when insurgent movements such as the Readjusters in Virginia during the early eighties and the fusionists in North Carolina during the nineties brought the Negro some gains, they served further to embitter the whites against him and to coerce white unity for the future.[7] And the Populists, who seemed on the verge of shattering the incipient solidarity of the region, constantly faced, in Professor Woodward's phrase, "the implacable dogmas of racism, white solidarity, white supremacy, and the bloody shirt."[8]

In withstanding the assaults of the Populists the Solid South had become institutionalized. Yet the significance of the Populist movement in the history of southern politics is not always appreciated. It invigorated the region's politics and brought into sharp relief longtime cleavages which the Redeemers had never been able to suppress completely. It brought to the surface for a moment a vigorous strain of radicalism long submerged in the stream of southern politics, led to a revival of Jeffersonian and Jacksonian principles, popularized the concept of positive government, and challenged the "New South" system and the mythology that helped uphold it. It left the region a constructive heritage, but it also contributed to the quickening pace of Negro disfranchisement and in the end served the needs of southern sectionalism.

The most distinctive attribute of political affairs in the South at the turn of the century was the overwhelming domination of the Democratic party. While in the upper South Republicanism remained strong enough to exert some influence on the practices of the majority party, the Democrats dominated state government in every commonwealth except

[6] Wilbur J. Cash, *The Mind of the South* (New York, 1941), p. 113.

[7] Helen G. Edmonds, *The Negro and Fusion Politics in North Carolina, 1894–1901* (Chapel Hill, 1951); Charles E. Wynes, *Race Relations in Virginia, 1870–1902* (Charlottesville, 1961).

[8] C. Vann Woodward, *The Burden of Southern History* (Baton Rouge, 1960), p. 150.

Kentucky, which came closest of all southern states to having a genuine two-party system.[9] The structure of political solidarity created by war and Reconstruction and made more inflexible by the divisions of the 1890s proved impervious to the solvent of independent party action in this period.

The Solid South was patently real in terms of the region's Democratic loyalties. Yet the South soon entered upon an era of almost unparalleled intraparty competition. One thing that stimulated this factionalism was the continued agitation of agrarian reform groups. Populist principles survived to leaven the factional politics of the early twentieth-century South, while the leadership of William Jennings Bryan and the Populist program strengthened the liberal wing of the Democratic party in most southern states. Paradoxically, at the same time that constitutional changes and new election laws were disfranchising Negroes and making it more and more difficult for Republicans to offer any real opposition, the adoption of the direct primary and other democratic devices encouraged ambitious politicians who could see little hope of advancing in the established hierarchies to launch insurgent movements within the Democratic party.

Another invigorating ingredient in this era was the growing influence of southern cities and the activities of an increasing number of middle-class men and women interested in civic reforms, humanitarian causes, and "good government." In addition, the enhanced stakes of public policy at the state and municipal levels promoted the political involvement of numerous economic groups—corporations, shippers, farmers, and labor organizations—determined to protect or advance their interests through state action. Also significant was the movement, in which the South played a vital role, to nominate the Virginian Woodrow Wilson for the presidency. The Wilson movement served to give the liberal factions a kind of national base and temporarily to sharpen the bifactional politics that had been developing in the South. Wilson's election also gave new pride and satisfaction to millions of Southerners, and the South assumed an influence in Washington it had not enjoyed since the 1850s.

All of these forces contributed to the widespread and rather durable bifactionalism that characterized the politics of southern states during the first two decades of the twentieth century. In a vague and imperfect way these contending factions separated progressives from conservatives, advocates of change from champions of the status quo, and politicians

---

[9] The only other southern state to elect a Republican governor between 1900 and 1918 was Tennessee, in 1910 and 1912, and that occurred only because of a bitter conflict within the Democratic party.

who appealed to the white masses from those who were supported by the "machines" and vested interests. But if factional competition within the one-party system was vigorous and if the progressive currents ran stronger in the South than is sometimes realized, it was nevertheless true that southern sectionalism lost little of its vitality and for the most part managed to assimilate the threats to its integrity, whether they were internal or external in origin. Although an extraordinary amount of competition existed in intraparty politics during the progressive era, and this competition reflected the historic divisions and changing character of southern society, it should not be supposed that this condition approximated a two-party system. The extent and significance of such intraparty division varied from state to state and from time to time, always subject to the vagaries of the amorphous and highly personalized politics resulting from the dominance of a single party. In such politics there were no effective means to recruit and train leaders and no reliable restraints to preserve factional discipline and program coherence for any length of time.

The war years diluted the bifactionalism of the earlier period, swept many of the old leaders from the scene, and brought other changes in state and local government. But the old factionalism did not entirely disappear. Toward the end of the 1920s the latent class conflict in Louisiana provided the setting for Huey P. Long, whose leadership brought a durable and well-disciplined bifactional system into existence. At about the same time the emergence of powerful new leaders in several other states, including Edward H. Crump in Tennessee, Harry Flood Byrd in Virginia, and Eugene Talmadge in Georgia, created fresh intraparty patterns that were to survive for decades. But whatever the politics in individual states, the passing years brought no real threat to the one-party system. The danger of outside intervention was virtually nonexistent, though it was a note often heard in campaign rhetoric. Meanwhile, one-party politics provided an outlet, however vicarious, for the lowliest white Southerner as well as his most influential neighbor.

The democratization of the white South around the turn of the century may have energized one-party politics, but it also contributed to the orchestration of sectional themes under the direction of demagogues and charlatans. The excesses and irrelevancies of such leaders were perhaps evidence of the difficulties they faced in attempting to break the political domination of the vested interests, especially in the lower South. While these "men of the people" helped give politics in the South whatever form and coherence it possessed, while they evoked a fierce loyalty from their supporters and doubtless acted as a "safety valve for discontent," they tended to bring forth, as Cash said of Coleman L. Blease, "the whole tradition of extravagance, of sectionalism and Negrophobia in Southern politics."[10]

The demagogues received much of their support from the rural South, which by the 1920s was assuming a more negative role in the region's politics than during the Populist and progressive periods. The political and social influence of the county-seat governing class (there were more than a thousand counties in the South in 1900) remained extraordinarily great; in most southern states no statewide political campaign and no important legislation could succeed without approval from these citadels of power. On the other hand, the widening rural-urban cleavage reflected the mounting fears and suspicions of the southern farmer, and men like Tom Watson, in V. O. Key's words, "turned the towns into whipping boys."[11] It was the rise of the city and the farmer's relative decline that caused many rural inhabitants to concentrate their reform energies on prohibition, religious fundamentalism, and cultural conformity. And it was these issues that precipitated the sharpest sectional conflict in the era of normalcy. The political outlines of this conflict were evident in the protracted struggle in the Democratic National Convention of 1924.

While the rural Deep South rebelled against the growing influence of the urban, Catholic, and "wet" East in the Democratic party, the Republican victories that disrupted the Solid South in 1928 occurred in the rim states of Virginia, North Carolina, Kentucky, Tennessee, Florida, Texas, and Oklahoma. The black belts and the areas of strongest rural, prohibition, and Protestant sentiment generally tended to support Alfred E. Smith in spite of their fears of his religion and leadership. Republican successes in 1928 came in those states with relatively few Negroes, traditional Republican strength, and economic interests that pulled them toward national integration.[12] In general these states were undergoing the most rapid economic and social change in the region. The "business progressivism" of the twenties manifested in many state capitols and the moderate increase in southern Republicanism in presidential elections

[10] Cash, *op. cit.*, p. 248.
[11] Key, *op. cit.*, p. 118.
[12] *Ibid.*, pp. 317–329. In his perceptive analysis of this election in the South, V. O. Key observes that "The whites of the black-belt counties were bound in loyalty to the Democracy by a common tradition and anxiety about the Negro. Whites elsewhere could afford the luxury of voting their convictions on the religious and prohibition issues." But he also notes that "A complex of factors—ruralism, cotton-growing, plantation organization, intense Reconstruction memories —as well as anxieties about the racial equilibrium characterized the Democratic areas." *Ibid.*, pp. 319, 329.

reflected these economic and demographic developments.[13] But the onset of the Great Depression, the election of Franklin D. Roosevelt in 1932, and the popularity of the New Deal destroyed any hopes the Republicans had of building on the southern defections of 1928. Republicanism in the region dropped during the thirties to the lowest levels since the Civil War.

The Wilson administration had earlier demonstrated how even a liberal Democratic regime in Washington might increase the South's attachment to the Democratic party. While Wilson's administration contributed to the liberalization of southern politics and tended to involve southern politicians in national affairs, it did not seriously challenge the South's political unity. Wilson discovered that it was necessary to cooperate with conservatives from the South in order to enact his legislative program, and the result in many instances was to strengthen the intrenched elements in the region at the expense of those challenging the status quo.[14] White Southerners in general, moreover, found much in the Wilson program to applaud and little that threatened the institutions and ideas that sustained the Solid South.

Franklin D. Roosevelt's leadership and program tended to broaden and nationalize the outlook of southern congressmen, forced New Deal issues into state and local political contests, and threatened the South's traditional social and economic structure far more than had the Wilson administration. Yet the section's response to Roosevelt and the New Deal was ambivalent. Southerners were "so painfully in need of succor," as Frank Freidel has said, "that they desperately sought federal aid; yet the New Deal inevitably threatened to upset the status quo and alter some of the cherished institutions upon which they fervently believed the very existence of Southern civilization depended."[15] At the same time, Roosevelt found it necessary to make concessions to southern leaders in Congress, who once more dominated committee chairmanships and exerted great influence on all parliamentary matters.[16] Although the

[13] For an able interpretation of progressive currents in the South during the 1920s, see George B. Tindall, "Business Progressivism: Southern Politics in the Twenties," *South Atlantic Quarterly*, LXII (Winter, 1963), 92–106.

[14] On this point see Arthur S. Link, "Woodrow Wilson and the Democratic Party," *Review of Politics*, XVIII (April, 1956), 146–156.

[15] Freidel, *F.D.R. and the South* (Baton Rouge, 1965), p. 35.

[16] According to James MacGregor Burns, Roosevelt was "the prisoner of the concessions he had made to the regulars—especially Southern Democrats—in gaining the nomination. He had recognized and hence strengthened conservative Democrats in Congress who had gone along with his program." Burns, *The Deadlock of Democracy: Four-Party Politics in America* (Spectrum edition, Englewood Cliffs, N.J., 1963), p. 173.

In the Seventy-third Congress (1933–1935) Southerners held nine of the fourteen

economic conservatism of these men led them increasingly to criticize the President and to vote against his proposals, there was no open break in the ranks of southern Democracy.[17] Roosevelt's growing preoccupation with the gathering war in Europe, the stimulus the war gave to southern patriotism and internationalism, and the mounting prosperity and economic development of the early 1940s combined to moderate southern discontent with parts of the New Deal. Depression, New Deal, and World War II had brought vast changes to all of America but, on the surface at least, the South's political solidarity seemed almost as great when the war ended as it had been at the dawn of the century.[18]

Perhaps it was fortuitous that just at this time a major study of southern politics should be getting under way at the University of Alabama, supported by a grant from the Rockefeller Foundation.[19] This project resulted in the publication of V. O. Key's magisterial volume, *Southern Politics in State and Nation* (1949), the most systematic and searching analysis of "the electoral process in the South" ever undertaken. For the student of southern political history one of the most valuable aspects of this remarkable book is the fact that it examined southern regional unity at its strongest, or at least before the crevices in the walls of the Solid South had become readily visible. For that reason it provides a convenient summary of all the factors which over the years had become institutionalized in the old order.

Key demonstrated that, three-quarters of a century after the end of Reconstruction, race and the position of the Negro dominated southern politics; the Negro question continued to suppress any meaningful political divisions among Southerners. Key showed that the areas of greatest Negro population and fertile soil—the black belts—had long served as the backbone of southern conservatism. He showed how the black counties in a state like Alabama allied themselves with the "big mules" of Birmingham and Mobile to dominate the state's politics, and how these elements used the South's strategic position in Congress, and particularly in the Senate, to promote political regionalism and prevent federal meddling

---

major standing committee chairmanships in the Senate and twelve of seventeen such chairmanships in the House. *Official Congressional Directory,* 73 Cong., 1 Sess. (Washington, 1933), pp. 175–180, 191–203.

[17] For evidence of southern disillusionment with Roosevelt and for the origins of the so-called southern Democratic-Republican coalition, see John Robert Moore, "Senator Josiah W. Bailey and the 'Conservative Manifesto' of 1937," *Journal of Southern History,* XXXI (February, 1965), 21–39.

[18] For the persistence of southern sectionalism, see Fletcher M. Green, "Resurgent Southern Sectionalism, 1933–1955," *North Carolina Historical Review.* XXXIII (April, 1956), 222–240.

[19] See Roscoe C. Martin's Foreword to Key, *op. cit.,* pp. v–viii.

that might threaten their control. The greatest cohesive factor among southern congressmen was "a common determination to oppose external intervention in matters of race relations."[20]

Despite the persistence of mountain Republicanism in Virginia, North Carolina, and Tennessee and a perceptible increase of Republican voting in presidential elections in such states as Texas, Florida, and Arkansas, Key noted the general continuation of the ancient prejudice against the Republican party. Although Republicans were strong enough in the upper South to force a measure of discipline and continuity on the majority party, they operated everywhere under serious handicaps. They were confronted with Democratic control of voting procedures, discrimination in the apportionment of legislatures, and congressional gerrymandering. In addition, the infrequency with which Republican primaries, candidates, and campaigns were offered limited the appeal of the party. Even had Republican leaders sought to attract a larger numbers of voters, on many issues they would have had to adopt positions out of line with the conservative state governments provided by the Democrats and with their own party's national conventions. Most southern Republicans did not really want to win elections, except in restricted local areas.[21]

As for the Democratic party in most southern states, Key described it as "merely a holding-company for a congeries of transient squabbling factions, most of which fail by far to meet the standards of permanence, cohesiveness, and responsibility that characterize the political party."[22] Whether the dominant party reflected the bifactionalism of Senator Harry Flood Byrd's Virginia or Florida's atomized "every man for himself" structure or some in-between position, one looked in vain for a continuing statewide organization with a recognizable program. Whether the basic conflict of the state's internal politics involved a clash of disparate geographic sections, the existence of a state machine, factions led by colorful personalities, a modified class politics, or a general free-for-all, the characteristic political system operated within a framework of limited suffrage, a low level of voter participation, the repression of meaningful issues, and the isolation of the South from presidential campaigns. While the white primaries were under mounting legal and political attack, they had been invaded by relatively few Negroes, and the restricted white electorates were guarded by the poll tax (in seven states) and a host of other suffrage qualifications. Rural dominance was widely apparent, made all the more incongruous by a substantial farm population too

---

[20] Key, op. cit., p. 352.

[21] "They have been big fish in little ponds and they have liked it." Alexander Heard, A Two-Party South? (Chapel Hill, 1952), p. 97.

[22] Key, op. cit., p. 16.

depressed to play any part in the political process, on the one hand, and powerful commercial farmers who dominated the American Farm Bureau Federation and allied themselves with business interests, on the other. And while growing industrialization and urbanization had brought new concerts of political power in the form of organized business, they had not introduced the urban masses to the practices of democracy. In contrast to the multiplicity of factions in state politics, the Democratic party in national politics was the Solid South, the instrument for conducting the region's "foreign relations" with the rest of the nation. "The suffrage problems of the South," concluded Professor Key, "can claim a closer kinship with those of India, of South Africa, or of the Dutch East Indies than with those of, say, Minnesota."[23]

While demonstrating the impressive continuity of southern sectionalism, Key seemed to find, in the region's recurring intraparty factionalism and particularly in the New Deal's impact, the promise of more rapid political change in the coming years. This acceleration would be the consequence of vast economic and social alterations clearly evident at the time Key wrote, and of the increasing intervention by the national government in the region's affairs. The forces of change, whether originating in impersonal economic factors or in the nation's new federalism, would inevitably upset—perhaps were already upsetting—the balance-of-power enclaves that had long prevailed in the southern states. And when that equilibrium was threatened, the champions of the status quo turned almost instinctively to the race question, the touchstone of white solidarity.

The year before the publication of *Southern Politics* the Truman administration's civil rights program and the forthright civil rights platform adopted by the Democratic National Convention precipitated the first sharp reaction. The Dixiecrat movement of 1948, which repudiated the Democratic ticket and carried four Deep South states, provided the southern unifiers with an opportunity for a kind of reconnoitering venture.[24] In 1948 they could scarcely have perceived the full potentialities of sectional defiance and southern white unity that eventually would be available to them. That came with the *Brown v. Topeka* decision in 1954 and the crisis that slowly built up during the years that followed. Since

---

[23] *Ibid.*, p. 661.

[24] The Dixiecrat movement gathered most of its strength from racial fears, though some Southerners found in it a means of expressing their hostility toward New Deal and Fair Deal economic policies without having to embrace Republicanism. See William G. Carleton, "The Fate of Our Fourth Party," *Yale Review*, XXXVIII (Spring, 1949), 449–459; Sarah McCulloh Lemmon, "The Ideology of the 'Dixiecrat' Movement," *Social Forces*, XXX (December, 1951), 162–171; and Emile B. Ader, "Why the Dixiecrats Failed," *Journal of Politics*, XV (August, 1953), 356–369.

1954, writes C. Vann Woodward, the South "has been more deeply alienated and thoroughly defiant than it has at any time since 1877." Tormented by a "minority psychology and rejection anxiety," it has been "reliving an old trauma." All of the old fears seemed suddenly to be realized in a kind of Frankenstein created for the South by unknowing and uncaring fellow Americans: "Negroes at the ballot boxes, federal bayonets in the streets, a rebirth of scalawags, a new invasion of carpetbaggers, and battalions of abolitionists and Yankee schoolmarms in the form of Freedom Riders and sit-ins and CORE and SNCC and COFO." In such a situation a besieged minority "could not afford the luxury of internal division."[25]

The old defense mechanism was quickly set in motion. The black belts and other traditional centers of southern unity reached out to solidify white sentiment in surrounding areas. In these subregions and throughout the Deep South the race question became the overriding issue in politics. Southern recalcitrance manifested itself in talk of nullification and "interposition," in "massive resistance," in a "Southern Manifesto" and lengthy southern filibusters in Congress, in tickets of unpledged presidential electors, in popular acclaim of a new group of Dixie firebrands, and in defeat of political leaders who offered any opposition to the program of resistance. So obsessed were southern legislatures with questions of race that by the end of 1956 no fewer than 106 prosegregation measures had been adopted in the eleven ex-Confederate states, and the legislative defiance continued without letup.[26] Meanwhile, the burgeoning White Citizens' Councils spread across the South, joined by a score of other voluntary defense organizations. Fiery crosses lit up the skies, schools and churches were bombed, and resistance in the Deep South reached the proportions of an insurrection. The moderation of the old-style paternalists was overwhelmed by the rampant Negrophobia—and the Gavin Stevenses surrendered to the Snopeses.[27] A sinister malaise rolled like a heavy fog over the land, bringing widespread racial estrangement, intimi-

[25] C. Vann Woodward, "From the First Reconstruction to the Second," *Harper's Magazine*, CCXXX (April, 1965), 128–129.

[26] For a survey of southern resistance, see Benjamin Muse, *Ten Years of Prelude: The Story of Integration Since the Supreme Court's 1954 Decision* (New York, 1964). By 1964, reported a writer for the Southern Regional Council, the number of laws enacted by southern legislatures to circumvent desegregation had reached 379. Margaret Long, "The Dream—Ten Years Later," *The Progressive*, XXVIII (May, 1964), 21–22. See also *Southern School News*, X (May, 1964), 1B.

[27] The ironic denouement of this tragedy, writes Walker Percy, was that "the Compsons and Sartorises should not only be defeated by the Snopeses but that in the end they should join them." Percy, "Mississippi: The Fallen Paradise," *Harper's Magazine*, CCXXX (April, 1965), 167.

dation of Negroes, and in some states an intellectual blockade that rivaled that of the 1850s.[28]

This was more than a matter of race. A good deal of the South's mass political protest was an expression of resentments and fears originating in stagnant and declining areas. In a more general way southern protest in the fifties and sixties was intensified because the region was propelled almost overnight into an urbanized and industrialized age. The resulting tensions produced political uncertainty, reinforced southern conservatism, and stimulated the nostalgia for traditional values and symbols.[29]

Many well-meaning Southerners rallied to the defense of the "southern way of life," and it was apparent that the old sectional shibboleths retained much of their magic. Yet there was an element of unreality, of parody, in the appeal to hallowed traditions of former years. Take the survival of the Confederate legend. "This legend," remarks Denis W. Brogan, "is now less an heroic memory than poison in the blood; it recalls less Chancellorsville, or even Nashville, than Oxford, Mississippi, with Ross Barnett as the poor man's Jefferson Davis."[30] If southern resistance to internal change and national conformity parodied the traditions which in an earlier day contributed to regional solidarity, it was also characterized by a foreknowledge of defeat that differed in a profound way from the expectations of the past. For however frenzied their defiance and however exhilarated they might have been during moments of tactical triumph, Southerners were not really hopeful. They did not expect to win. In a sense the South was only playing a role, a role to which it had long been accustomed. The classic pattern of that role, according to

[28] One feature of this resistance was a vigorous effort in several states of the lower South to restrict Negro participation in politics by tightening voter registration laws and purging the voter lists. In many instances the local registrars who applied these measures hardly needed additional weapons to discriminate against prospective Negro voters. See, for example, Joseph L. Bernd and Lynwood M. Holland, "Recent Restrictions Upon Negro Suffrage: The Case of Georgia," *Journal of Politics*, XXI (August, 1959), 487–513. The voting rights legislation of 1965 was designed to counter these disfranchising tactics.

[29] The South's emergence as the section most strongly opposed to foreign aid and most other "international" programs in Congress seems to be a political manifestation of the fears and uncertainties produced by these social and economic changes. There is a decided correlation between the areas of strongest southern "unilateralism" and those most concerned with race politics. See Charles O. Lerche, Jr., "Southern Congressmen and the 'New Isolationism,'" *Political Science Quarterly*, LXXV (September, 1960), 321–337, and *The Uncertain South: Its Changing Patterns of Politics in Foreign Policy* (Chicago, 1964).

[30] Brogan, "The Impending Crisis of the Deep South," *Harper's Magazine*, CCXXX (April, 1965), 148.

Joseph Margolis, was fixed far back in the section's history. It was a role "involving open and organized antagonism construed as the devoted defense of principle, defeat construed as invasion, moral criticism construed as the imposition of penalties, and finally continuing loyalty to a lost cause construed as the solidarity of a cultured and homogeneous people in occupation."[31]

Champions of the status quo and of southern political unity could find little reassurance in the changes in the region's politics since World War II. In desperation they themselves set the example of disrupting the Democratic South in 1948 through third-party action, and many of them eventually shifted to the Republican party. The 1950s brought the two-party system in presidential elections to the South; in presidential elections since 1948, every southern state except Arkansas and North Carolina voted Republican at least once. In the meantime, southern influence in the Democratic party continued to decline, and southern congressmen were repeatedly unable to prevent the passage of civil rights legislation which the national party had recommended. Negro voting in most southern states became an important new factor in political life, and in the early 1960s the reapportionment of state legislatures set in motion by the federal courts foretold a drastic shift in the locus of political power in state government. In one way or another all of these developments threatened the old-time southern sectionalism.

But if the Solid South had disappeared in presidential contests and if the currents of southern politics were being altered by rapid social and economic changes, it was still possible in the mid-sixties to speak of political sectionalism below the Potomac. In the nation's political arithmetic the South remained a significant factor. Except in a few scattered localities, the Republican party had not seriously challenged the intrenched Democrats at the congressional, state, and local levels.[32] Most Southerners continued to think of themselves as Democrats. As late as 1961, 60 percent of the white respondents in a survey carried out by Professors Donald R. Matthews and James W. Prothro characterized themselves

[31] Margolis, "The Role of the Segregationist," *AAUP Bulletin, XLIII* (December, 1957), 610–614.

[32] In 1965 the thirteen southern states had only 3 Republican Senators and 18 Republican Representatives (out of 119) in Congress. Oklahoma had the only Republican Governor in the region. Although every southern state legislature had at least one Republican member, the total number of Republicans in the region's thirteen legislatures was only 44 senators and 137 representatives. See *Congressional Quarterly Weekly Report, XXII* (November 6, 1964), 2644, and *ibid.* (November 20, 1964), 2709.

as Democrats, as compared with 14 percent who thought of themselves as Republicans.[33]

The tangled skein of traditional loyalties, institutionalized inertia, and vested interests make it difficult for Republicans to extend their challenge below the presidential level. Considerations involving offices and patronage restrain many politicians from leaving the Democratic party; local political elites are naturally determined to maintain their control;[34] and favorable public policies and beneficial concessions often dampen the desire of businessmen for change.[35] The disproportionate power of rural areas and the lack of organization among industrial and urban masses facilitate the domination of state and local government by business interests and other conservative elements. The result is that the most affluent and powerful Southerners, many of whom have long criticized Democratic policies emanating from Washington, find little reason to complain about state and local policies. Nor have they been inclined to support Republican candidates for Congress.

Many Southerners think of the Democratic party in terms of its southern and congressional wing. Southerners constitute the bulwark of what James M. Burns describes as the congressional Democratic party, "the John Garner-Howard Smith-Harry Byrd-John McClellan congressional Democrats" in contrast to "the Roosevelt-Truman-Stevenson-Kennedy presidential Democrats."[36] The typical southern congressman is a conservative, and his powerful position makes him both a source of federal money and an effective instrument in the fight against the national party's liberalism. Southern congressional influence is reflected in the

[33] Matthews and Prothro, "Southern Images of Political Parties: An Analysis of White and Negro Attitudes," in Avery Leiserson (ed.), *The American South in the 1960's* (New York, 1964), p. 84.

[34] The political power and patronage at the courthouse level in such a state as Texas (with 254 counties) is a weighty factor in resisting change and perpetuating the one-party system.

[35] In Arkansas, for example, the utilities, bankers (some of whom have the use of state deposits without paying any interest), wholesale and retail liquor dealers (who benefit from a fair trade law and guaranteed markups), the American Farm Bureau Federation, and local officials like the county judges (who oppose stringent state regulation of purchases) all act as a drag on positive government at the state level.

[36] Burns, *op. cit.*, pp. 197, 200. "The congressional Democratic leaders," writes Burns (p. 316), "have an ideal strategy: they can oppose the presidential Democrats in elections and in Washington, all the while benefiting by the victories of liberal congressmen in the North, who will return to Washington to form a coalition in Congress with the congressional Democrats so that the latter may retain their chairmanships and their control of Congress." For Burns's analysis of the southern influence, see *ibid.*, 271–274, 311–316.

fact that in the current Congress Southerners serve as chairmen of ten of the sixteen standing committees in the Senate and thirteen of twenty such committees in the House.[37] The so-called "conservative coalition" of southern Democrats and Republicans is still an important force in Congress. Southern Democrats and northern Democrats took opposing stands on 24 percent of the 1964 session's roll-call votes on such issues as foreign policy, civil rights, welfare programs, and reapportionment. Although the conservative coalition was evident on only 15 percent of the roll-call votes that year, it had appeared on 28 percent as recently as 1961.[38]

The politics of race, as might be expected, continues to inhibit a more realistic division among Southerners and to perpetuate sectional attitudes and practices. It has been the principal factor in frustrating the liberal inclinations of a sizable group of southern congressmen. In the Deep South the consequences of intense Negrophobia included both the Dixiecrat successes of 1948 and the Goldwater victories of 1964, in addition to a virtual monopoly of state politics. The "New Know Nothingism" went far to gloss over the economic and social cleavages in these states and to impede the halting process of political transformation. Small white farmers and members of labor unions frequently succumbed to the blandishments of racist demagogues, and in some areas yesterday's liberalism became today's reactionary politics.

In Alabama the old regional factionalism rapidly receded as the northern and southeastern parts of the state joined the black belt in their racial apprehension.[39] In Louisiana, where the electorate had long tended

[37] In addition Southerners serve as chairmen of the Select Committee on Small Business in both houses and as Democratic Whip and secretary of the Democratic Conference in the Senate. *Official Congressional Directory,* 89 Cong., 1 Sess. (Washington, 1965), 243–247, 255–263. In the Eighty-fourth Congress (1955–1957) Southerners held eight of thirteen standing committee chairmanships in the Senate and ten of fifteen in the House. *Ibid.,* 84 Cong., 1 Sess. (Washington, 1955), 207–211, 217–223.

[38] In 1961 the coalition won almost 50 percent of these votes in the Senate and 70 percent in the House. See "On Conservative Coalition," *Congressional Quarterly Weekly Report,* XIX (November 3, 1961), 1796–1805; " 'Conservative Coalition' Appeared on 15% of Roll Calls," *ibid.,* XXII (November 27, 1964), 2741–2750; and "Democrats from North and South Split on 24% of Votes," *ibid.* (December 25, 1964), 2835–2840.

[39] The penalities of being "hoisted on one's own rhetoric" in a politics of race is well put by Everett C. Hughes: "To be elected to office a man declares that he will resist racial change to the death; thus he has made compromise, the essence of politics, impossible. If he retreats, he will be destroyed, politically and perhaps in other ways by the extremists whose cause he has espoused." Hughes, "The Sociological Point of View," in Robert B. Highsaw (ed.), *The Deep South in Transformation: A Symposium* (University, Ala., 1964), p. 72.

to divide along class lines based on economic issues, the race question disrupted the South's most durable and ideological bifactionalism; the northern hill parishes, stronghold of the Long faction, eschewed economic concerns in order to concentrate on race.[40] In Georgia the old intraparty cleavage disintegrated under the impact of the race issue, the effects of the county-unit system, and the emergence of Herman Talmadge as the state's dominant political leader.[41] Even in Texas, where racial matters are relatively unimportant, the race issue inhibited the natural tendency of East Texas politicians to support liberal policies. Meanwhile, Virginia and Arkansas succumbed to the politics of race, showing that the virus of political racism was not limited to the lower South. In some states outside of the Deep South the civil rights movement brought a reaction that hurt liberal candidates. While the passage of comprehensive civil rights legislation has freed southern congressmen in some respects, they remain acutely sensitive in this area, always ready to rally to the defense of the "southern" position.[42]

• • •

The course of southern sectionalism since Reconstruction can be roughly divided into three phases. During the first, from the 1870s to the end of the century, regional unity was still being forged. Despite the declining threat of federal intervention, Republicanism remained significant in many areas, and independent movements reflecting longtime social and geographic divisions disrupted the one-party harmony. In turning back

[40] The religious issue has also been a factor in recent Louisiana politics, separating the Protestant parishes of the north from the Catholic parishes of the south. A Catholic candidate ran strongly in the Democratic gubernatorial primary in 1960 and 1964, in addition to John F. Kennedy's appearance on the national ticket in 1960. Race and religion may well have interrupted the shift to rational Republicanism in Louisiana. See Robert J. Steamer, "Southern Disaffection with the National Democratic Party," in Allan P. Sindler (ed.), *Change in the Contemporary South* (Durham, N.C., 1963), pp. 160–170.

[41] Joseph L. Bernd, *Grass Roots Politics in Georgia: The County Unit System and the Importance of the Individual Voting Community in Bifactional Elections, 1942–1954* (Atlanta, 1960).

[42] Former Representative Frank E. Smith of Mississippi, himself a victim of the politics of race, has recently written: "With the rare exception of a few who represent urban or border districts, all members of Congress from the South for the past fifteen years have been identified as segregationists and opponents of civil rights legislation. . . . The extremist members are not only accepted as the spokesmen for the South, they are also in a position to keep forcing the Southern position to even further extremes. All other members are their prisoners, because no one can afford a vote which does not coincide with the racist opposition to all civil rights." *Congressman from Mississippi* (New York, 1964), pp. 117–118.

the greatest of these insurgent movements, Populism, the champions of Democratic solidarity revived to fever pitch the question of the Negro's role in southern life. They ushered in the second major epoch in the history of modern southern sectionalism, the first three decades of the twentieth century. Although various internal differences were manifest in state and local politics during this period, in national politics southern unity was at its peak. The Wilson administration threatened southern political influence only indirectly, if at all, and the South enjoyed the new experience of contributing substantially to the legislative program of the national government and receiving significant federal appropriations without any real threat of outside intervention.[43] Near the end of this period, in the election of 1928, the gradual growth of the Democratic party outside of the South and the economic development of the peripheral states of the section brought a temporary disruption of the Solid South. Ironically, the social and political fears of the Deep South weakened the status of the national Democratic party throughout the region and made it possible for the more diversified rim states to vote Republican.

The New Deal brought the South into still another phase in the evolution of its sectionalism. Momentarily, the Great Depression and the Roosevelt administration reversed the secular trend toward Republicanism on the basis of economic and demographic changes; but in the long run the developments of the 1930s and 1940s encouraged the fragmentation of the Solid South. For one thing, the changing nature of the national Democratic party and the shrinking importance of the South in it began to eat away at the old assumption that Democratic control and defense of the "southern" position were synonymous. Moreover, while the New Deal brought desperately needed federal money to the South, it also brought increasing federal intervention and the slow alteration of internal social and economic relations. The economic expansion of the war years and the postwar prosperity encouraged the region's reaction against the national standards and welfare programs associated with the New Deal. Yet the South remained wedded to the Democratic party until mid-century, when the overt threat of a federally supported movement for Negro rights brought a recrudescence of sectional feeling and resort to all of the old sectional defenses. Paradoxically, this protest was itself the opening wedge in the shattering of southern solidarity and the growing attractiveness of the Republican party.

[43] There was probably a vague uneasiness in the minds of some southern politicians during the Wilson era concerning the future control of the Democratic party and the possibilities of federal legislation in the interest of truly national purposes.

The potent influence of race, the strategic role of southern congress-men, the predominance of Democrats in state and local politics, and the fact that a Southerner now occupies the White House are all likely to impede the spread of more competitive politics in the South. Nevertheless, it is clear that the region's political solidarity has grown weaker in recent years, and at some point between the forging of the Solid South during the quarter-century after Reconstruction and the middle of the twentieth century the old southern sectionalism reached its zenith and began a slow and uncertain decline. While this was happening, the circumstances that nourished political regionalism underwent a bewildering change. The role of the Democratic party as the guardian of southern solidarity and the role of the Republican party as the perennial threat to southern interests were reversed. The present South no longer has a clearly defined economic interest that sets it apart from the rest of the country. White attitudes toward the Negro are widely shared from Virginia to Texas, but individual states and subregions have differed enormously in their political responses to crises in race relations, and Negroes are steadily increasing their leverage in southern politics.

Despite the great transformation of the South since 1945, its political metamorphosis will not be accomplished overnight. This is particularly true of the Deep South, where political affairs are still dominated by racism, demagogic leadership, and economic and cultural backwardness. The most durable political changes seem to be taking place in the upper South and in states such as Texas and Florida, which have experienced rapid economic development while being relatively unconcerned about the race issue. Southern congressmen continue to display a conspicuously regional outlook, though this too is changing in the outer South and the metropolitan areas. For the region as a whole this much can be said: the nationalizing influence of the federal government and of the national parties, the emerging role of Negroes and other less-advantaged groups in political life, and the state-by-state removal of the race issue as the major determinant in politics will eventually complete the erosion of southern sectionalism.

4. The Ideology of White Supremacy

GUION GRIFFIS JOHNSON

To understand the importance of white supremacy in the thinking of the average white Southerner even today, one must appreciate the complex of ideas that was fashioned into a veritable monolith during the late nineteenth and early twentieth centuries. In the paper reprinted below a North Carolinian who has devoted much of her life to the study of race relations presents an excellent survey of the formation and crystallization of white supremacy ideology during the period between 1876 and 1910. She shows the similarity between white supremacy ideas and proslavery thought, describes the mounting strength of the movement to proscribe the Negro in various ways, and reveals the interaction between South and North in the tragic era of Jim Crow's triumph. Some southern whites conceded the possibility of Negro progress, but by 1910, writes Mrs. Johnson, the ideology of white supremacy had been established as an absolute.

Although she concentrates on the mind of the South, Mrs. Johnson suggests that the rest of the nation contributed to the southern victory in race relations. While northern attitudes toward the Negro were generally more tolerant, many Northerners shared the negative assumptions of southern white supremacists and tended to accept the finality of the southern solution to the race problem.

THE AMERICAN CIVIL WAR, AS IS THE CASE IN MOST WARS, HAD BEEN a conflict of ideologies[1] as well as a trial at arms. The ideological conflict had revolved chiefly around the function of government, the nature of the union, the innate capacities of mankind, the structure of

Originally published as "The Ideology of White Supremacy, 1876–1910," in Fletcher Melvin Green (ed.), *Essays in Southern History* (Chapel Hill, 1949), pp. 124–156. Reprinted by permission of the University of North Carolina Press. The footnotes and portions of the original essay as indicated have been omitted.

[1] Ideology, as used in this essay, signifies a system of thinking, however vaguely expressed, which attempts to define and to justify personal and group relations of

society, and the economic laws which control it. The triumph of the federal government automatically established the *de facto* status of that cluster of ideologies which shall be referred to loosely as representing the point of view of the North and the *de facto* destruction of those ideologies typical of the South.

The history of Reconstruction amply bears out the fact that neither the North nor the South was consolidated in a united front on any of the great questions which had been the subject of controversy. The passage of the Fourteenth Amendment, for example, made it necessary for a number of northern states hastily to change their laws in order to permit an equality of civil rights to Negroes, and it was not until the passage of the Fifteenth Amendment that Negroes won the ballot throughout the North. The act of writing into the Constitution the Fourteenth and Fifteenth Amendments was in itself an ideological revolution. This revolution established the *de jure* status of the position which the North had assumed in the pursuit of the Civil War, and the Amendments were in themselves a logical consequence of this position.

• • •

The discussion in this essay will be confined to an analysis of the value premises with respect to the Negro as set forth by southern whites in their efforts to negate the assumption of equality implied in the Fourteenth and Fifteenth Amendments. This is not to ignore the economic realities of the period, but to emphasize the fact that the status of the Negro rapidly became after 1865 as it was before that time the *raison d'etre* of any controversy which arose involving the general welfare of the South or the relation of the South to the federal government.

• • •

Between the anti-slavery and pro-slavery dichotomy there was obviously little hope for a logical solution acceptable to both sides. The South, with a ballot purged of the old slaveholding regime, had ratified the Fourteenth and Fifteenth Amendments which declared the Negro to be entitled to equal citizenship, but it was not until 1876 that the South at last made its peace with Congress. . . . After eleven years of attempting to bring the South into conformity with the national idea of equal rights,

---

whatever nature. The ideology is usually a set of value-loaded premises from which a platform of social dynamics may be formulated either through orderly political action or through extra-legal means. It is the content of thinking with which this essay is concerned and not the end results of these patterns of thought.

the federal government had retired from active participation in the experiment of the social revolution, leaving behind a Negro political machine protected by a legal equality and rewarded with federal patronage.

The period of conflict had produced a temporary consolidation of interests among southern whites. The old controversies between upper classes and lower classes, low country and up country, commercial and agrarian interests were to reappear time and time again only to be whipped into line by the cry of Negro domination until at last the Negro had been removed as an important factor in southern politics. There were still southern men who could lift their voices in behalf of the Negro, but the number was steadily growing fewer as the composition of the upper classes was steadily changing from the old planter aristocracy with its strong paternalistic motivation, to the new-rich, recruited from "tradespeople" and "mechanics," with their anti-Negro neurosis.

In the North the reaction had set in soon after the passage of the Fourteenth Amendment. The strong equalitarian sentiment of the negrophiles and the general feeling that the southern freedom had become the wards of the nation had given rise to a profound sympathy for the Negro in the abstract, but the actual status of the northern Negro was little changed for the better. As the rumor of misgovernment and fraud under Negro domination circulated in the North, the doctrine of the immediate fitness of the Negro for all the rights of citizenship came more and more to be questioned, and the way was rapidly being prepared for *laissez faire* in the South. It came to be said in the North that the equality of man could be achieved only through the slow processes of time and that the Negro offered a flat denial to the American assumption that all who came to this country's shores would first be assimilated and then absorbed.

The philosophy of the anti-slavery school bore in itself the seeds of *laissez faire*. If the Negro had only to exercise liberty in order to know how to use it wisely, federal intervention in his behalf was obviously unnecessary. Having been guaranteed the rights of citizenship, the Negro was now upon an equal footing with every other citizen of the United States and must not expect special favors. "It is not well for these people to be protected at every turn," wrote a federal agent in 1865 after his experience in dealing with the freedmen in Louisiana; "it is only by being cheated a while that they will learn to take care of their own interests." In 1908 Charles Francis Adams expressed the same idea from a political platform in Richmond, Virginia. The third generation of freedmen was now rising. ". . . from this time on," said Adams, "it is but reasonable to demand of those composing it that they work out their own destiny. It is for the Afro-Americans, as for the American descendant of the Celt, the Slav, or the Let, to shape his own future, accepting the common lot of mankind."

Even before the passage of the Fourteenth and Fifteenth Amendments, many political, financial, and religious leaders in the North had accepted the theory of rugged individualism as applied to the Negro. Now that he was no longer a slave, Pompey in the cotton field, it was argued, had as much a chance of making his own way as an Andrew Carnegie just off an immigrant ship. Both stood penniless in the land of opportunity. A northern man who had watched the experiment of free labor in Louisiana before the close of the war summarized in 1865 the dominant economic theory of the time as applied to the Negro. "The prevailing superficiality of thought" with respect to "the necessary antagonism of labor and capital" in the South would not, he declared, be assumed by "democratic thinkers in this country in any other relation of society than this; but as soon as it comes to considering the freed slave, in his new relation as a hired laborer, the liveliest suspicions are aroused." He then analyzed the "facts" which were rapidly being accepted in the North.

The fact is,—and this must be the foundation of all philosophy upon the subject,—the negroes are just what we should expect them to be after generations of slavery. If they were not, as a rule, lazy, dishonest and licentious, the chief argument against slavery would lose its weight.

The talk of dividing the confiscated and abandoned lands or the public land in the South among the freedmen he thought to be equally absurd.

Another subject, upon which there has been great confusion of mind and endless debate, is the tenure of land. We pass over the absurd assumption, often put forth, that the freed people are by right the owners of the land upon which they have toiled. It is the practical question, whether it is wise to divide lands among them as a free gift, that we wish to consider. We believe that no possession will benefit them which they have not themselves earned . . . they must earn the right to possess land, by steady, thrifty industry . . . why should a worthless vagrant, because he is a negro, receive the gift of a farm, the value of which a hard-working farmer's son in New England would think himself fortunate to acquire in ten years? Let the thing settle itself.

* * *

Here was a clear statement of policy outlined according to the accepted theory of clasical economics. The assumptions of this theory had been the basic philosophy which had guided the government since the time of Alexander Hamilton. The widespread acceptance of the theory, despite the agitation of extremists, spelled the ultimate defeat of equalitarianism as embodied in the Reconstruction Amendments, for it was obvious to these extremists at the time (hence the advocacy of subsidies to the freedmen and active government intervention in their behalf) that it was only by a firm policy of support from the outside that the *status quo* in the South would be overthrown, the organic law of the nation to the contrary notwithstanding. In a society such as the South where economic interests were based upon a system of labor, where profits of labor were in part dependent upon cheap labor, the changing of the status of labor which demanded a diminution of these interests necessarily involved a conflict between the new status and the old interests. The old interests, of course, were in a much better position to bargain and obtain their ends than was labor once federal intervention had been removed. *Laissez faire* now became the federal policy in the South despite frequent waving of the bloody shirt for political purposes, or, in the words of the time, "the South was left to work out its own problems."

The basic economic philosophy of the South was this same philosophy of rugged individualism. Of the classical economists, perhaps Malthus, whose theories were widely accepted in the ante-bellum South, continued most to influence southern thinking after the war. Upon the basis of the Malthusian doctrine, supported by the writings of Thomas Carlyle, southern whites erected their economic philosophy concerning Negro labor. The basic assumption was that the Negro would not work without compulsion. From this premise, southern whites derived three important corollaries: (1) the Negro needs the direction of the white man in order to be industrious and actually prefers it to the supervision of another Negro; (2) without this supervision and compulsion the Negro degenerates; (3) the Negro is inherently "lazy, shiftless, and licentious."

Southern whites held with the North that Negro labor should compete in the open market with white labor without the advantage of favoritism which federal intervention had given. Men who, like Edmund Ruffin, had contended before 1860 that slave labor was as efficient as free white labor now tended to argue that free Negro labor was as efficient as free white labor only when directed by whites. It was this latter contention which southern whites used in defense of the Black Codes passed immediately after the close of hostilities. Those, however, who like Hinton Rowan Helper of North Carolina had thought that Negro labor was inferior to white labor, came now to complain bitterly of the inefficiency of free Negro labor and to throw out inducements for immigrant labor to come South. When no such flow of white labor followed these overtures, it came to be said that "bad labor drives good labor out."

For example, Philip Alexander Bruce, a Virginia historian, thought in 1889 that an easy solution of the southern race problem would be the inducement southward of white foreign immigration. The inefficient Negro laborer could not compete on equal terms with the white laborer, and economic competition alone would solve the Negro problem. But fewer white immigrants were coming South than before the war; cheap Negro labor made the region unattractive to them. The shiftless, self-indulgent Negro laborers were breeding more rapidly than the more frugal, self-denying whites and might "by the irresistible pressure that will result from an enoromus numerical disproportion between the two races" eventually drive the whites out or produce an open contest for possession of the land. From these assumptions, Bruce arrived at a position similar to that which Lincoln had applied to the nation as a whole. "The South," declared Bruce, "cannot remain permanently half black and half white." Throughout the period the question of the relative efficiency of Negro labor was to be raised until at last Negro migration into the war industries of the North and West began after 1917 to drain off the surplus.

If it was necessary, as the southern ideology contended, for the whites to have constant and immediate supervision of the blacks in order to force Negro labor to be efficient, it was also necessary that the whites be able to maintain this supervision without being confronted with the embarrassing assumption that the Negro was politically equal. The elimination of the Negro voter was worked out slowly and with it the curtailment of his civil rights. It was not until 1890 . . . that the first serious attempt arose to disqualify the Negro. A Mississippi constitutional convention led the way in devising means of depriving the Negro of the vote without seeming to contravene the Fifteenth Amendment and at the same time without wholly eliminating illiterate white voters. The Mississippi Constitution included a variety of alternative qualifications including a poll tax receipt, property ownership, and an educational or understanding test of reading or reasonably interpreting any clause of the federal constitution to the satisfaction of the registering officer. Seven states followed the example of Mississippi between 1895 and 1910. The literacy and property tests automatically disfranchised large numbers of Negroes and the discretionary power of the registering officer might complete the work. The so-called grandfather clauses adopted by scme of the states were designed to protect illiterate whites. . . .

• • •

The South defended disfranchisement by an elaboration of the Calhoun doctrine that the Negro is unsuited to a participation in the equality on which the union rests. Suffrage, then, became a privilege and not a right. It should be enjoyed by those—the educated, tax-paying, property-owning, and virtuous citizenry—most capable of exercising it judiciously for the good of the whole. This position marked a return to the theory of the federal period which had with few exceptions based suffrage upon a property qualification. . . . Thus in its determination to maintain a biracial social structure, the South was forced constantly to penalize the whites who rested at the lowest end of the economic scale and to load with an additional weight the already important factor of wealth.

This aristocratic conception of race was usually explained in the terms which had been employed for many years to defend absolutism. The group of Virginia citizens who extended a platform to Charles Francis Adams in 1908 stated the formula of biracialism much as John Adams had defended the property qualifications of the suffrage: "The race question has been solved in Virginia in a manner which assures the supremacy of intelligence; gives to people of all races a fair opportunity to work out their destiny upon their merits, and offers a just reward to good citizenship." In 1889 James Bryce approved the southern position in his *The American Commonwealth* by declaring, ". . . in the hands of the Negroes at the South, or the newly enfranchised immigrants of the larger cities, a vote is a weapon of mischief." He thought the great American assumption that citizenship automatically fitted one for intelligent participation in government to be absurd and illogical. . . .

The process of limiting the civil equality of the Negro in the South began earlier than did the attempt to seek constitutional means of depriving him of the ballot. The Federal Civil Rights Act of 1866 had been general in its terms as were also the provisions of the Fourteenth Amendment, but the Civil Rights Act of 1875 enumerated specific rights. All persons within the jurisdiction of the United States should be entitled to the full and equal enjoyment of the accommodations, advantages, facilities, and privileges of inns, public conveyances on land or water, theaters, and other places of public amusement, subject only to the conditions established by law and applicable alike to citizens of every race and color regardless of any previous condition of servitude. The law carried provisions for specific punishments and specific modes of redress.

In five different cases having to do with the civil rights of Negroes which reached the Supreme Court in 1883, the Court took the position that individual discrimination against Negroes was not prohibited by the Thirteenth and Fourteenth Amendments. Indeed, that seems to have been the prevailing opinion of Congress at the time of the passage of the Amendments. . . . The effect of the test cases in the eighties was to declare that the federal government cannot prevent the curtailment of the civil rights of Negroes by individuals unless such individuals are acting under the sanction of a particular kind, and the federal court could declare state statutes in such instances unconstitutional. Within these limits the states might proceed to define and to secure civil rights for Negroes.

The definitions which the South employed looked steadily toward favoritism in behalf of the whites. After 1883 few of the southern states passed civil rights acts as such but depended upon the courts to determine the rights of citizens in public places. The first of the racial separation laws looked toward the continuation of the old ante-bellum laws against interracial marriage. The so-called Jim Crow laws, calling for racial separation in railroads and streetcars, began with a sweeping statute in 1875 in Tennessee abrogating the rule of the common law giving a right of action to any person excluded from any hotel, or public means of transportation, or place of amusement, and it even gave public conveyances the privilege of refusing to carry Negroes. This law was set aside, and legislatures thereafter were more careful in wording their statutes. All of the southern states fell in line in the passage of Jim Crow laws in the eighties and nineties, and the concept of racial separation also found expression in legal action to prevent the eligibility of Negroes to be served in white hotels, barber shops, restaurants, and in any but restricted areas of public amusement. Specific laws made the education of Negro and white children in separate systems mandatory. As a matter of course the poorer accommodations fell to the lot of Negroes. They lived in the worst residential districts; their amusements were such as they could provide for themselves; they were either excluded entirely or segregated in public gatherings; they were segregated on public conveyances; their schools received the lowest allotment of public funds; and they continued to fill the lowest occupations in the field of labor.

Thus when the old social and economic structure fell with the Civil War, the South immediately began the erection of a new structure upon the basis of the old philosophy. By the turn of the twentieth century that adjustment had become fixed in a biracial social and economic order. As stated by Bishop Charles Betts Galloway at the seventh annual meeting of the Conference for Education in the South held in Birmingham in 1904, the position of the southern whites was as follows:

First.—In the South there will never be any social mingling of the races. Whether it be prejudice or pride of race, there is a middle wall of partition which will not be broken down.

Second.—They will worship in separate churches and be educated in separate schools. This is desired alike by both races, and is for the good of each.

Third.—The political power of this section will remain in present hands. Here, as elsewhere, intelligence and wealth will and should control the administration of government affairs.

Fourth.—The great body of the Negroes are here to stay. Their coerced colonization would be a crime, and their deportation a physical impossibility. And the white people are less anxious for them to go than the Negroes are to leave. They are natives and not intruders.

This solution of the race problem scarcely deviated in philosophy from the major assumptions of the slavery regime. The Negro was presumed to be an inferior type of man, but he was wholly acceptable within a given sphere of activity; "he was all right in his place." Any relationship which brought the inferior Negro except in the capacity of a menial into association with the superior white man tended to elevate the inferior and automatically to degrade the superior. Political, religious, or educational equalities were tantamount to social equality, and social equality would inevitably lead to intermarriage and the deterioration of the white race. The extremists would conclude from these assumptions that the Negro must be removed from American civilization or be ground down so effectively that there would never be any temptation to cross the race line.

Southern whites felt that the Fourteenth and Fifteenth Amendments negated the major assumption of Negro inferiority. So long as the amendments remained a part of the federal constitution, they were sleeping thunder which might be hurled against the "domestic tranquility" of the South at any moment by a Congress or a Supreme Court favorable to the Negro. The South, therefore, was driven back into the defensive position which it had occupied since 1820. Southern leaders must now rationalize the caste status of the Negro as it had once rationalized his slave status.

The caste status to which the Negro had been assigned since the colonial period but which had often been softened by the personal relationships of slavery became frozen after emancipation by the fewer and fewer contacts possible between whites and blacks except in economic relationships. Once the property status of the Negro was removed the kindliness of the white man toward the oppressed race must depend entirely upon humanitarian impulses *per se*. The white South which had declared in 1860 that slavery was the cornerstone of its social structure quickly realized that emancipation had not destroyed that cornerstone. The South before 1860 knew what the status of a free Negro was and it also knew what it meant to lose property in slaves. After 1865 a mass of white men who had lost property in slaves was left to confront a mass of free Negroes. It was only logical that the old relationship should continue as before; that the dominant white race should seek in every possible way to rule the subordinate Negro race as before. While emancipation may have lost to the planter his particular set of Negroes, it did not deprive him of dependent Negro labor. Negro labor was as much dependent upon the white employer as before. Public subjugation came now to be substituted for the old private subjugation under slavery.

The processes of public subjugation had begun long before 1865, for no sooner had Negro slaves been imported in this country in large numbers than the theory of "the taint of Negro blood" began to be enunciated. Most southern states, in an attempt to define who might be enslaved, soon found it necessary to make "the Negro" a fixed legal term. South Carolina, however, steadfastly refused to say what amount of Negro blood would bring one within the proscribed term. . . . It was not in fact until the last decade of the nineteenth century that South Carolina at last put a legal penalty upon the possession of Negro blood.

The usual test applied by the southern states to decide whether persons came within the legal term was to declare a person of color to be one who was descended from a Negro to the third generation inclusive though one ancestor in each generation may have been white. . . .

The literature attempting to define and analyze the caste status of the American Negro is extensive, but it was not until 1853 that a young octoroon, William B. Allen, professor in radical Central College in Mc-Grawville, New York, analyzed the status from the point of view of the proscribed caste. . . .

In 1869 Charles Sumner sought to analyze the basis of caste in a scholarly lecture in Boston. He thought the theory of American caste to be similar to that of the divine right of kings. In America the theory had been converted into "a claim of hereditary power from color." This outworn theory of absolutism should be discarded, he thought, for the more fundamental concept of the common humanity of man, a fact to which all fields of science pointed: ethnology, geology, paleography, anatomy. When the mass of mankind was considered, the importance of color and other ethnological differences disappeared; the fact that all mankind was capable of changing from a lower to a higher level of civilization was the important consideration.

During the height of the agrarian controversy in the South, a southern man, George Washington Cable of Louisiana, also spoke out against the American caste system. Like Sumner he thought the American proscription of the Negro arose from the old theory of divine rights, but he also thought that the Americans had given the theory an Oriental emphasis. "Its principle declares public safety and highest development to require the subjugation of the lower mass under the arbitrary protective supremacy of an untitled but hereditary privileged class, a civil caste." It was not an aristocracy which the South was attempting to set up, "for an aristocracy exists, presumably, at least, with the wide consent of all classes, and men in any rank of life may have some hope to attain to it by extraordinary merit and service; but a caste; not the embodiment of a modern European idea, but the resuscitation of an ancient Asiatic one."

Cable declared that the Negro as a free man was never given a chance to prove his capacities. . . . For this reason, one heard much of "Negro supremacy," "a black oligarchy," "the Africanization of the South," and "race antagonism" which is "natural, inborn, ineradicable," and some writers had the temerity to "stand up before the intelligent and moral world saying, 'If this instinct does not exist it is necessary to invent it.' "

Cable thought that the "tap-root of the Negro question" and, therefore, of the caste system itself was fear. Although he never specifically defined the basis of this fear, the implication throughout his discussion was that this fear was twofold. It rested upon the economic fear of loss of services in the labor of the Negro and upon physical fear of the Negroes in case they should outnumber the whites and, realizing their strength, decide to take revenge for long-continued mistreatment. . . . No economic theorist, but a humanitarian after the school of Heber and Ruskin, Cable saw in the Negro "a kindly race of poor men" whom progress, speeded up by conscious human direction, might develop into industrious citizens. Cable was denounced as a sentimental theorist, and public opinion finally drove him from the South.

Numerous theories, already well-worn in the ante-bellum period, were at hand to justify the caste system. Among the patterns of thought most frequently exhibited in the writings and platform oratory of the time were the ideas clustering around the concepts of (1) retrogression, (2) progress, (3) paternalism, (4) romanticism, and, for lack of a better term, (5) negrophobia.

The theory of retrogression, widely popularized by Thomas Carlyle's *The Nigger Question,* which had been written after emancipation in the West Indies, was used in the ante-bellum period as a justification of slavery and it became now a convenient justification of white supremacy. It was argued that the Negro as a freeman could not stand up under the competition of civilized life and would retrogress to savagery and meet the fate of ultimate extinction. This assumption had been based primarily upon Malthusian arguments, but, even before Malthus, the natural scientists had outlined the concept of retrogression. At the time of emancipation it was widely predicted that the Negro would rapidly die out and become as rare in American life as the Indian. . . . When, however, the census of 1880 showed a large increase of Negroes, in some areas a doubling of the population in a decade, the news aroused consternation in many quarters and produced a quick revision of concepts.

While some were unwilling to accept the count of the 1880 census as accurate, others abandoned the theory of extermination of the Negroes through natural causes but they did not cast aside the doctrine of retrogression. Indeed, the fact of a rapidly increasing Negro population made the predictions of the theory seem even more alarming, for an essential premise was the cultural deterioration of the Negro when removed from direct supervision of the dominant race. "The time has come for honest, manly effort," declared Bishop T. U. Dudley of the Protestant Episcopal Church of Kentucky. "Separated from us, their neighbors and their friends," the Negroes "must retrograde toward the barbarism whence they are sprung, and then, alas, we might be compelled to wage relentless war against them for our own preservation."

Philip Alexander Bruce, with ancestry in the old planter aristocracy of Virginia, was one of the first Southerners to make a serious study of the problem from this point of view. His *The Plantation Negro as a Freeman,* written in 1889, was an exposition of the southern situation in the light of a rapidly regressing Negro population. Believing that an examination of Negro character and society "without partiality and without prejudice" would be the only approach to a solution of the problem, Bruce described Negro family life, character, education, religion, and superstitions. He appraised the Negro as a citizen, a laborer, landowner, and criminal. His conclusion was that ultimately, and at no distant date, the Negro would "revert to the African original." "The return of the race to the original physical type involves its intellectual reversion also. . . . Every circumstance surrounding the Negro in the present age seems to point directly to his future moral decadence. . . . The influences that are shaping the character of the younger generations appear to be such as must bring the blacks in time to a state of nature. . . ." Such a condition was further complicated by the high fertility rate of Negroes. . . .

The Negro might be expected to increase at an alarming rate another half century, "because, during that period of time, the soil must remain comparatively cheap and abundant, and the negro be in sufficient demand as a laborer to supply him with all that is necessary to his existence." The unlimited increase of the blacks was "pregnant with innumerable calamities." "It virtually means that a period will come when there will be a sharp contest between blacks and whites for the possession of a large part of the Southern States. . . ." The whites might kill off the blacks, or they might in disgust migrate and leave the blacks in barbaric enjoyment of the southern region. The only real solution, he thought, was immediate and complete deportation. . . .

In accordance with the Malthusian system, Bruce believed that a barbaric race might be elevated to a higher cultural level only when supervised by a civilized race under a paternal system of compulsion. Wherever he found whites to be in a considerable majority, he discovered retrogression to be going on at a slower rate. Instead of calling for deportation as the only remedy to prevent race war, Bruce might have argued as logically the spread theory which was used at the time of the Missouri Compromise and which was to reappear in southern thinking in the twentieth century. . . . Bruce also assumed that Negro personality traits would forever prevent the black man's becoming assimilated as a workable part of American society. . . .

Guided by apprehensions based upon the theory of retrogression, a movement was started in the late nineteenth century to bring the whites and blacks of the South into more cordial relationships so that the pessimistic outlook which such men as Bruce foresaw might be prevented. Bishop Dudley urged such a policy in 1885. He wanted the Negro welcomed back to the polls and to the white churches. "The separation of the Negro race from the white race means for the negro continued and increasing degradation and decay. His hope, his salvation, must come from association with that people among whom he dwells, but from whose natural guidance and care he has been separated largely by the machinations of unscrupulous demagogues." When the "machinations of unscrupulous demagogues" continued to drive the blacks and whites further apart, and foreign observers as well as Southerners continued to point out that "there is less chance than there ever was of their working together peacefully for good; and increasing racial antagonism, nourished by both sides, grows daily," a definite movement toward interracial cooperation was launched through the combined efforts of southern leaders and northern philanthropists. Begun first as conferences on southern education, the movement, after the Atlanta riot of 1906, became a definite program to bring southern white and black leaders in closer touch so that they might discuss problems of mutual importance. The interracial movement as an organization with regional, state, and local branches did not come into existence until the third decade of the twentieth century.

No American writer of the period who tried seriously to analyze the race problem failed to find some comfort in the hope of education. The extent of hope usually depended upon the writer's concept of the theory of progress, and the theory of progress was itself undergoing a vast change at the very time that equalitarianism was being incorporated into the federal constitution. The hypothesis of progression from a lower to a higher state was expressed first by the moral philosophers and then by the natural scientists. From this position it was but a step to the application of the theory to all plant and animal life including man. If particular races of men seemed less advanced than others, it was because they had not progressed as far on the scale of evolution. The theory of progression had already affected northern thinking before the period of Reconstruction. Such men as Charles Sumner and Carl Schurz accepted it as proof that the Negro possessed the ability to develop and lacked only the opportunity to prove it. To the theory of progress they added the immediacy concept of the extreme natural rights wing of the anti-slavery school. But the progression theory was also capable of proving the incapacity of the Negro for immediate citizenship.

It would be difficult to determine who contributed most to American thinking on progress as applied to the Negro. Comte had outlined the theory of progress in the philosophical school and Maillet and Lamarck had devised scientific theories of development. The works of Charles Darwin, *The Origin of the Species,* published in this country in 1859, and *The Descent of Man,* published in 1871, seem to have influenced most the thinking of social scientists in the period following Reconstruction. . . . The Darwinian hypothesis explained the origin and perpetuation of species of animals and plants by a process of natural selection and survival of the fittest. Man was protected in this process of selection and survival by certain inborn instincts. By implication, acquired characteristics might also be inherited.

• • •

Separate Negro congregations under the supervision of white ministers were encouraged in the South during the slavery period on the assumption that the black man was not sufficiently acquainted with American institutions to understand the intricacies of denominational creeds and the attempt was made to evangelize rather than to ritualize the Negro. Northern missionaries who flocked to the South in the closing days of the Civil War encouraged the withdrawal of the former slaves from connections with their masters' churches and the Negroes themselves showed an inclination to set up their own church organizations. The Methodist Episcopal Church, South, was one of several denominations that made some effort to retain their Negro congregations, but when this effort failed, Atticus Greene Haygood, president of Emory College and later a Methodist bishop, placed the full responsibility for withdrawal upon the Negro's race instinct.

This instinctive disposition to form Church affiliations on the color basis may be wise or unwise. But it is in them—deep in them. The tendency is strengthening all the time. This instinct will never be satisfied till it realizes itself in complete separation. Whether we of the white race approve or disapprove matters little. . . . We may, all of us, as well adjust our plans to the determined and inevitable movements of this instinct—that does not reason, but that moves steadily and resistlessly to accomplish its ends. It is a very grave question to be considered by all who have responsibility in this matter: Whether over-repression of race-instincts may not mar their normal evolution—may not introduce elements unfriendly to healthful growth—may not result in explosions? . . .

Here was a convenient theory, based, as it was thought, solidly upon objective science which relieved churchmen of the burden of applying Christian ethics to the lower caste. It was possible actually to interpret the Golden Rule in terms of segregation. Yet, religious philosophy did not, except in the mouths of extremists, deny the concept of the Fatherhood of God and the brotherhood of man. The Negro was generally conceded to be one of God's children, but the theory of race instinct and the concept of retarded races made it possible to hold that the full implications of brotherhood could not apply to the Negro. If brotherhood *could* not be applied, it was an easy step to the conclusion that brotherhood *should* not be applied and that if it were applied, even on rare occasions by opening the doors of the white church to a visiting Negro minister or to an unsegregated audience, such application was tantamount to social equality. . . .

Not all southern theologians condoned this generally accepted caste position of the white churches. Pride of race, declared Bishop T. U. Dudley of the Protestant Episcopal Church of Kentucky, "is but a pretext to excuse the conduct which, in our heart of hearts, we know to proceed from the old root of bitterness—the feeling of caste which demands that the liberated slave shall be forever a menial. I charge the Christian white men of the South to mark that the effect of this separation, on which we have insisted, has helped to drive these people into a corresponding exclusiveness, and is constantly diminishing the influence of our Christian thinkers upon their beliefs and their practice."

Even Bishop Dudley would admit that the practices of Negro churches were becoming "more and more like the African original." Likewise northern missionaries who had in the beginning attributed the undesirable traits of the Negro to the evils of slavery now placed less emphasis upon slavery and more upon "barbarism." The "wild ravings" of the Negro ministers and the emotional behavior of the congregations became another proof that the Negro was an African and not a "lamp-blacked white man." Percy Stickney Grant's *Socialism and Christianity* of 1910 illustrates the shift in ideologies which had taken place following the Civil War.

When, in 1866, we came to deal with a race which had no such traditions or political ancestors as the American colonists—to a race sadly near an unpoetic state of nature—"natural rights" were granted, "equality" was affirmed and "fraternity" demanded. . . . We are now (in the generation after the war) confronted by our failures, but are also, luckily, at the same time attended by a new philosophy that explains our failures and bids us not to be discouraged. The theory of evolution takes for granted human inequality and consequently knows nothing of natural and universal rights. In place of jumps it discloses steps; in place of catastrophes and sudden transformation, slow processes.

The physical and cultural inferiority of the Negro should be taken for granted, he argued, and means employed to "oil the wheels of progress." The Biblical concept of brotherhood and equality now became in the light of evolution the concept of brotherhood and inequality. . . .

Once the present inferiority of the Negro was admitted, the southern position became more tenable, and once it was admitted that there was a grain of truth in the southern position the easier it was to accept the whole of it. Thus, for almost two generations after Reconstruction the attitude toward the Negro on the part of northern Christians may be described as "patient helpfulness" and on the part of southern Christians a stout defense of segregation in the sanctuary "because it is desired alike by both races, and is for the good of each."

The concept of progress resolved itself into a controversy similar to that which had existed before 1860: Was the Negro permanently inferior to the Caucasian or could he be brought up to the level of the "higher" race? Was it possible for a retarded race to skip some of the steps toward advancement and thereby ultimately catch up with the "superior" race? Or must a backward race repeat the historical experience of the superior race in order to progress to a higher level and thus be forever behind? The southern position on white supremacy seemed to imply permanent inferiority, but whenever the question was discussed in the pulpit or the press the Negro was usually given to understand that his race might eventually by hard work and self-denial, win civil and economic equality— but never social equality. Those who believed in permanent inferiority tended to reject the Negro as a permissible component of southern population and called loudly for expulsion. This position will be discussed under the category of negrophobia.

The writings of Edgar Gardner Murphy, an Episcopal clergyman of Montgomery, Alabama, were typical of scholarly southern thinking of the period. To Murphy, the Negro was "a backward and essentially unassimilable people" whom "the consciousness of kind," a phrase which he borrowed from the Columbia University sociologist, Franklin H. Giddings, would forever set apart from the whites. Yet the Negro had it within his power to work out his own salvation and eventually to win the respect of the dominant race. By using "the positive liberties and advantages of education and of industry, of religion and of political freedom," the Negro in America might, Murphy thought, "through the acceptance of a programme of positive progress, . . . enter into a larger heritage than is open to any like number of his race in any quarter of the world. Important are some of the advantages which he has not; but more important are the many advantages which he has." The freedmen in 1865 were by no means in a state of development worthy of being brought within the democratic assumptions of the constitution. . . .

Murphy denied, however, that the fundamental question at issue was the capacity of the Negro race. The fundamental was the attitude of the dominant race toward the Negro. These antipathies should be explained and an attempt made to understand them in the hope of redirecting them for the good of society. The state should begin a positive policy of development, and this policy should be applied to both races. The black race should be educated to the level of the white race and the white race should be educated to a better understanding and appreciation of the blacks. Murphy sought to allay the fears of the whites by assuring them that the operation of the principle of the consciousness of kind would forever prevent widespread social mingling and amalgamation.

Thomas Nelson Page, whose romantic novels of ante-bellum life did much to perpetuate the fiction of the golden age of the plantation regime, also thought that the Negro might be developed through education, but he would not admit that the race was as capable of progress as did Murphy. He would stop, in fact, only one step short of permanent inferiority, reluctantly admitting that the concept of permanent inferiority would close the door of hope forever to the Negro who was also one of God's children. Page's estimate of the history of the Negro race and its capacities to develop strongly resembled ante-bellum ideology. . . . "In art, in mechanical development, in literature, in mental and moral science, in all the range of mental action, no notable work has up to this time come from the Negro."

The white novelist could not find an instance where the Negro race had risen of its own efforts, but he would not say that "because a Negro is a Negro he is incapable of any intellectual development. On the contrary, observation has led me to think that under certain conditions of intellectual environment, of careful training, and of sympathetic encouragement from the stronger races he may individually attain a fair, and in uncommon instances a considerable degree, of mental development." He did not think that the formal education which the Negroes had been receiving since emancipation was the type needed to achieve the elevation of the race, and the race, he declared, must either be elevated or deported. . . . The Negro needed, he thought, a training different from that of the whites, character training especially. ". . . the Negro must be taught the great elementary truths of morality and duty. Until he is so established in these that he claims to be on this ground the equal of the white, he can never be his equal on any other ground. . . . Until then, he is fighting not the white race, but a law of nature, universal and inexorable—that races rise or fall according to their character."

It was typical of the romantic school of writers, such as Thomas Nelson Page, to compare the rising generation of Negroes with the Negroes born in slavery only to find that those born in freedom fell far short of the old ideal. . . . Nevertheless, there were both romanticists and paternalists among southern whites whose attitude on the Negro problem, while contributing nothing dynamic to the discussion, often helped to ease the friction of the times. Page referred to the practice "so commonly to be found in the South" among the upper classes of treating their Negro retainers, even "the weakest and worst of them with . . . mingled consideration and indulgence." The South had been turning toward romanticism during the last two decades of the ante-bellum period. The regional fiction of the time indicated the trend. The movement was the effect of Victorianism, or sentimental humanitarianism, which may be traced in other parts of the country as well as in the South. . . .

The movement in the post-war South was the defense of the old aristocracy against the forces which had uprooted the social structure. The romantic school turned wistful glances back to slavery, found it good, and with it "de old darkey" of plantation days. Writers of this school stressed the good conduct of the slave during the war, fondly recalled the "black mammy" of their childhood, and the "pickaninny" who entered into their youthful sports. They usually attributed the "bad conduct" of the Negro during freedom to fundamental errors taught him by northern emissaries who knew nothing whatever of the true nature of conditions. These errors were: "first, that the Southern white was inherently his enemy, and, secondly, that his race could be legislated into equality with the white." Such writers as Joel Chandler Harris not only dramatized the Negro of slavery, but excused his faults since emancipation and hoped that time would eventually teach him the error of his ways. . . .

The recollections of slavery days to be found in the memoirs of this period were written chiefly in the romantic vein, and southern historians have also helped to perpetuate the tradition. A flood of romantic novels cast a halo around the plantation with its benign master and genteel mistress and shed a beneficent glow upon the slave.

Romanticists tended toward paternalism when dealing with the Negro. This spirit of kindliness, sometimes sorely grieved at the conduct of the Negro but usually explanatory and tolerant, sprang directly from the paternalistic philosophy of the patriarchal state fostered by the theologians of the ante-bellum period. The correlative rights and duties which the paternalists stressed in the post-war years were strongly reminiscent of Filmer and Burke. The whites had the right to control the government by reason of their superior intelligence and wealth, but they were also obligated to protect the Negroes and lift them up to a higher plane of civilization. In return it was the duty of the Negroes to look to the whites for guidance and to accept cheerfully the status which the whites assigned them. The role of the Negro should be implicit acceptance of the biracial social structure; he must always "keep his place." The role of the whites should be that of *noblesse oblige*. . . .

• • •

Arrayed against the paternalists and all those who were willing to concede that the concept of progress applied to the Negro as well as to the whites was that still larger group of white Southerners who maintained that the Negro was permanently inferior and, therefore, a menace to American sociey. This position led some to an unreasoning fear of the Negro which amounted to a phobia. Others were willing to tolerate the Negro so long as his services were cheap and he "kept his place." Given the fact of present degradation, most Southerners argued *a priori* that the Negro was and had always been inferior. Alfred Holt Stone, planter in the Yazoo-Mississippi delta, whose magazine articles on the status of the Negro in the South were written in the early years of the twentieth century, based his entire philosophy upon the theory of permanency of type. He declared that the racial status of the Negro had been fixed several thousands of years ago ". . . the Negro is one of the oldest races of which we have any knowledge, and . . . its very failure to develop itself in its own habitat, while the Caucasian, Mongolian, and others have gone forward, is in itself sufficient proof of inferiority. . . . if we blot out the achievement of the American Negro who has passed through slavery, what has the race left to boast of? And if we go one step further, and from the achievements of the 'American Negro' obliterate all that the American mulatto has accomplished, what ground indeed would be left to those whose sentiment and sympathy have apparently rendered them so forgetful of scientific truth?"

From this pseudo-scientific approach, Stone summarized and justified the prevailing public opinion. The Negro was an inferior type of man with predominantly African customs and character traits whom no amount of education or improvement of environmental conditions could ever elevate to as high a scale in the human species as the white man. Many were the complaints of "the burden" which the South had to bear from "the menace" of its black population. It was pointed out that when the world came to look upon the Negro as the African that he really was, a better understanding of the South's plight might be obtained. This was the position of E. H. Randle of Virginia, writing in 1910 *Characteristics of the Southern Negro* in reply to Andrew Carnegie's optimistic article on the Negro which appeared in the *North American Review* of June, 1908.

The first important thing to remember in judging the Negro, Randle thought, was that his mental capacity was inferior to that of the white man. The Negro mind seldom developed "beyond that of the twelve-year-old white child, although there seems to be much less difference in the mental capacity of the children of the two races. . . ." He declared that education did not improve the Negro. "We have tried that for nearly a half century," he wrote, "and the contrary is the result. He has exchanged common sense for a small quantity of parrot book-learning; energy for laziness, efficiency for shiftlessness—with a moderate number of good exceptions. The lands have declined most where there are the most negroes." . . . The Negro was an encumbrance because he drove away northern and foreign white immigration, because it was an increasingly heavy tax burden to attempt to educate and to police him, and because he was inefficient as a laborer.

Randle saw a dark future ahead. ". . . think of the black belts where there are many negroes to one white man. When most of them get a smattering of education and begin to want to hold the county offices, and to possess the lands; stirred up by one of their number or some bad white man, they may organize on a large scale and start out to kill and possess." . . . This was the same fearful cry of a Negro insurrection which had gone up in the South since the eighteenth century.

The corollaries of the assumption of permanent inferiority which were accepted in the ante-bellum period were still held to be incontrovertible. It was argued that race mixing was harmful and that the mulatto, although he might not be the physical inferior of the Negro, was certainly the trouble maker in race relations, and, therefore, an objectionable member of society. It was said that if one made a concession of equality on any ground, the Negro would accept it as unlimited equality. The lesson of Reconstruction had been: "Give the Negro a political inch and he will take a social ell." The only solution to the race problem, therefore, was either to force the Negro always to keep his place or to rid the country of him entirely.

Southern whites who let their minds dwell long upon such a dismal picture reacted emotionally. Schizophrenic thought and behavior patterns were the result. Frenzied mobs lynched a Negro on slight evidence of guilt and there were those in the market place heard to say that "the only solution to the Negro problem was a first class lynching Monday of every week." Such extreme statements did not necessarily mean that those who uttered them were consistently cruel to Negroes. If they employed Negro labor they were likely to ameliorate their relationships with kindliness, saying that this procedure brought best results. Others were less expedient and pursued an uncompromising attitude toward the Negro at all times. Still others, the extremists, would not permit Negroes about them under any circumstances. . . .

The negrophobist had short patience with the "sickly sentimentality" of the romanticist and the paternalist who were constantly pointing out the duties which the white people of the South owed the Negro because he was the basis of their labor, and, therefore, the "mud-sill" of their civilization; because he was a weaker race, and, therefore, "a ward of the white people." Nor did he have any patience with those who argued that progress through education would eventually raise the average intelligence of the Negro. The phobist had thought from the time that education was first agitated that it "would ruin the Negro for work," but the Reconstruction legislatures had passed the Negro education bills with the argument that education would make the Negro "a better man, a better citizen and a better Christian." The result of education had confirmed the worst fears of the phobists. The Negroes had shown, the phobists declared, an increasing tendency to get out of place, to push the southern white man off the sidewalk, and, what was far less endurable, to despoil the white woman. Dunbar Rowland, director of the Mississippi Department of Archives and History, addressing the Alumni Association of the University of Mississippi in 1902, pointed out that "thoughtful men in the South" were beginning to lose faith in "the power of the education which had been heretofore given to uplift the negro" and to complain of the burden thus placed upon "the people of the South in their poverty." He argued that the Negro did not advance because he lacked the ability to do so; for the South had given him every opportunity to rise. . . .

The most extreme form which negrophobia took in this period was Charles Carroll's restatement of the Pre-Adamic theory of the origin of the Negro race in his two volumes, *The Negro a Beast* (1900), and *The Tempter of Eve* (1902). Carroll's assumption that the Negro was created prior to Adam and, therefore, was not of the genus *homo sapiens* bore close resemblance to the outline of the theory which Buckner H. Payne, writing under the signature of "Ariel," had set forth in 1867 in *The Negro: What Is His Ethnological Status?* Carroll departed from Payne, however, in his assumption that the Negro was the serpent mentioned in the Bible as the tempter of Eve. In 1860 S. A. Cartwright of Mississippi, accepting the conclusion of Adam Clark, the English Biblical scholar, that the tempter of Eve was an orangutan and not a serpent, also had declared the tempter of Eve to have been a Negro.

A large part of Carroll's *Tempter of Eve* was devoted to a lengthy effort to prove from geological and ethnological sources as well as from Biblical data that the betrayer of the human race had been a Negro woman. Amalgamation, he argued, was cursed of God because it gave rise to a creature who was the offspring of *homo sapiens* and a beast. This spurious issue, like the pure Negro stock itself, was devoid of a soul and, therefore, outside the pale of redemption. . . .

Negro writers frequently pointed to such extravagant statements as these from "the crazy Carroll" as well as to the widespread publicity given to all Negro crime as a deliberate campaign against the Negro in an attempt to justify white supremacy and Negro exploitation in the eyes of the world. George Henry White, the last Negro to represent North Carolina in Congress, paid his respects to this propaganda of hate in 1900 on the floor of the House.

Possibly at no time in the history of our freedom has the effort been made to mould public sentiment against us and our progress so strongly as it is now being done. The forces have been set in motion and we must have sufficient manhood and courage to overcome all resistance that obstructs our progress. . . .

It is easy for these gentlemen to taunt us with our inferiority, at the same time not mentioning the causes of this inferiority. It is rather hard to be accused of shiftlessness and idleness when the accuser of his own motion closes the avenues for labor and industrial pursuits to us. It is hardly fair to accuse us of ignorance when it was made a crime under the former order of things to learn enough about letters even to read the Word of God.

While I offer no extenuation for any immorality that may exist among my people, it comes with rather poor grace from those who forced it upon us for two hundred and fifty years to taunt us with that shortcoming.

White supremacy had come now to be accepted as an absolute. It found respectable advocates in the North as well as in the South, in Europe as well as in the United States, in scholarship and in public opinion. But the Fourteenth and Fifteenth Amendments had thrown—and still continue to throw—the South upon the defensive by upsetting the legality of the status which the whites had assigned to the Negro during the more than two hundred years of slavery. With the principle of equality incorporated into the government as a part of the organic law, it was necessary for those who found the old status of inferiority, degradation, and exploitation disrupted to begin a new period of justification. All of the old assumptions used to justify the legal enslavement of the Negro were used to defend his civil enslavement. The work of justification was considerably speeded up by the appearance and widespread acceptance of the theory of positivism as expressed by Comte, the theory of evolution as expressed by Darwin, the theory of progress developed by Spencer, and by the continued acceptance of the theory of *laissez faire* in government and in business.

In the South itself little argument was needed to justify white supremacy. The controversy during the slavery regime had silenced opposition for almost thirty years before the conflict at arms. Occasionally during the Civil War and for almost twenty years thereafter it was possible to protest against the lowly status assigned the Negro, but, after the emotions aroused during the controversies of the agrarian revolt, it became increasingly difficult to question the wisdom of caste relationships. The taboos of race relations which had been established during slavery were the taboos of freedom. The Negro had a definite and inferior place to keep; so long as he kept that place he was acceptable. But he must never aspire to rise outside his own racial structure; no white man who wished to retain his superior caste position among other white men must ever suggest that the Negro deserved a higher status than that assigned him. As in the late ante-bellum period so in the period following Reconstruction there was little tolerance of debate upon "this delicate situation." . . .

The period between 1876 and 1910 had written the name of the Negro off the registration books and removed the Negro as a minority pressure group in southern politics. By means of state laws the caste status of the Negro was established in public as well as private relationships. There were few voices of protest throughout the land. When the caste position of the Negro was challenged, the points at issue were fundamentally the same as those of the slavery period: the status and capacities of the Negro. Three groups of thinkers in the South—the romanticists, the paternalists, and those who accepted the theory of progress through education—held out some hope to the Negro, although they either neglected to define what this future higher status should be or they exhibited considerable confusion of thought on the subject. All tended alike to measure the Negro upon the Malthusian scale of personality traits and to find, when the Negro fell short of the ideal, that the black man had serious character defects in comparison to his Caucasian brother. The Negro was, in other words, still considered to be a "peculiar" type of man, and the negrophobists would declare that he always would remain so. White supremacy was, from this point of view, the determination of the dominant race "to ward off political ruin and to save society from destruction."

5. Southern Education, the Race Issue, and Intersectional Cooperation

LOUIS R. HARLAN

Professor Harlan of the University of Cincinnati received his A.B. degree from Emory University and his Ph.D. from Johns Hopkins, where he studied under C. Vann Woodward. As a leading student of American Negro history and the history of the South since the Civil War, he is the author of *Separate and Unequal: Public School Campaigns and Racism in the Southern Seaboard States, 1901–1915* (1958) and his current interest is a biographical study of Booker T. Washington.

The following paper is concerned with one area where Northerners responded to southern arguments, the movement to establish a genuine system of public education in the South.

Unofficial leadership in southern education was provided by the Southern Education Board, "an intersectional partnership of moderate progressives" established in 1901. Professor Harlan emphasizes the way in which such "progressive" endeavors were influenced by the white supremacy movement, approaching its greatest strength in this period. He describes the role of northern philanthropists in the southern educational revival and analyzes the compromise effected between the "best North" and the "best South." The northern businessmen and their southern allies were basically conservative and, even in matters involving Negro rights, they sought not to foster a new equality but only to restrain rampant demagoguery and racial violence. They were timid and shortsighted, argues Harlan, who is sharply critical of their policies, which he believes resulted in widespread discrimination in the southern public schools. The intersectional accord reflected in this chapter

Originally published as "The Southern Education Board and the Race Issue in Public Education," in *The Journal of Southern History,* XXIII (May, 1957), 189–202. Copyright 1957 by the Southern Historical Association. Reprinted by permission of the Managing Editor. The footnotes in the original essay have been omitted.

of southern history, like the debate over imperialism a few years before, suggests the prevalence of racialism among most Americans and a relatively benign attitude in the North toward the South during the first part of the twentieth century.

WHEN THE SOUTHERN EDUCATION BOARD WAS CREATED IN 1901 to direct a region-wide public school crusade, it at once encountered a powerful movement which had been accumulating force for a decade. Disfranchisement of Negroes in state after state was accompanied or followed by new segregation laws, discrimination of various sorts, and extralegal violence. Sometimes called the white supremacy movement, this current of extreme racialism enveloped all other movements in the region within its context, tingeing them with its attitudes and deflecting them from their original directions into its own stream. "These new antipathies are not defensive, but assertive and combative," Edgar Gardner Murphy noted at the time; "this popular temper is . . . frankly and ruthlessly destructive." Southern progressivism could not avoid or evade the white supremacy issue, nor could Southern prohibitionism or the Southern education movement.

The Southern Education Board, with eleven Northern and fifteen Southern members in its thirteen-year history, was an intersectional partnership of moderate progressives, moderate in the North on the delicate racial and sectional issues, and progressive in the South in the limited sense that it offered education as a key to regional progress. In challenging racialism by good will, tact and hard work, the Board's efforts were a test of the efficacy of moderate progressivism in a field where the Radicals of Reconstruction had signally failed. The Northerners on the Board were from New York rather than Boston. Robert C. Ogden was manager of John Wanamaker's New York department store. George Foster Peabody, a Wall Street banker, and the young railroad president William H. Baldwin, Jr., had long been associated with Ogden as trustees of Negro industrial schools. These men financed the Board's modest budget, with help from Andrew Carnegie and the General Education Board. Walter Hines Page and Jabez L. M. Curry, Southerners transplanted in the North, served as intersectional diplomats. Booker T. Washington was the agent for Negroes, but did not attend the Board meetings.[1] Most of the Southern members were college presidents. The veteran campaigners Charles D.

[1] Washington met frequently with the Northerners, and spoke on the same platforms with the Southerners in the North and South, but did not attend the Board or Conference meetings. Ogden failed in an effort to get Washington on the program of the Conference for Education in the South.

McIver, Edwin A. Alderman, and Charles W. Dabney had been partners in the earlier North Carolina school crusade. Edgar Gardner Murphy, on the other hand, had attracted the philanthropists' attention by organizing an intersectional conference on Southern race questions at Montgomery, Alabama, May 8–10, 1900. These were the chief policy-makers, though other Southerners were later added.

As Ogden explained the attitude of the philanthropists at a Southern gathering, "While we were originally interested in the South through negro education, our impulses have risen from negro education to the question of the entire burden of educational responsibility that you have throughout this entire section of the country." This change of perspective grew out of sober thought about the significance of the white supremacy movement. As early as 1896 Ogden predicted that the ensuing ten years would cover the Negro's crisis, "and within that period it will be determined whether as a mass his race is to rise or fall in this country. I very much fear the fall." The new philanthropists were not as concerned about Negro civil rights as were the humanitarian radicals of an earlier generation. William H. Baldwin's hard-boiled philanthropy assumed that the Negro "will willingly fill the more menial positions, and do the heavy work, at less wages," leaving to whites "the more expert labor." Baldwin's advice to the Negro was quite specific: "avoid social questions; leave politics alone; continue to be patient; live moral lives; live simply; learn to work . . . know that it is a crime for any teacher, white or black, to educate the negro for positions which are not open to him."

Though these philanthropists may have been complacent about an inferior status for Negroes, they were perturbed by the social and economic hindrances placed on Negroes by the dominant whites. After several experiments within the Negro community, they concluded that the key to Negro problems lay within the white community. There had to be a working compromise between the "best North" and the "best South." The "best North," in Ogden's scale of values, was men like himself, conservative business and professional people; the "best South" included educators and a remnant of upper-class paternalists, "a minority powerful to restrain if not always powerful to accomplish."

If race prejudice was due to ignorance and economic competition, the philanthropists reasoned, then through public schools the whites might learn racial tolerance along with skills which would widen their opportunities. An educational movement of constructive character, moving in a path parallel to the insistent white supremacy demands, could so harbor strength by avoiding direct clashes as to outdistance and check the rival force.

The regional approach of the Board is significant. A single, pervasive social institution, the public school, was the lever by which it hoped to move the region, to solve all of the other complex problems arising from Southern poverty, ignorance, and racial tension. The Board undoubtedly viewed the South as an underdeveloped region. Its task was to furnish technical assistance and a little money if the South would supply the educational enthusiasm and local leadership. Massive economic aid would have had to be federal aid, because of the sheer size of the school systems, and that was apparently out of the question after the Blair education bill was defeated in Congress in the eighties.

The Southern education movement began in 1901 with a Pullman-train journey of influential and philanthropic Northerners to North Carolina, the first of an annual series of such excursions at Ogden's expense, and a public meeting with its governor, Charles B. Aycock, and other members of the Conference for Education in the South. Just elected on a platform coupling Negro disfranchisement and universal education, Aycock represented the conservative wing of the white supremacy movement. A tacit bargain with him underlay the whole educational movement and dictated its tactical methods. The philanthropists acquiesced in disfranchisement and Jim Crow laws and undertook to promote their views in the North, while Aycock openly pledged that the schools of the disfranchised Negroes would have protection from hostile state legislation through the power and prestige of his high office.[2]

Ogden's guests, on their return to the North, indicated a complete surrender to white supremacy. "We have to get rid of our more or less vague idea that all men are created free and equal," announced editor Lyman Abbott of the *Outlook*. The Rev. Charles H. Parkhurst preached at the Madison Square Presbyterian Church that "we learned to look upon matters more in the way in which the Southern mind regards them." Good Southerners advised the Negro to "keep quiet," said Parkhurst, who had been convinced that "the less the negro talks about his civic rights under the Constitution, particularly the right of suffrage . . . the sooner he will attain to all the rights that justly belong to him." Walter Hines Page of *World's Work* admitted that race friction was getting worse, but thought it could not be "allayed . . . by anything whatsoever except the training of the inefficient and the ignorant." Page stressed a positive approach to the Southern problem. "The statesman-schoolmaster," he affirmed, "is the man to build our hopes on." These spokesmen for the philanthropic capitalist did not so much change Northern opinion as indicate its final capitulation to racialism. Others had already taken the same

---

[2] Actually, Aycock did little to protect Negro school funds at the county and district levels, and, according to the state school superintendent, James Y. Joyner, less was spent on Negro rural schools in 1905 than in 1895.

path to reunion, and racial discrimination was spreading in the North.

Seeking to cushion the shock of racialism and keep public education open as an avenue of Negro advancement, the philanthropists offered the Negro charity rather than full-fledged philanthropy. They were willing on the Negro's behalf to renounce some of his claims to equal status and opportunity. Not being Negroes themselves, they were probably not fully aware how disappointing such a compromise was to many Negroes, nor how vulnerable the complete loss of political power made the Negroes. And they fatally miscalculated in assuming that the upper-class wing of Southern racialism, because it spoke the language of conservatism, would be their effective partner in protecting Negroes. People who were disturbed by the collapse of the Reconstruction settlement undoubtedly sighed with relief that the Negro was keeping education as a solace and hope, and that all they needed to do to further Negro progress was to ride on Ogden's train to hear Southerners speak at educational conferences. But they were misled in this facile optimism.

The Southern Education Board members agreed that for the first two years, at least, "we would not emphasize the *negro* too much," according to Dabney, who ran the Board's propaganda bureau at Knoxville. "In the excited state of public sentiment," he wrote, "this was considered wisest." The Southern campaigners preached in general terms the education of all the people and fairness to Negroes. But as Alderman stated their position in a Northern magazine, the education "of one untaught white man to the point that knowledge and not prejudice will guide his conduct . . . is worth more to the black man himself than the education of ten Negroes." As Charles B. Aycock simplified the doctrine: "Education of the whites will provide education for the negroes." Exactly how this magic would work was never clear, but its Southern advocates insisted that education for Negroes was also essential. They said nothing about desegregation, and as little as possible about "separate but equal" education, a doctrine then popular only among constitutional lawyers.[3]

The Northerners took Dabney to task in 1903 for ignoring the Negro entirely in the propaganda he spread over the South. In Mississippi, for example, Negro education was not mentioned at a time when James K. Vardaman was trying to destroy the state's Negro school fund. "When I reminded them that a year ago all of them . . . were proclaiming the same principles and policies, I was greeted with silence or explanations," Dabney wrote home. "Recent events have re-excited them about the negro's interests and put them to thinking how they can help to maintain them against the white aggressors." Dabney considered resigning, but the other Southerners patched up the intersectional compromise again.

[3] The Southerners' stand on school segregation was rigid.

Spokesmen for Negro schools watched from the sidelines with attitudes fluctuating between suspicion and hope. "The fact that it is controlled by Mr. Ogden & Peabody will make it necessary to devote much thought to Negro as well as white education," Principal Hollis B. Frissell of Hampton assured Booker T. Washington in the first year. But Negro college graduates and some Northern liberals were alienated by the fact that the Northern members, who sat on all of the leading philanthropic boards interested in the South, channeled these funds into Negro industrial institutes and white colleges. And Washington himself wrote privately that the Southern educational campaign meant "almost nothing so far as the Negro schools are concerned." He charged the "the Southern members . . . do not put themselves on record in a straight and frank manner as much as they should."

One might expect the General Education Board, with its millions, prestige and relative independence, to balance the caution of the Southern campaigners with its own boldness. But Wallace Buttrick, its executive secretary, was equally cautious and perhaps a bit frightened by the emotional timbre of Southern racialism. After a grass-roots conference in the South with North Carolina county school superintendents, Buttrick decided that equal treatment for Negroes would make whites cold toward philanthropy. "As a matter of absolute justice they ought to participate proportionately with the whites," he said in a confidential report. "But we are confronted 'with a condition and not a theory.' . . . We shall err and invite defeat, if, in the present state of public sentiment, we demand too much from the white people of the South."

Ogden restrained his own sincere impulse to speak up for Negro education partly from loyalty to his vulnerable Southern allies. He was constantly aware of the danger that the whites might divide educational tax funds so that Negro schools would receive only the returns from Negro taxes, and his Southern friends convinced him that if this question were submitted to Southern voters, the demagogues would win. "For these men to openly attack you," warned Murphy, "would not only be 'unpleasant' but would 'drive to cover' men . . . on whom we—and the negro—*must* depend for fairness and patriotism." "I feel 'like a dog' to have to say these things," Murphy protested, "but I *know* our people." The philanthropists assumed that Southern sensitivity would permit discussion of racial issues only by Southerners. But they might well have risked their timid millions, and the added capital of good will so painstakingly accumulated by intersectional conciliation, in bold leadership on the Negro's behalf in ventures their Southern colleagues could not risk. They decided instead to intensify their original efforts for general popular education. Such action had much to be said for it, but as far as Negro education was concerned it was simply evasion. The real dilemma of the public school campaigns was that white educational sentiment, as it grew, increased the temptation to take the Negro's share of school funds. Educational promoters were tempted to promise taxpayers a fiscal saving through racial discrimination. The philanthropists, seeking Southern allies against the demagogues who exploited lower-class prejudices, actually joined forces with the upper-class conservatives who quietly administered school discrimination.

"Within the saving limits of established principles," said Ogden, "I strive to be, in this Southern Education matter, all things to all men that peace may in the future reign throughout the length and breadth of our land." He sometimes went to great lengths to promote intersectional harmony. He appeared at the New York Union League Club to scotch a proposal to reduce Southern congressional representation as a reprisal for disfranchisement.[4] Avoiding visits to Negro colleges and warning friends against accepting professorships there, he advised Negro leaders to employ "concession, moderation and patience." The editors and public figures who accompanied him southward were counseled to be as "wise as serpents" and as "gentle as doves." "I pursue my own course quietly," he wrote a liberal Southerner, "always, however, adapting myself to the standards of the environment in which I may be found." But adaptation to the environment of Southern racialism weakened the philanthropists' position as guardians of Negro interests.

It was clear by 1906 that racialism continued to dominate Southern affairs. The Northerners and Murphy held a caucus, and at the next Board meeting Peabody broached the topic of a special campaign for Negro education. The Southern members tried to delay action. "We should avoid anything like a crusade," said Alderman; "guard against going into it with heat." When Peabody replied that it was "about time for a crusade of the right kind," Alderman rejoined: "Southern men have shied from this subject. It has been touching a sore tooth. . . . We want now to influence public sentiment: stop being silent, but be wise; go forward, but with forethought, not so spectacularly as to set back the movement." This discussion made clear the Board's dilemma, that a crusade for Negro education would jeopardize the crusade for white education. Yielding reluctantly to the superior power of the white supremacy movement, the Board continued its strong efforts for a middle path between equalitarianism and racialism, and resigned itself by default to the growth of separate and unequal schools.

Pressed from the South by an opposition led by the *Manufacturers' Record,* organ of industry in the South, Page told a Southern newspaper re-

---

[4] Ogden was denounced for this by Negro leaders.

porter: "You will find when the wood pile is turned over not a nigger, but an uneducated white boy." "There is a man," he said, "and it is the man we want to reach." Ogden himself yielded to the temptation to describe his movement as "almost exclusively in white interest." Believing that commerce and education could go hand in hand, Ogden was sincerely puzzled by the attacks from the New South. His guests were being called "picturesque junketers," "Pullman car philanthropists," and "the swell-belly parade." The conciliatory methods may have won over some moderate Southerners, but the language of the opposition press could hardly have been stronger if the movement had been bolder.

The Southern attacks did not conceal the movement's conservatism from the more doctrinaire liberals. Ogden's characteristic methods seemed to Oswald Garrison Villard of the *Nation* "too complacent and too conciliatory; as if there was some lack of the fiery indignation of the reformer." Negro leaders who shared Villard's distrust of the philanthropists and their allies formed in 1906 the militant Niagara Movement, out of which grew the National Association for the Advancement of Colored People, a protest group with a long-range objective of full democratic equality with whites. Warned by Hollis B. Frissell that the new movement stressed "the rights rather than the duties of the colored people," the philanthropists received it with cold silence and expressed private disapproval. Washington, whose leadership was challenged, went further. Maintaining an unmistakably hostile public silence,[5] he privately ordered his assistant, "Telegraph . . . newspaper men that you can absolutely trust to ignore [the] Niagra [*sic*] movement."[6] His efforts at suppression extended to buying up hostile Negro newspapers.

Washington's own racial policy was failing tragically at the time he was trying to prevent alternative policies. His own school and his Southern supporters were under attack. Southern officials were giving Negro schools a smaller and smaller proportion of tax funds. The General Education Board refused to aid Negro high schools, and the Peabody Fund was dissolved without giving Negro schools a proportionate share of the principal. Even in education, the traditional touchstone of Negro advancement, the conservative Negro leader had little to conserve, as he made clear at a gathering of Southern professors in 1915. "We are trying," he said, "to instil into the Negro mind that if education does not make the Negro humble, simple, and of service to the community, then it will not be encouraged.

Perhaps the Southern Education Board can better be judged on the

[5] Washington's public remark that "a hungry race cannot live upon 'principles' " was in reference to educational policy rather than public affairs, but perhaps it reveals his frame of reference.

[6] The spelling error was probably that of a Southern white telegrapher.

basis of general trends in the South than on its discreet utterances. There really was a Southern educational awakening between 1900 and the first World War. Annual expenditures for education quadrupled, kept well ahead of the rise in property values, and acted as a springboard for further increases in the next decade. Though other improvements did not always keep pace with physical expansion, and though the lag behind non-Southern schools continued, Southern whites had better schools and more books, necessities of life in a state of civilization. The Southern Education Board played an important part in the work which brought about this public school expansion.

On the other hand, the Board's efforts seem to have had almost no effect on the Negro schools. Nor did the Board brake or deflect the course of racialism. "Passionate and rapidly developing enthusiasm for white education is bearing sharply and adversely upon the opportunities of the negro," the sensitive Murphy noted. "There is not only no chance to help the situation of the negro educationally, but it is steadily growing worse, and their schools, upon every sort of pretext, are being hampered and impoverished where they are not actually abandoned." Marked financial discrimination against the already conveniently segregated Negro schools apparently developed from a conjunction of motives: increased white desire for education, white racial hostility, and efforts of taxpayers to limit taxation. It is misleading to think of the dual system of education as a financial burden when the two systems were grossly unequal. Discrimination against Negro schools represented a fiscal saving and was a basis for compromise between taxpayer and tax-layer. The educational campaigns themselves drove the wedge of inequality between the two systems. Discrimination varied from place to place, but it was almost universal, flagrant, and increasing. In South Carolina, for example, in 1900 the white child of school age received about $5.75 for every dollar expended per Negro child, whereas in 1915 the ratio was about $12.37 to one dollar. By other measurements such as school property, transportation, attendance, pupils per teacher, and high school opportunities, the contrast was even more striking.

Educational reform within the context of racialism partook of racialism, whatever may be the long-range effect of expanded education on white attitudes. Discrimination in education was a cancerous growth out of reform. The Southern Education Board's sympathetic and gentle approach to the race issue in Southern public education lacked moral firmness and was therefore weakened by compromise.

6. *The Progressive South*

ARTHUR S. LINK

Despite its pervasive conservatism, the modern South has not been un-affected by such reform movements as Populism, progressivism, and the New Deal. Nor have southern congressmen always come down on the side of obstructionism and reaction; they have contributed from time to time to the formulation of constructive policies for the nation.

The following essay is by Princeton University's Arthur S. Link, who in addition to being a distinguished Wilson biographer and editor of the Wilson Papers, has long demonstrated an interest in the South's role in national affairs and may be considered the first modern scholar to emphasize the im-pact of the progressive movement below the Potomac. Here Professor Link argues that a group of agrarian liberals from the South pushed a reluctant Wil-son further than he was originally prepared to go, thus contributing to several important domestic reforms during the first Wilson administration. He thus reminds us that one of the elements in southern political thought is a strain of agrarian radicalism, which on occasion has had more than regional sig-nificance. His analysis also throws light on the broad division within the ranks of the southern congressmen during this period and outlines the nature of southern progressivism at the state and local levels during the progressive era.

T HE ELECTION OF WOODROW WILSON AND DEMOCRATIC MAJORITIES in the House and Senate in 1912 confronted the Democrats of the South with their most serious challenge since before the Civil War. They had come to power more because of the disruption of the Republican party than because their party now represented the majority opinion of the country, and the future of the Democratic party for many years to come would depend upon their performance during the next two years. But the question whether they were not too much rent by personal fac-

Originally published as "The South and the 'New Freedom': An Interpretation," in *The American Scholar*, XX, No. 4 (Summer, 1951), 314–324. Copyright © 1951 by the United Chapters of Phi Beta Kappa. Reprinted by permission of the publishers.

tionalism and too sectionally conscious to govern in the national interest remained yet to be answered.

Southern Democrats in 1913 controlled practically all important congressional committees; they had a large majority in the Democratic caucuses in both houses; they had a president apparently responsive to their wishes, and they had a goodly representation in the cabinet. Judged by all superficial appearances, at least, the South was "in the saddle." These, however, were only the outward signs of control. The fact that Southerners happened to be chairmen of certain committees may or may not be important. The important question is whether they used the power they possessed to achieve political and economic objectives that the South especially desired, and whether they helped to shape the character of Wilsonian reform.

Wilson came to the presidency in 1913 with a clear conception of what the Democratic party should do to right the wrongs that special privilege had allegedly perpetrated through the Republican party. He would have the Democrats revise the tariff to eliminate all features of special privilege to domestic industries, bring the national banks into effective cooperation and control, and work out a new code for business in order to restore competition and make impossible the misuse of power by the giant corporations. This was the sum and substance of the "New Freedom." The political and economic millennium was to be achieved by these simple expedients, all of which were based upon the assumption implicit in Wilson's campaign addresses of 1912, namely, that the limits of federal authority under the Constitution would not permit, and wise statesmanship would not desire, the extension of federal authority directly into business operations or the use of that authority to change the social and economic relationships then existing among the various interest groups.

Wilson originally conceived of the New Freedom as the political means of implementing the doctrines of laissez-faire, by removing all kinds of special class legislation. It was, therefore, a program intended to meet the needs primarily of the business community. There was nothing in it for the farmers or laborers directly, although these groups presumably would benefit from lower tariff rates and the restoration of competition in business. But Wilson had no more idea of legislating to advance the interests of these particular groups than he did of granting subsidies to American manufacturers. It can be said, in brief, that the Wilsonian program had the one supreme objective of taking the government out of the business of subsidizing and directly regulating economic activity and taking the country back to some mythical age when there was a perfect natural identification of economic interests.

The most significant fact about the first Wilson administration is that the New Freedom, as it was originally conceived by its author, survived for only a few months. It required only short contact with reality to convince Wilson that his elaborate doctrines of 1912 were inadequate to deal with such great concentrations of economic power as existed at the time. More important as a factor in moving him away from his laissez-faire position, however, were certain powerful political forces over which Wilson and his administration had no control and which, as it were, seized control of administration policy and pushed it far beyond the bounds that Wilson and his advisers had originally thought desirable. In effect, what occurred from 1913 to 1917 was that Wilson adopted many of the assumptions and almost the whole platform of Theodore Roosevelt's New Nationalism.

This metamorphosis in the Wilsonian program is the key to understanding the first Wilson administration. The Southern contribution toward bringing the administration to an advanced position with regard to the exercise of federal authority was considerable, but the character of this contribution was different from what has been generally assumed. The Southern Democrats in Congress were divided roughly into two factions. First, there was what might be called the administration faction, consisting mainly of committee chairmen like Oscar W. Underwood and Carter Glass, who, by and large, represented a political tradition and constituencies whose interest were more or less divergent from those of the more numerous Southern group. Members of the administration faction were for the most part conservatives, although most of them had no fundamental political principles, were loyal party men, and would follow Wilson's lead. Secondly, there was a larger faction that represented more accurately the political traditions and economic interests of the South—the spokesmen for the agrarian interests of the South, men like Claude Kitchin, Otis Wingo, James K. Vardaman and Robert L. Henry.

The Southern Agrarians of the Wilson period were the direct inheritors and now the prime articulators in the Democratic party of the philosophy underlying the Agrarian crusade—namely, that it was government's duty to intervene directly in economic affairs in order to benefit submerged or politically impotent economic interests. As it turned out, the existence and power of the Southern Agrarian group had important consequences for the Democratic party, the Wilson administration, and the nation. Whereas the administration faction usually followed the regular party line, the Southern Agrarians were often far to the left of it; and in the end they helped to make Wilson an advanced progressive and helped to commit his administration to a broad program of welfare legislation.

The program of the Southern Agrarians was aimed at benefiting the farmers almost exclusively. Although this had been true also of the Democratic program in 1896, Bryan and progressive Democrats in the North and West had moved beyond the almost pure agrarianism of 1896. There was a growing concern for the plight of submerged groups from about 1890 to 1913 and a consequent rise of a great movement for social justice. This phase of progressivism had not been totally absent in the South, but the Southern states were still overwhelmingly rural, and most Southerners had no conception of the grave social and economic problems raised by industrialization and urbanization.

Hence Southern progressives were more concerned with strengthening the political and economic position of the farmers, through regulation of railroads and corporations, a low tariff, the direct primary, and the like, than with tenement reforms, minimum wage legislation, or workmen's compensation legislation. But the important point about the Southern Agrarian program is not that it was limited in scope, but that its advocates were an important element in the Democratic party and that they were now in a position to give voice to their own demands.

The brief period when the philosophy of the New Freedom had any real authority was the few months in 1913 when the Underwood tariff bill was under discussion in Congress. There was little disagreement among Democratic congressmen, progressive or conservative, over the provisions of the bill, except for minor differences on the wool and sugar schedules. There was a much greater difference of opinion between the conservatives and the agrarian radicals, however, on the question of the reorganization of the banking system and the control of the money supply. It was here that the Southern Agrarians, acting with their colleagues from the West, first helped to move their party away from laissez-faire toward a dynamic concept of government.

In line with his New Freedom principles Wilson was inclined to favor the banking and monetary system proposed by the National Monetary Commission, one providing for a reserve association or associations owned and controlled by the bankers themselves. The original Glass bill, which had the tentative endorsement of the administration, provided for such an arrangement. But even before the federal reserve bill emerged from the House Banking Committee, there occurred a momentous struggle within the party councils that was not ended until the Agrarian leaders had won all their important demands. Secretary of State Bryan and Louis D. Brandeis persuaded the President that a banking bill which did not provide for exclusive governmental control, on the top level, was not only unwise but also would never be approved by the House caucus. This was true, incidentally, regardless of the position Bryan might have taken in the controversy.

Wilson was won over by the persuasive arguments of Bryan and Brandeis and the threats of the radicals. Thus the Glass bill, as it finally emerged from the House committee, provided for a decentralized reserve system, for government issue of federal-reserve currency, and for an over-all supervision and limited control of the new system by a central reserve board composed exclusively of presidential appointees. It marked, to all practical purposes, the demise of the New Freedom and the beginning of the rise to dominance of the progressives in the Wilson administration.

Bryan and the Western Democrats were now satisfied, but not the Southern Agrarian leaders. In spite of the radical changes that had been effected, the new banking system still would operate exclusively for the benefit of the business community. Here was the rub, as far as the Southern radicals were concerned. After tariff reform had been accomplished, their main objective was the establishment of a system by which farmers could obtain easier and cheaper credit. When the Glass bill was published, and the Southern Agrarians discovered that it included no provision for agricultural credit, they rose in rebellion and declared that they would help the Republicans defeat the measure if the administration did not concede their demands. The fight between the administration forces and the Southern Agrarians was bitter, and for a time threatened to defeat banking reform altogether. Suffice it to say that, in spite of the ridicule of the Eastern press and in spite of the opposition of the administration and of Wilson's spokesmen in the House, the Federal Reserve Bill as finally passed by Congress contained ample provisions for short-term agricultural credit. And this was true because Wilson realized that he must give in to the demands of the Southerners.

The philosophic foundations of the New Freedom were dealt another heavy blow during the formulation of an antitrust policy by administration leaders. It was Wilson's original idea that all that was required was to define precisely what constituted an unfair trade practice or illegal restraint of trade, so as to remove all element of doubt from the laws. The enforcement of the antitrust laws would be delegated, as before, to the Justice Department and the courts. Some of the Southern radicals proposed more drastic remedies, such as prescribing by law the percentage of the total production of a field of industry which one corporation would be allowed to control, or a high excess profits tax which would increase in direct proportion to the size of the industry; but they made no determined fight for these proposals. Wilson, therefore, gave the job of drawing up the measure to Representative Clayton of Alabama, chairman of the Judiciary Committee, and the bill that came out of his committee was simply a synthesis of current ideas, most of which were already embodied in the laws of many states. In addition, Representative Covington of Kentucky drew up at Wilson's request a bill providing for an interstate trade commission, which was to be an enlarged Bureau of Corporations and without any real authority over business practices.

Thus far Wilson had proceeded in line with his New Freedom concepts. At this point, however, an important turn in administration policy occurred. Brandeis, George L. Rublee, and Representative Stevens of New Hampshire visited the President and persuaded him to change the character of his antitrust program entirely. Under their direction, the Clayton bill was rewritten so as to provide for greater flexibility in defining an unfair trade practice and, more important, the interstate commerce commission was reconstituted as the Federal Trade Commission and given apparently vast authority over the day-to-day operations of the business world. The Covington bill had provided for nothing more than an investigatory body to serve as an adjunct of the Justice Department. In the revised bill, the Commission was established as an independent regulatory agency, empowered to supervise business practices and to issue cease and desist orders when it found that corporations were engaging in unfair practices. This last change marked the complete adoption by the Wilson administration of Roosevelt's program for the regulation of business.

The Southern leaders in Congress had nothing to do with bringing about this profound change in Wilson's antitrust policy. The Southern and Western Agrarian radicals, acting with a small Labor bloc in the House, worked hard, however, to have a provision inserted in the Clayton bill exempting farm and labor unions from the operation and application of the antitrust laws. This had been one of the major objectives of the American Federation of Labor since 1906 and had been given Democratic approval in the platforms of 1908 and 1912. Although Wilson was rapidly abandoning his New Freedom assumptions, he was not yet ready to go so far as to approve what was obviously legislation in the interest of particular classes. Since the first days of his administration he had resisted bitterly this move, and a bill specifically exempting farm and labor unions from antitrust prosecutions, which had been passed by the House in the previous session, was blocked by administration pressure. When the Clayton bill was under discussion in the House committee, however, the Agrarian and Labor bloc declared that they would guarantee its defeat unless Wilson gave in to their demands.

Thus faced with another major revolt within his party, Wilson resolved his dilemma by resorting, it must be admitted, to one of the most artful dodges in the history of American politics. The famous labor provisions of the Clayton bill were drawn by Representative E. Y. Webb of North Carolina, who had succeeded Clayton as chairman of the Judiciary

Committee, and represented Wilson's attitude perfectly. On the face of it, the new provision did indeed seem to give the exemption and immunity from antitrust prosecutions that the farm and labor spokesmen were demanding. Actually, this was not the case at all. Farm and labor organizations were not to be construed by the courts as being, *per se,* combinations in restraint of trade, but they were in no way freed from the threat of prosecution if they violated the antitrust laws.

Wilson had completed his program of domestic reform by the fall of 1914. In his letters and public statements at the time, he made it clear that he thought everything had been done that was necessary to clear away special privilege and put all classes on an equal footing. Under the operation of the beneficent new laws, Wilson was sure that the nation would enjoy a long period of prosperity and economic freedom. As we have seen, he had been forced partially to abandon his earlier position and to make important concessions in order to get his program across. He was reconciled to the concessions he had been compelled to make, but he was absolutely determined to draw the line at the point it had reached by the fall of 1914.

In fact, a pronounced reaction against progressive policies had set in among Wilson and his advisers during the spring of 1914, and relations between the President and progressive leaders became exceedingly strained at this time. The following year, 1915, was practically barren of progressive accomplishments, except for the La Follette's Seamen's Act, which the administration had opposed and which Wilson almost vetoed. There were, however, several great political forces at work which were so strong that Wilson would be compelled to accommodate his program to satisfy their demands. One was the well-organized Agrarian movement for the establishment of a federal system of long-term rural credits. Another was the movement in behalf of federal social legislation, which was rapidly gaining momentum during this period. Another was the movement for women's suffrage, which was becoming so powerful that it would soon be dangerous for any politician to oppose it. Finally, there was the fact that the Progressive party was obviously disintegrating after 1914 and that the only hope the Democrats had of obtaining a national majority in 1916 was in winning a large minority of the former Bull Moosers to the Democratic side.

Wilson resisted this movement to extend the intervention of the federal government into the fields mentioned here as long as he could do so safely. Then, when it became evident that the Democrats could win the election of 1916 only by adopting the New Nationalism, lock, stock and barrel, Wilson capitulated and supported the very demands he had so long opposed, as strongly as if he had been their originator. We do not have the space to discuss this last and most important phase of Wilsonian reform in any detail, except to consider the extent to which the Southern leaders contributed to the administration's final, complete surrender to the New Nationalism.

The main objective of the Southern Agrarian progressives after 1914 was the adoption of a federal rural credits bill. The first nationwide movement for long-term federal rural credit facilities had been inaugurated by the Southern Commercial Congress in 1913, and during the next year or two there was widespread discussion of the subject all over the country. In the spring of 1914 a joint subcommittee drew up the bill which was finally passed in 1916 and which would have passed in 1914 had not Wilson let it be known that he would veto the bill if Congress enacted it. Both Wilson and the Agrarian leaders proclaimed themselves advocates of a rural credits measure. What, therefore, was the root of the difference between them? Wilson would not agree to the establishment of a system involving direct subsidies or financial support by the government, and Wilson, Secretary of Agriculture Houston, and Carter Glass were insistent that the government should do no more than provide for the structure of a rural credits system, with capital and management to be provided by private sources. The Agrarian spokesmen, on the other hand, contended that any system which was not operated and financed by the government was bound to fail. But as this involved the direct intervention by the government in behalf of a special class, Wilson was absolutely adamant against it. The result was an impasse, with both sides holding out stubbornly for their own proposals until 1916, when Wilson accepted the Agrarian proposal for reasons of political expediency.

It was, in fact, in agricultural legislation that the Southern Agrarians had the greatest influence in the shaping of the later Wilsonian program. Their greatest contribution was undoubtedly the forcing of the Rural Credits Act of 1916, but they were also able to obtain the adoption of the Lever Warehouse Act in 1914, the Smith-Lever Act for rural extension work of the same year, the Smith-Hughes Act for vocational education, and the program of federal subsidies for highway improvement in 1916.

Southern influence was practically negligible, however, in the formulation of the remaining great social and economic legislation of 1916—the federal Workmen's Compensation Act, the Child Labor Law, the Adamson Act, and the act establishing the Federal Tariff Commission. But there still remained three other areas of legislation in which the influence of the Southern Agrarians was decisive and which merit notice here.

The first involved the question of what sort of military and naval bills Congress should enact in 1916. On this controversial subject the Southern progressives joined with radicals throughout the country in resisting the administration's designs greatly to increase the navy and to establish a large volunteer army. They were not successful in blocking the movement for a large navy, because the pressure here was too great. But they were signally successful in blocking Wilson's plans for military preparedness, indeed, in emasculating them.

The second field of legislation in which Southern progressive influence was decisive was the area of federal fiscal policy. Before the outbreak of the World War, Wilson and McAdoo were able to keep a firm grip on the formulation of tax policies, and their influence was conservative indeed. The tax structure that the Republicans had erected and which was weighted so heavily in favor of the upper classes was left practically undisturbed by the Wilson administration. An income tax provision was included in the Underwood Tariff Law, to make up the anticipated deficit resulting from the lower duties, but the rates were very low and the administration was quick to make it clear that it had no intention of using the income tax to effect a redistribution of wealth.

The outbreak of the war in Europe in the summer of 1914 caused a temporary disarrangement of the finances of the United States and resulted in a sharp decline in imports, which meant that the administration was faced with an alarming decline in revenues. To meet this emergency, McAdoo proposed a series of new excise taxes and a tax on freight shipments, such as had been applied during the Spanish-American War. The Southern and Western Agrarians rebelled at the administration's emergency tax program, claiming that it would throw the whole burden of carrying the country through the crisis on the masses and demanding instead an increase in the income tax. They were successful in eliminating the tax on freight shipments and in getting most of the new taxes put on alcoholic beverages and other luxuries. Even so, they did not like the emergency tax law and vowed that they would continue to fight all such consumption taxes.

With the opening of Congress in December, 1915, the Southern progressives found themselves virtually in control of the House Ways and Means Committee. Long before the new session convened, a majority of the committee declared in writing to the new chairman, Claude Kitchin of North Carolina, their determination to overhaul the tax structure and make it more democratic. The result was that during the winter and spring of 1916 the control of federal tax policy was literally taken out of the hands of the administration leaders and assumed by these Southern Agrarians and their Western allies. It was obvious by this time that some kind of preparedness measures would be adopted, and that either the government would have to find new sources of revenue or else resort to borrowing. The Republicans proposed a bond issue; the administration proposed new consumption and excise and increased income taxes. The Ways and Means Committee, however, replied with one of the most startling and significant tax bills in the history of the country. The Southern Agrarians, who had bitterly resisted the preparedness movement, saw now that new defense measures were inevitable; but they were determined that the people of the East, who had been most vociferous in support of preparedness, should pay for it. Kitchin said as much, in fact, before the House caucus when he explained the new tax bill, which greatly increased the income tax, levied the first federal inheritance tax in our history, and placed an excess profits tax on munitions manufacturers.

The last area in which Southern influence was decisive in determining the policies of the Wilson administration was the federal government's policy toward Negroes. Here the Southern contribution was definitely retrogressive and proved that it was impossible for white Southerners of all shades of opinion to get much beyond the rationale of slavery. Suffice it to say that Wilson practically sacrificed the Negroes on the altar of political expediency, by allowing segregation in the government departments, dismissal and downgrading of Negro civil servants in the South, and the like, in order to win Southern support for his program.

Yet in spite of this and other blind spots in the Southern progressive program, it must be concluded that the contributions of the Southern Agrarians were undoubtedly in many ways decisive in moving the Wilson administration away from a static laissez-faire program, to which it was originally dedicated, toward a dynamic, positive program of federal action. Although their program was limited in scope and motivated largely by class interests, the Southern progressives could claim as much credit as could several other major groups for the amazing metamorphosis in Democratic policy that occurred from 1913 to 1916. This is the real significance of their contribution.

7. The Conservative South

FRANK FREIDEL

Franklin D. Roosevelt's election as President in 1932 gave southern congressmen their second major opportunity in the twentieth century to play a significant part in the legislative program of a national administration. Roosevelt's leadership, like that of Wilson, tended to nationalize southern politics and broaden the outlook of southern congressmen. But, unlike the New Freedom, the New Deal threatened the power structure of the South with revolutionary social and economic changes, and in time many Southerners, both in and out of Congress, became critics of Roosevelt's administration.

Professor Frank Freidel of Harvard University has published several volumes of his multivolume biography of Roosevelt and his knowledge of the Congresses of the New Deal era enables him to make an authoritative evaluation of the role of the southern delegations in a national context. The next paper, first read as one of his Walter Lynwood Fleming Lectures at Louisiana State University, illuminates the relationship between the President and the southern congressmen, and between the New Deal and the South. Describing the New Deal's impact on the area, he reveals something of the desperate need an impoverished region had for the kind of aid offered by the New Deal and explores the ambivalent attitude of many southern leaders toward Roosevelt and the administration. In addition to clarifying the importance of Roosevelt's leadership and sketching the interplay of regional needs, conservative traditions, and the innovations of the 1930s, Freidel's paper is particularly useful for its explanation of the growing opposition of southern conservatives to New Deal reforms.

I N THE FALL OF 1932 THE SOUTH, HAVING HELPED ELECT THE President of its choice, Franklin D. Roosevelt, waited eagerly for his promised New Deal, with no more certainty than the rest of the nation as to what that New Deal might be. A majority of Southern

Originally published as "The New Deal versus Bourbonism," in *F.D.R. and the South* (Baton Rouge, 1965), pp. 34–70. Reprinted by permission of the Louisiana State University Press.

Democratic politicians had first rallied behind Roosevelt at the beginning of 1931 to meet the threat of continued Eastern conservative domination of the Democratic party; out of the despair of acute economic crisis, that same majority awaited his actions during the long interregnum between his election in November, 1932, and his inauguration in March, 1933. Never again would he enjoy such unanimous and unquestioning support from the Southern political leaders, except momentarily in the war crisis of December, 1941. The majority temporarily blanketed serious differences in the views of Southern politicians, both within the organizations of each of their states and among their constituents. Above all they were, for the time being, amenable to change; and, as yet, none fitted the cruel portrait of those of their number in the United States Senate which the political scientist V. O. Key has reported:

Commonly a southern Senator is caricatured as a frock-coated, long-maned, and long-winded statesman of the old school who conspires in the cloakroom with Republicans to grind down the common man. He is supposed in return to receive generous campaign contributions from Wall Street as well as kudos from the conservative columnists who praise him as a constitutional scholar, a man of statesmanlike vision, and an embodiment of the virtues of the Founding Fathers. While there is in all this enough truth to embarrass good southern Democrats, the report of the Southern Democratic-Republican congressional coalition has been not a little exaggerated.

Whether active in state politics or members of one of the houses of Congress, whether of Bourbon or agrarian ideological antecedents, most of the leaders of Southern democracy developed, in time, an embarrassing ambivalence toward Roosevelt and the New Deal. The South was so painfully in need of succor that they desparately sought federal aid; yet the New Deal inevitably threatened to upset the status quo and alter some of the cherished institutions upon which they fervently believed the very existence of Southern civilization depended. All but a few of them fell under the spell of Roosevelt's charm and yet abhorred some of the changes his administration brought to the South.

Roosevelt faced a dilemma, too. He was a Yankee, not a Southerner; and while he held the South, his adopted section, in genuine affection, his attitude toward inviolable Southern institutions was intellectual rather than emotional, pragmatic rather than dogmatic. To him the greatest challenge facing the South was the alleviation of poverty, not the maintenance (or, for that matter, the elimination) of white supremacy. Therefore, he stood for change, even while he depended upon Southern leadership in Congress to whom change was sometimes painful or even intolerable. These leaders, indoctrinated in traditions of party loyalty, for the most part gave him emphatic support, far beyond their convictions, on issues and for much longer than might have been expected. Gradually, as they voted measure after measure to comprise the New Deal, they became more and more restive. The Southern majority in Congress was eroded and finally, in 1937, shattered. It was not until that year that the caricature which Key reports would serve as more than a crude political cartoon of a handful of Southern Senators. Roosevelt, for his part, labored to maintain the majority, at times trying to be above faction and somehow to remain a neutral in the struggles between the Bourbons and the New Dealers. Of course he could not be neutral, and this was his dilemma. He could not hold indefinitely the support of Southern leaders and yet seek to remake the South. In certain respects he was willing to modify or water down the New Deal in its practical operation in the South, but these concessions brought about a furor in the North. Even more than the pressure from Northerners, Roosevelt's own firm convictions kept his an energetic New Dealer in his Southern policies. That is to say, he was the champion of the impoverished; and these impoverished, more concerned with their immediate personal welfare than with constitutional questions and long-range tendencies, gave Roosevelt their hearts and their undying loyalty. Regardless of how their leaders might warn them, they were ready again and again—provided they held the franchise—to vote for President Roosevelt.

That was the basic political pattern of the New Deal South. Here is how it gradually emerged.

In the winter of 1932-33, the South was politically triumphant but economically prostrate. If, as has been argued, it had not been struck by the Depression as badly as other sections, this was true only because so much of the South had been so blighted in the 1920's that its economy had less distance to plummet. True, the South was still predominantly rural and small farmers could grow some of their own food, but since 1929 many of them had been slipping from a subsistence to a near-starvation level. The twelve-cent cotton of 1929 had been bad enough; in total the farmers received only $1,245,000,000 for their crop. The five-cent cotton of 1932 was a complete calamity; the crop brought $374,-000,000. Forced farm sales in Mississippi were double the national average. In Georgia, gross farm income dropped from $206 per person in 1929 to $83 in 1932. Throughout the South innumerable farm families received less than $100 in cash during an entire year. Coal miners were destitute; steel workers were in worse straits than their fellow workers in the North; some textile workers enjoyed employment but worked nineteenth century hours for subsistence wages. Added to the distress were all the festering problems that had plagued Southern economy in the 1920's and long before. Only a drastic program of recovery and reform would be likely to bring the South its full share of national prosperity. Further, it would have to be a program especially tailored to fit the distinctive functioning of Southern economy. Yet during the months of the interregnum Southern leaders in Congress were envisaging a most limited program while President-elect Roosevelt was quietly planning a national one into which the South must fit.

The planning of the leaders in Congress is interesting in retrospect. They were strong men who had harried President Hoover unmercifully for several years. They were firm in their rather conservative principles. They were ready to listen respectfully to Roosevelt as the head of their party and the future President, but obviously they expected the molding of policy to be largely in their hands. They seem to have taken an older view of the Presidency, one prevalent during the nineteenth century, in not expecting Roosevelt to assume firm and detailed legislative management.

During these months when most Americans were crying for strong leadership, Roosevelt did not disabuse the Southern leaders but seemed rather willing to concede them great power. He conferred with them on several occasions and agreed on their program. How little they had to offer is shown by their bills: limited farm relief, legalization of beer with mild alcoholic content, some public works spending, and a balanced budget. Above all they wanted a balanced budget through a cutting of government costs and a raising of taxes. Roosevelt gave them enthusiastic support on these points in conference and correspondence. To Senator Pat Harrison of Mississippi, ranking Democrat of the Senate Finance Committee, he wrote concerning the Lame Duck session from December to March:

"I have not bothered you in any way about the appropriation bills, because I have had the utmost confidence that you will do the right thing with them. . . .

"It is my thought, however, that you will do everything possible to cut the total of each bill even below the revised budget figures of the President.

"At the same time I deem it of first importance that the budget should be honestly balanced, even at this short session."

Roosevelt's only demurrer came when Speaker Garner and Senate Majority Leader Robinson, thinking they acted under Roosevelt's mandate, endorsed President Hoover's proposal for a national manufacturers' sales tax.

When the anathema of Southern conservatives, Senator Huey Long of Louisiana, pushed his way into Roosevelt's hotel suite, asserting he was going to "talk turkey," he received the same affable treatment. Long came out smiling: "I think we've got a great President. Every man, woman and child in the land would be delighted if they knew what I know after this conference. He is for feeding the hungry in a land of plenty. He is for clothing the naked in a country with an overproduction of clothes. He is for housing those without shelter."

No one paid much attention to Long's pronouncements even though the New Deal ultimately was to take shape far closer to Long's views than those of the conservatives. Already, insiders were whispering that Roosevelt was a soft, malleable man who tended in conversation to nod agreement with whomever he was talking to. Soft he was not, as time demonstrated; but his impression of giving assent was one of his habitual ways of disarming opponents. It was only later that it became apparent to Long that Roosevelt was indeed going to operate through the existing power structure in the Senate; Long was not in that structure. Long once told an audience that President Hoover had been a hoot owl, and that Roosevelt was a scrootch owl, explaining that a hoot owl knocked a hen off the roost and seized her. "But a scrootch owl slips into the roost and scrootches up to the hen and talks softly to her. And the hen falls in love with him, and the first thing you know, there ain't no hen."

In those first months of 1933 Southern leaders heard the soft talk but did not foresee the consequences; it is no wonder they thought they could pretty much shape a New Deal to suit themselves. Senator Cordell Hull of Tennessee went so far as to recommend to Colonel E. M. House, who informed Roosevelt of the suggestion, that a Congressional advisory system be established:

"The Governor should avail himself of the best expert assistance both in and out of Congress in dealing with each serious problem arising. . . . To avoid confusion, misunderstanding and jealousy, the Governor, in inviting and assembling persons for the purpose of conference, should ordinarily invite those in Congress according to rank, and then supplement by inviting any person or persons known to be expert on a given point or line."

Hull seems not only to have expected Roosevelt to be a weak President but also to have feared that he would be an excessively conservative one, and he sent Josephus Daniels to sound Roosevelt out. Roosevelt assured Daniels, "Put it down that my administration will be progressive with a big P."

Roosevelt overdid his simulated willingness to oblige. As Hull granted at the beginning of January, 1933: "No political party at Washington is in control of Congress or even itself. There was never such a call for leadership by one individual in high place. This need is most glaring when we realize that there is no cohesive nation-wide sentiment behind any fundamental policy or idea today. The election was overwhelmingly a negative affair, but if we Democrats succeed at Washington, the next election will be overwhelmingly an affirmative affair."

Even as Hull wrote, Roosevelt was at work with his Brain Trust (not one of whom was a Southerner) planning a program which would rally nationwide support. He wanted legislation which would provide positive aid to each of the great sections of the country and to every one of the main economic groups. The South was prominent but not dominant in his plans. The Cabinet which would help administer the program would include three Southerners: Hull, in the most prestigious position as Secretary of State; Daniel Roper of South Carolina (who had once been McAdoo's mainstay) as Secretary of Commerce; and Senator Claude Swanson of Virginia (for reasons that will become apparent) as Secretary of the Navy. It would also include three Republicans. Through happenstance it developed a regional imbalance which weighted it toward the Northeast. When the Cabinet was announced, Southerners were delighted by the recognition they had received and were not inclined to be critical.

As for the Southern leadership in Congress, Roosevelt presumably gave it almost complete freedom during these months because he did not want to disturb the unified support he could expect from it. Interestingly enough, Southern members of Congress were so besought by their constituents for aid and were so divided among themselves that, far from resenting Roosevelt's dramatic emergence on March 4, 1933, as a powerful positive leader, they welcomed it, momentarily at least, with heartfelt gratitude. Senator Josiah Bailey of North Carolina, very soon to become a conservative, constitutionalist thorn in Roosevelt's side, confided to a constituent that Congress by itself could not act, that the nation needed a President of almost dictatorial vigor.

The one dramatic advance indication that Franklin D. Roosevelt would indeed be a strong President in the progressive tradition came on January 21, 1933, when, in the company of Senator George Norris, he visited Muscle Shoals on the Tennessee River, where most of the water of the Tennessee River poured uselessly over the spillways of Wilson Dam. There he announced his support for a program to utilize this wasted power and develop in many ways the resources and economy of a large region. Speaking extemporaneously that evening in Montgomery, Alabama, he proclaimed the sort of large vision for which the New Deal became notable:

Muscle Shoals is more today than a mere opportunity for the Federal Government to do a kind turn for the people in one small section of a couple of States. Muscle Shoals gives us the opportunity to accomplish a great purpose for the people of many States and, indeed, for the whole

Union. Because there we have an opportunity of setting an example of planning, not just for ourselves but for the generations to come, tying in industry and agriculture and forestry and flood prevention, tying them all into a unified whole over a distance of a thousand miles so that we can afford better opportunities and better places for living for millions yet unborn in the days to come.

The Roosevelt who could speak thus was the President to whom the South, like the rest of the nation, turned in hope on March 4, 1933, when he asserted in his inaugural address: "This great Nation will endure as it has endured, will revive, and will prosper. So, first of all, let me assert my firm belief that the only thing we have to fear is fear itself. . . . In every dark hour of our national life a leadership of frankness and vigor has met with that understanding and support of the people themselves which is essential to victory."

In the days that immediately followed, Southerners in Congress enthusiastically backed their new President as he proposed measure after measure to enact the limited program they had sought during the Lame Duck session: the budget cuts and the weak beer plus emergency legislation to re-open the closed banks. There was nothing in these measures to threaten states' rights and Southern ways; one of the most ardent Brain Trusters, Rexford G. Tugwell, remembers that he thought the President was following too closely Wilson's New Freedom and tried to exhort him toward Theodore Roosevelt's New Nationalism.

No great amount of exhortation was necessary even though, as governor, Roosevelt had been one of the most eloquent exponents of states' rights. He also liked to plan, and the emergency seemed to call for planning. The entire nation, including the South, was hysterically behind the new President; so the sweeping program of the Hundred Days came through Congress with incredible ease.

It was ironic that the proud Southerners, most of them dedicated to the preservation of their region's ways of life and who by long seniority had come by 1933 to hold the key committee chairmanships and almost monopolize the leadership of Congress, thus enacted the greatest array of reform legislation in the nation's history. Through 1936, they, to a remarkable degree, moved White House proposals through Congress and remained at least outwardly loyal to the President. From the left, there was sporadic sniping from Senator Huey Long, allied with a handful of Midwestern and Western progressives. From the right, a conservative trio opened fire: Senators Carter Glass and Harry F. Byrd of Virginia and Josiah Bailey of North Carolina, abetted at times by others. But even so firm a conservative as Pat Harrison fought for most of the President's measures; and Senate Majority Leader Joseph Robinson of Arkansas—

reputedly a man with no taste for New Deal innovations—continued to be loyal to the day of his death at the climax of the Supreme Court fight.

The reasons for Southerners' going along with the President during the monumental Hundred Days were pretty much national rather than peculiarly Southern. A despairing nation regained its confidence during the first several weeks of the New Deal—and nothing much more than confidence. With public opinion so overwhelmingly in favor of the President, criticism seemed almost unpatriotic; those days were obviously the time for Roosevelt to act. Congressmen from the North and the West as well as from the South could be counted upon to be swept along in the New Deal tide. Roosevelt, who had long since studied the political timing of Theodore Roosevelt and Woodrow Wilson and who as governor of New York had developed his own effective techniques for dealing with reluctant legislators, in the spring of 1933 emptied his full bag of knowledge. He was deliberately slow in handling patronage in one of the last periods of American history when it was of vital consequence to Congressmen. Fifty per cent of Roosevelt's mail when he took office concerned patronage. One Senator kept a running tally of the job applications that piled up in his office—by November, 1933, more than fifteen thousand. In addition, the President was flattering and ingratiating to the Congressmen in many ways, giving them the recognition they had lacked during the previous twelve Republican years. Starting with this overflowing reservoir of support, gradually as he obtained measure after measure he called upon their strong ties of loyalty to vote for matters they normally would have oposed. In time, recognition became less novel to Southern Congressional leaders, and Roosevelt seemed less eager to go through the motions of seeking their counsel. Gradually, more and more of the talk they heard back home from those they respected (and upon whom they depended for political support) became less and less enthusiastic toward the New Deal. Slowly the reservoir emptied—but only slowly.

Certain special Southern factors tied these Congressional leaders to President Roosevelt long after their first enthusiasm had dwindled. First is one which Arthur Link, historian and Wilson biographer, has long since suggested concerning Wilson and his Congressional leaders and which applied equally to Roosevelt: that these Southerners especially felt personal ties of loyalty to each other and to the Democratic party. They had long been in the minority; they enjoyed power and wished to retain it through continuing in the majority. Their strong inclination, through tradition, was to give the President what he wanted. Realistically they could see that the best way to keep the Democratic party in power in the thirties was not to undercut too seriously their popular President, Second, and much more important, the Roosevelt measures represented a giant, nationwide cornucopia from which federal aid poured into the desperately Depression-ridden South. Distressing though this aid was to many of the Southern élite, Southern politicians concerned themselves more with channeling, rather than stemming, the flow. They did not want to join Republicans in curtailing it altogether. Never previously had so much been done for the South. Third and finally, the early Roosevelt measures gave some of the Southerners the impression that he was indeed reviving the New Freedom. Many Southern Congressional leaders had helped Wilson fabricate his program. Roosevelt's bills confirmed the handiwork of which they were so proud.

From the outset, Senator Glass expressed in fiery language his distaste for the New Deal; but Glass, an elder statesman, stood almost alone. The leader who might have been most able to build Glass's sentiments into a stubborn opposition was Garner, who, happily for Roosevelt, had been relegated from his seat of power as Speaker of the House to relative impotence as Vice-President and President of the Senate. During the first few years, Garner was loyal enough to line up votes for White House programs and to confine himself to "Don't-rock-the-boat" admonitions to Roosevelt. Even though there were wide doctrinal differences between Roosevelt and Garner, they remained tied by personal loyalty and affection. During the Congressional campaign of 1934, Garner spent his time at home at Uvalde, Texas, hunting and fishing. He assured Roosevelt that Texas was in splendid shape economically, that he saw no need for heavy federal spending. Yet, after the election, he wrote the President:

"Upon my return home this morning, after getting lost in the woods and having to climb a tree to get my bearings, I found your favor of the 13th. . . . I feel like a cur dog in not having been around where I could have been more helpful than I have, but, as I have said to you before, I think my greatest contribution can be while the Congress is in session in keeping contact with the Senate and House. I have had some experience and, I might add, what seems to be luck in that particular. As your messenger I will try to hypnotize, mesmerize and otherwise get our friends to approach matters in a helpful way."

Roosevelt replied: "It will be fine to see you both in Washington soon after my return there. That story about your falling out of the tree and killing a deer was garbled in transmission. As we get it now, we are led to believe that you got tired of shooting deer and that you climbed a tree, fell out of it on top of the deer and choked it to death. You must have been reading about that Abernathy man who used to choke wolves to death with his bare hands."

As Speaker, Garner undoubtedly would have maintained for a while, at least, the same sort of pleasant, personal relationship; but later in the New Deal, things might have been different. When Garner as Vice-President began covertly to rally the opposition, Roosevelt could limit his relations with the Vice-President. As Speaker, Garner could not have been so easily cut off or ignored. He once reminisced: "Theodore Roosevelt had Cannon to check him in all but the first two years of his administration. I would have liked to play that part in Franklin Roosevelt's administration. I think I could have talked him out of a lot of things. That could have been my contribution. I would have had no desire to dictate his decisions. I would not have tried to tell him what he could do, but there would have been times when I would have told him what he could not do."

As it was, Roosevelt's first speaker, Henry Rainey of Illinois, was acquiescent; and of the three succeeding Southern Speakers—Joseph Byrns of Tennessee, William Bankhead of Alabama, and Sam Rayburn of Texas —none was ready to function as an Uncle Joe Cannon in the Franklin D. Roosevelt administration.

Senator Joseph Robinson, whom (as I have mentioned) many observers had expected to become an obstructionist, remained loyal, as did his lieutenants, Alben Barkley, Pat Harrison, and James Byrnes. It is difficult to say why Robinson remained cooperative. Roosevelt was not always as considerate of him as he should have been and did not always inform him in advance about his legislative plans. It may be that Robinson cooperated simply out of political upbringing because first and foremost he put party loyalty ahead of every other consideration. This is a more generous estimate of Robinson than some that could be heard in Washington during the 1930's. A story was told that Robinson, after several years, groaned to Carter Glass, "Oh, you can't imagine the hell I have to go through." Glass is supposed to have replied, "In your case, Joe, the road to hell seems to be lined with post offices." One political commentator at the time asserted that while Robinson's friends had not received any large patronage plums, they had obtained altogether some two thousand minor offices.

In Alben Barkley, one is confronted with a man who was more liberal in his leanings and to whom most of the New Deal legislation was obviously acceptable. Barkley was in the Southern tradition and did his best to maintain amenities; he commanded personal loyalty among many Southern Senators. Being himself in favor of the New Deal, he was Roosevelt's logical choice as a successor to Robinson after Robinson's sudden death in the summer of 1937. The White House applied pressure, and it is revealing that Barkley in his autobiography solemnly maintains the fiction that Roosevelt did not intervene. For the President to have intervened as he did was costly since it led to a serious defection on the part of the vanquished and his allies. His reason for intervention was the ill-concealed conservatism of Barkley's rival, Senator Harrison.

Harrison not only did not like most New Deal measures but also was rumored to be definitely obligated to Bernard Baruch. As majority leader he might well have dragged his heels or failed to exert the extra effort required to obtain various White House measures. Roosevelt apparently considered the nominal support Harrison would have given him as majority leader to be less desirable than the election of Barkley, entailing the rather obvious hostility of the defeated Harrison as chairman of the Senate Finance Committee. In any event, but only after a very close ballot, Barkley became majority leader, giving Roosevelt his support; and Harrison openly expressed his opposition by sabotaging several of Roosevelt's financial measures from his position as chairman of the Finance Committee.

The last of these Senate figures of real consequence to the President was James Byrnes of South Carolina. Byrnes, a younger man of personal charm and intellectual vigor, was ambitious. Unlike the others he was a city boy, having come from Charleston, and his viewpoint—at least through 1936—seemed to be more national than Southern. His aspiration would seem from hindsight to have been national also: he wanted to become President. In any event, throughout the first four years he was on warm terms with both the President and a number of the Brain Trusters. It would not seem unreasonable to assume that at the time he was a New Dealer. In any event, he was a most valuable lieutenant of the President.

In the House, divisions of much the same sort could be found: traditional Southerners who were mildly opposed to the New Deal; traditional Southerners who accepted the New Deal, possibly because of party loyalties and partly because of economic benefits going to their areas; and some modern young Southerners, like Maury Maverick and Lyndon B. Johnson, both of Texas, who were ready with fire and enthusiasm to espouse the New Deal causes.

Among the older Southern leaders there were certain characteristics held in common that seemed to predominate. A number of these men seem to have had a rural background and to have been of humble origin. Several of them were of families who had moved from Tennessee farms to Texas in an effort to better themselves. They were men who had received relatively little schooling and who had struggled hard to acquire what education they had. They were particularly sensitive to the interests and needs of their farmer constituents and, in some instances, were agrarian in their points of view. Some of them also enjoyed their relationships with bankers and utilities executives. They gloried in Southern traditions and do not seem to have been especially involved in the industrialization of the South. They particularly savored the honors and prestige associated with Congressional leadership. Frequently they indulged in honorifics. Joseph Alsop has pointed out that one way of telling the folks at the annual barbecue that the county boss was a fine fellow was to say, "The recording angel all-wise and all-seeing will some day take his golden pen with its diamond point, dip it in the bright cerulean of the spacious firmament, and write the name of Lucius Quintus Cassius Jenkins with the great names of Washington, Jefferson, Lee, and Davis." Ironically, those very men who were the subjects of such oratory believed every bit of the hyperbole.

Roosevelt knew precisely how to ingratiate himself with these leaders; he did it by providing patronage to their areas and bestowing honors upon them as frequently as possible. Even an old recalcitrant like Glass, full of venom against the New Deal, was mollified considerably by Roosevelt's assiduous courtship in the form of jollying notes and flattering attention in public. Roosevelt, in February, 1933, had offered Glass the position of Secretary of the Treasury, quite possibly hopeful that Glass, a financial conservative, would not accept. On the one hand, Roosevelt refused to guarantee to Glass that he would not tinker with gold; on the other hand, he assured Glass that he would appoint the other Virginia Senator, Claude Swanson, to the Cabinet, making it possible for Glass's disciple, Harry F. Byrd, to move into the Senate even without Glass's appointment. Glass obtained his honor of being offered a post he did not really want and his desire to move his ally into the Senate; Roosevelt retained his freedom to stem deflation. Throughout the New Deal the Glass-Byrd state machine in Virginia was so strong that it could and did defy the President with impunity. In 1936, when Joseph P. Kennedy offered to contribute to Glass's senatorial campaign, Glass expressed his appreciation, but declined, since he had no opposition and no need for campaign funds. Nevertheless, neither of the Virginia senators openly opposed Roosevelt in any of his three campaigns for reelection.

Within these bounds the Southern leaders gave Roosevelt surprisingly little trouble. During much of the New Deal he was free to concentrate upon developing other lines of support—to keep behind him the Western progressive Republicans and gradually increase the enthusiasm of urban Northerners. Since Western progressivism at only a few points conflicted with Southern interests, Roosevelt had few problems there. It is interesting to note again, however, that Huey Long participated with several progressives in the Senate in voting against some of the early New Deal measures which were repugnant to the old progressive tradition. More significant as an indication of the trouble that was brewing was Roosevelt's courtship of the Northern urban vote, including the Negro vote; but during the first term this attracted relatively little attention in the South.

During those first years, most Southerners—like all Americans—were deeply concerned with how the New Deal was affecting them, and it was this which shaped their attitudes toward Roosevelt. From the outset most of the economic leaders of the South were not pleased. In many ways they had capitalized upon the separate and unequal role of the South in the national economy. Most of the old disorders against which Southern leaders had so long complained were still plaguing the South: it was discriminated against in freight rates; it lacked its fair share of capital and industry; and it was predominantly agrarian. Northern corporations drained profits out of the South, and in times of economic distress they sometimes closed their Southern factories first. The Southern economy in both its private and public sectors was the poor country cousin. Unfortunately the "country cousin" had tried to support himself by working for lower wages. Both agriculture and industry in the South maintained their existence only through providing the most meagre return to farmers and workers. Southern states lured Northern industry to their areas not only by the promise of low wages but also by tax concessions which precipitated an undue share of the cost of government onto people who were already underpaid.

The New Deal did not threaten to readjust tax apportionment in the South; but it did carry the threat of wiping out wage differentials, the foremost being the National Recovery Administration which would establish a national minimum wage of presumably forty cents an hour and a maximum work week of forty hours. Within an hour after President Roosevelt had signed the enabling legislation in June, 1933, a cotton textile code was presented to the N.R.A. in which manufacturers proposed a forty-hour week, the maintenance of no more than two shifts, and a minimum wage of $11 per week in the North and $10 per week in the South. William G. Anderson of the Bibb Manufacturing Company, Macon, Georgia, in presenting the case for Southern textile manufacturers, enthusiastically described services that owners provided for workers in company towns. Speaking elsewhere, Anderson had suggested that a textile worker's family of four could live on a food budget of $1.35 a week, and that by increasing the budget to $1.68 "such luxuries as meat, coffee, and sugar could be included." Claiming that a $10 weekly wage was too low, William Green, president of the A.F. of L., cited figures of the Bureau of Labor Statistics showing that for all regions of the United

States, based on 1932 prices, the bare subsistence wage for a family of five was $26.77 per week. Green cited President Roosevelt's statement when he signed the Act: "No business which depends for existence on paying less than living wages to its workers has any right to continue in this country." The figure was set in the final code at $13 per week with a dollar differential for the South. Conditions were such in North and South alike that the code was a boon to workers. It was one of the most successful of the N.R.A. codes.

In a cotton mill at Greensboro, Georgia, for example, the N.R.A. raised the hourly wage of workers about five hundred per cent, Arthur F. Raper has reported. Unfortunately, producing with obsolete machines, the mill had been competitive only because of its low wages; within six months it installed new machinery which required twenty fewer employees to operate.

Throughout the South, and to an even greater degree than in the rest of the country, employers fired workers of marginal usefulness, required the same work output in a shorter number of hours, and engaged in subterfuges (such as kickbacks from salary checks) in order to keep their labor costs from soaring. The N.R.A. legal adviser in Arkansas, Brooks Hays, found one garment factory paying its Negro help $5.00 to $7.00 per week. A competitor complained, "That plant is playing havoc with the garment trade from South Carolina to California." Oftentimes it was the Negroes in the mills or those serving almost as the personal retainers of small-town merchants who lost their jobs.

At the outset, before these aspects of the N.R.A. became apparent, the South shared the national enthusiasm over the promise of easy, perhaps even instant, recovery. William W. Ball, who perpetuated the thinking of the plantation South in the Charleston (South Carolina) *News and Courier,* cheerfully informed a friend in the spring of 1933:

I knew, everyone knew, that a crisis was present March 4, 1933, but I could not have believed then that one-fifth of the power would be granted to Franklin Roosevelt that has been given him. . . . It is a queer condition—the country has been (is still going) through a revolution and not one man in 5,000 perceives it. In 60 days our business laws have changed more than in 60 years—and what the results will be no one can foretell. One of the explanations of the serenity with which the American people receive these things and submit to them is that Roosevelt is a mild and serene gentleman— his personality is soothing and does not excite alarm. . . . The great men in business, especially in the great towns, are oppressed with the sense of incapacity, or guilt, or both. . . . The "captains" of finance and industry have been exposed as empty-pates, and the "umble"-ness and filthy veneration with which millions of petty Americans have hitherto looked upon them has vanished. The "captains" are bare in nakedness as greater fools even than knaves.

By the end of 1933, Ball was sounding the alarm against the New Deal, but even then he granted that the N.R.A. had substantially helped the textile business by leading manufacturers "to a reduction of working hours which . . . I suspect, [they] really wanted but lacked the will voluntarily to adopt by concert of action."

Almost at the outset of N.R.A. operations, Senator Glass, himself the owner of a Lynchburg, Virginia, newspaper, was furious over the threat of N.R.A. interference. In August, 1933, he wrote Walter Lippmann:

Of course, it was supremely desirable that there should be complete co-operation with the federal administration in the effort to restore prosperity and to abate the wretchedness of the prevailing depression; but in my view, the methods employed have been brutal and absolutely in contravention of every guaranty of the Constitution and of the whole spirit of sane civilization. The government itself has resorted to blackmail, boycott, and to a species of threats that will forever mark a black page in the history of the country. I had a personal interview with General [Hugh] Johnson [the Administrator of the program] last week, at which I plainly told him that his blue eagle was fast becoming a bird of prey and that he was creating a reign of terror among thousands of struggling small industries which are threatened with bankruptcy by reason of the brutal methods employed. I personally know this to be a fact with respect to my own state and its industries, and I have no reason to think it is different in any other state. Thousands of the very concerns which are publicly exhibiting the blue eagle are privately cursing the symbol as a black buzzard.

Some disgruntled workers, both white and black, who had failed to gain expected benefits from the N.R.A., applied new meanings to the initials: "No Roosevelt Again," "National Run Around," or "Negro Removal Act." Nevertheless, most workers in the South, whether in mills or mines, retail stores or lumber camps, were more optimistic. An Arkansas lumberjack when asked about his work replied, "There wouldn't be none, I reckon, if it weren't for that there Blue Eagle of Mr. Roosevelt's. Leastways if it weren't for that bird there wouldn't be but a mighty few hands a-working. . . . We ain't a-complaining none, but at the same time, Mister, we ain't none of us a-thanking nobody for it except the President."

In May, 1935, the N.R.A. code system was ended by an adverse Supreme Court decision; it was more or less accidental that the case coming before the Court involved New York poultry rather than Southern lumber. What was the N.R.A. balance sheet for the South? Overall, it was undoubtedly disruptive and unenforceable. Yet it did bring some order into two of the sickest industries, textiles and bituminous coal. It did bring the beginning of the end for child labor. It made a start toward putting a floor under wages and a ceiling over hours. It stimulated the movement away from unskilled labor toward skilled workers, even as it put more money into the pay checks of the skilled. It painfully prodded the South away from its "country cousin" differential toward the promise of a larger sharing in the national income.

Overshadowing the N.R.A. and enduring in one form or another long after the N.R.A. was gone was President Roosevelt's agricultural program. First, last, and always, this program meant for the South the raising of the price of cotton. The original Agricultural Adjustment Act, compounded in the spring of 1933, comprised, above all, the programs of the more substantial farmers of the South, the Middle West, and the Far West. Through a complicated mechanism it was intended to limit production and boost prices of cotton, some grains, and livestock. Other commodities from time to time were affected. The program was supported largely by the American Farm Bureau Federation (made up of those farmers who, despite the collapse of agricultural prices, could still pay ten dollars a year for dues). Its president, Edward A. O'Neal III, who since 1899 had been farming near Florence, Alabama, in the heart of the Black Belt and who had maintained for years a cordial relationship with President Roosevelt, effectively presented the Farm Bureau program. By coincidence, in the Senate the chief champion of the farm program was another Alabaman, John H. Bankhead. Although a lawyer whose clients had included railroads, mines, and corporations, Bankhead had announced when he was elected to the Senate in 1930 that Alabama needed a farm senator; and he undertook to be one. He, rather than Senator Ellison D. Smith of South Carolina (nicknamed "Cotton Ed") became the great advocate for the cotton interests, from the grower through the manufacturer. All cotton legislation, indeed all farm legislation, affecting the South became his particular concern. Moreover, he and his brother, Representative William B. Bankhead, who became Speaker of the House in 1936, were sympathetic not only with the planters but also with the small farmers and the sharecroppers. It was a sympathy that President Roosevelt himself emphatically shared. Roosevelt enjoyed relaxing in the magnificent country home of Cason Callaway, one of the largest of the textile manufacturers and a benefactor of Warm Springs, listening to the singing of Negro musicians dressed like old-time plantation hands. Also, Roosevelt dreamed of turning the miserably debt-ridden small farmers, sharecroppers, and field hands, as well as a considerable number of the unemployed in the cities, into self-sustaining, self-supporting small farmers, each on his own homestead. It was one of Roosevelt's oldest and most enduring dreams.

It was not part of the dream of either President Roosevelt or Senator Bankhead that the first cotton program should result, as it did, in benefiting the large growers and in helping the smaller growers and the sharecroppers not at all or even affecting them negatively. Roosevelt wanted to help everyone connected with cotton, not just the larger and stronger producers.

In its total effect on the South, by the fall of 1933 the cotton program did bring some measure of recovery to farmers, if no more than to return their incomes to the miserable 1929 level. Thanks to the plow-up of part of the crop, the price went up from five cents a pound almost to the twelve-cent level of 1929. In the next several years, acreage quotas kept the price up, reaching about fifteen cents in 1936. At this point, the skill of the growers in taking poorer land out of production and heavily fertilizing the remaining land or in switching to machine tilling sent the pre-acre cotton yield to spectacular heights, led to bumper crops and, once more, to collapsing prices. New programs late in the thirties helped rescue the growers, but these programs most benefited a limited number of planters. When in 1940 Senator Byrd proposed that the subsidy be restricted to $5,000 per year per farmer, he evoked little enthusiasm among Senators from cotton states even though, step by step, he raised the figure to $50,000.

What could be done for the poorer Southerners? Norman Thomas, indignant that the A.A.A. contracts contained an escape clause by which Arkansas landlords were dispossessing sharecroppers, went to the White House in 1935, carrying one of the contracts:

If you ever had dealings with Mr. Roosevelt, you know that he really handled interviews his own way. He tried to keep the conversation in his own hands. He did it rather charmingly. . . . And so it was this time. He began to tell me about his wrath about some chamber of commerce at some meeting. And so at last I took a deep breath and I said, "And so are the Southern planters," and managed to get in and tell him briefly what was on my mind. Then I asked him if he had read the contract. He said that he hadn't. . . . So I said, "Would you mind reading the clauses I have marked?" He said, "Certainly." I handed it to him, and he read it. . . . Roosevelt handed it back to me, half laughing, and said, "That can mean everything or nothing, can't it?" I said, "In this case, Mr. President, nothing. Over at the Agricultural Department they have just fired Jerome Frank and Gardner Jackson, and another man. The reason they were fired wasn't wholly on this, but part of the reason was that they had tried to make this contract mean something."

The President wasn't happy about my saying that, and a little impatiently he interruped my explanation why they had been fired and said, "Oh, Norman, I'm a damned sight better politician than you are."

I made the obvious retort, "Well certainly, Mr. President. You are on that side of the table and I'm on this."

He brushed that aside and went on to say, "I know the South and there is arising a new generation of leaders in the South and we've got to be patient."

That was his point.

Roosevelt was patient: trying not to stir the wrath of the more conservative Southerners in Congress and working carefully with Senator Bankhead and more enlightened Southerners to push programs for the rural unfortunates. He depended upon scholars like the remarkable University of North Carolina group, headed by Professor Howard W. Odum, to spell out the facts and upon other Southerners like Will Alexander, later head of the Farm Security Administration, and Aubrey Williams of the National Youth Administration, to put the programs into successful operation. These programs provided work relief through the W.P.A. (in which the Southern differential was about 50 per cent below Northern levels), through the Civilian Conservation Corps, and through the N.Y.A. They also provided loans to move farmers from poor land and out of shacks and locate them on good land in good bungalows. They helped to make good farms even better, especially through the construction of check dams and contour plowing to stop erosion. They electrified Southern farms through T.V.A. and the Rural Electrification Administration.

Some of these programs flourished; the T.V.A. was notably successful and had behind it the hearty support of most Southern political leaders. Some of the programs floundered; Paul Conkin's *Tomorrow a New World* is a brilliant but sad analysis of the expensive mismanagement of community projects, useful primarily in providing campaign provender for the Republicans. The scale of even the more effective programs was not sufficient to do more than nibble at the prevailing poverty. Bankhead wanted to put a billion-dollar bond issue behind the loans to tenant farmers; Roosevelt, fearing a Congressional battle, cut the figure to an appropriation of fifty million.

Obstacles were everywhere. There was the resistance of private power companies to public power, of large landowners to resettlement programs, of employers of seasonal farm labor to W.P.A. competition even on the Southern differential. Roosevelt himself could not be considered as overpaying his three Negro, Warm Springs farmworkers who, in 1938, received $20 per month each. This is an instructive backdrop to his wrath against Governor Gene Talmadge, who in 1935 complained to Harry

Hopkins about the payment rates of the federal aid programs. Pathetically inadequate though the W.P.A. stipends were, Talmadge denounced them as being so dangerously high that recipients would not take farm employment. Hopkins showed Talmadge's letter to the President, who wrote a tart reply, but, apparently not wanting to give Talmadge the satisfaction of receiving a letter from the President, sent it to Hopkins to sign:

I take it, from your sending the letter of the gentleman from Smithville to me, that you approve paying farm labor forty to fifty cents per day. Your correspondent does not mention the hours of work per day, but I assume that the forty or fifty cents is paid for working at least ten and possibly twelve hours. If one of these farm laborers were employed three hundred days a year, which means six days a week excluding Sundays and holidays, he would make, at forty cents a day, one hundred and twenty dollars a year; or if he were paid fifty cents a day, he would make one hundred and fifty dollars for his work. In view of the fact, however, that this type of employment is generally seasonal, I take it that the man described would actually have to live on from sixty to seventy-five dollars a year.

Somehow I cannot get it into my head that wages on such a scale make possible a reasonable American standard of living.

Efforts to inagurate public housing programs in the cities led to parallel protests. The first federal slum clearance project was undertaken in Atlanta, Georgia, where Charles F. Palmer, impelled at first, he says, by economic motives although obviously he has always been strongly humanitarian, fought against stubborn and versatile opposition to wipe out obnoxious slums and build low-cost Techwood Homes. In the process he changed from a skeptical Republican to an admirer of Roosevelt. At Thanksgiving time, 1935, the President went to Atlanta to dedicate Techwood and, in doing so, reminded his Southern audience of the considerable evils of the so-called prosperity of the 1920's, of the substantial recovery made in the first two and a half years of the New Deal, and of the surge of reform that had accompanied it. Challenging those who were resisting change, he asserted: "Recovery means something more than getting the country back into the black. You and I do not want just to go back to the past. We want to face the future in the belief that human beings can enjoy more of the good things of life, under better conditions, than human beings ever enjoyed in the past."

But the stirrings of change were creating much alarm among many Southern leaders; in the years ahead they sturdily met the challenge of President Roosevelt and engaged him in strenuous combat.

8. The South and Isolationism

ALEXANDER DECONDE

In one sphere, that of foreign relations, southern congressmen gave the Roosevelt administration strong support. During the late 1930s and the 1940s it was frequently said that the South was the most internationalist part of the country, and historians and other writers recalled the southern region's staunch advocacy of Woodrow Wilson's League of Nations and its patriotic response in the Spanish-American War. In recent years the South has shown an unmistakable tendency to move away from its earlier internationalism.

The author of the following essay is Professor of History at the University of California, Santa Barbara; his major works include the books: *The American Secretary of State: An Interpretation* (1962) and *History of American Foreign Policy* (1963). Here he re-examines southern foreign policy attitudes in the twentieth century and concedes that the South has been strongly internationalist during certain periods such as the late thirties, citing such factors as party loyalty, dependence upon foreign markets for agricultural exports, and ethnic and cultural considerations as explanations. But he argues that the South is not intrinsically less isolationist than other sections; on the contrary, he asserts that in some periods the region's racialism and provincial outlook have made it decidedly isolationist. DeConde's essay summarizes the most significant influences on southern attitudes toward world affairs since 1900 and suggests the importance of sectionalism in making America's foreign policy.

RECENTLY STUDENTS OF AMERICAN POLITICS AND FOREIGN POLICY have shown concern over the South's "shift away from internationalism" toward what many of them call a "new isolationism." In the summer of 1957 *Newsweek* magazine said that the South's over-

From *The Journal of Southern History, XXIV* (August, 1958), 332–346. Copyright 1958 by the Southern Historical Association. Reprinted by permission of the Managing Editor. Most of the footnotes in the original paper have been omitted.

turning of "its treasured tradition of internationalism" marked a turning point in Southern history. Before the Second World War, it pointed out, 69 per cent of the South's representatives in Congress supported every internationalist measure proposed and another 29 per cent voted for at least three fourths of the measures. But in the past six years more and more Southerners in Congress have been voting against foreign-aid bills, and many of them have even revolted against the Reciprocal Trade Agreements Act.

Explicit in the concern for the South's new attitude toward foreign policy is the assumption that the South[1] immediately prior to the Second World War, and even earlier, was the most internationalist and the least isolationist section of the nation. Surface evidence, the usual general criteria for measuring intangibles like "internationalism" and "isolationism," and the weight of tradition appear to support the assumption. Yet there is reason to question the generally accepted aphorism that the South was basically less isolationist and more internationalist than other sections of the country.

This paper questions that aphorism. It advances, as a partial and tentative thesis, the idea that the South's "internationalism" did not represent a fixed attitude toward foreign policy and that its "isolationism" is not a new and sudden phenomenon. The South's relative lack of isolationist bias in the period of American neutrality during the Second World War, it appears, reflected special ethnic, cultural, economic, and political conditions that prevailed among its people. Its "new isolationism" has grown from the same roots. The South's "isolationism," in fact, in many ways appears more deep-rooted than its "internationalism."

Before the period of the Second World War, a high point in Southern internationalism, the South was not notable for its internationalism. Its attitude on race, in fact, fostered a kind of isolationism that today, when most of the world's newly independent nations are composed of dark-skinned peoples, hampers American foreign policy and international co-operation.

For over a half century Southerners opposed recognition of an independent but black Haiti; only after the South seceded did the United States recognize the Negro nation. Partly because white men would have to sit with Negroes as equals, Southerners were reluctant to support international co-operation with newly independent Latin American nations in the Panama Congress of 1826. In 1919 Senator James A. Reed of Missouri appealed to Southern prejudices in condemning the League of Nations. In the League, he said, "dark" peoples would outnumber whites in the

---

[1] The "South" in this essay refers to the eleven former Confederate states plus West Virginia, Kentucky, and Oklahoma.

ratio of three to one. Senator Cole L. Blease of South Carolina, a notorious rabble-rouser and Negro-baiter, in 1926 assailed the World Court because it would, he alleged, "throw the destinies of Southern women and Southern men into the lap of a black man." And as late as 1943 some Southern members of Congress, for reasons of race, opposed admission of Chinese into the United States on a quota basis.

Before 1938 the South did not differ markedly in sentiment from other sections on issues of preparedness and neutrality. In some respects, according to public opinion surveys, it lagged behind the rest of the country. It placed a greater value on neutrality than did other sections, and it favored withdrawing American troops from the Far East lest the United States become too involved with Japan. Southerners in the days before Pearl Harbor were, in comparison to other Americans, less favorable to participation in an international organization for peace than they were for going to war.

Yet a prominent Southern writer in the period of American neutrality during the Second World War said the South was "less isolationist by nature than the Mid-West and Far West." Although the generalization is unsound, the foreign policy attitudes of the South and West, notably of the Midwest, in that period offer some reason for so superficial a generalization. The Middle West, according to public opinion polls and the votes of its representatives in Congress, was the most isolationist section of the country. It wanted to stay out of the war. The South, its sentiment measured by the same criteria, was the least isolationist and the most internationalist section. More than any other region the South favored aid to Great Britain and France and active intervention in the war.

So clear and overwhelming did the Southern sentiment for intervention appear that many considered it one of the distinguishing features of the South's unique sectionalism. In the neutrality period of the Second World War the South, even more than the Midwest, offered one of the most significant manifestations of sectionalism in foreign affairs.[2]

But in the period of neutrality during the First World War the South's internationalism and its attitude on intervention did not appear as clearcut. Although pro-Allied sentiment in the South at that time appeared stronger than in other sections of the country, a poll of newspaper editors in the fall of 1914 showed a higher percentage of Southern editors favoring neutrality than those of any other section. And on April 5, 1917,

[2] In his perceptive presidential address to the Southern Historical Association in Knoxville in 1952, C. Vann Woodward pointed out that in the world crises following the Second World War the South has responded to the slogans of nationalism with a zeal that exceeded that of other sections of the country. "The Irony of Southern History," in *Journal of Southern History,* XIX (February, 1953), 8.

when the House of Representatives passed the war resolution, only four of the fifty dissenting votes came from the South.

Later, when President Woodrow Wilson fought for the League of Nations, he received his fullest support in the Senate from Southerners. The South solidly supported the League of Nations. Wilson was a Southerner and a Democrat, and so the South backed his foreign policies and the League of Nations more as a matter of partisan loyalty than from predilection for international co-operation. The South took up the League cause, the Montgomery *Advertiser* admitted, "largely because Southern Democrats regard the Treaty [of Versailles] and its ratification as a Democratic issue." The Greenville (South Carolina) *Piedmont* expressed the same idea. "The South is heart and soul for the Treaty," it said. "It hasn't read it, but it has read some of the speeches of them darned Republicans."

Yet in the period of neutrality of the First World War more Southerners opposed intervention and Wilson's foreign policies than they did intervention and President Franklin D. Roosevelt's foreign policies in the period of neutrality of the Second World War. In an editorial of March 11, 1917, the Greensboro *Daily News* said the rich and the heads of corporate industry wanted war, not the great, silent masses. It was persuaded from its readers' letters, it said, "that the masses of people of this section have little desire to take a hand in Europe's slaughter and confusion." This was an isolationist view that other Southerners shared.

Several Southerners in Congress, such as Claude Kitchin of North Carolina, majority leader in the House of Representatives, and Senator James K. Vardaman of Mississippi, opposed Wilson's foreign policy and upheld traditional isolationist views.[3] Vardaman belonged to that "little group of willful men" who in February 1917 successfully filibustered against Wilson's Armed Neutrality bill and was one of the six senators who voted against war with Germany. But his opposition to White House policy led to his defeat for re-election in 1918. Kitchin's constituents in North Carolina's second congressional district did not get rid of him for his isolationism. They continued to return him to Congress in 1918, 1920, and 1922 with the usual large majorities.

In his opposition speech of April 6, 1917, to Wilson's request for war, Kitchin insisted that the President's foreign policy had been pro-British from the outbreak of hostilities. "We are to make their quarrel, right or wrong, our quarrel," Kitchin said. "We are to fight out, with all the resources in men, money, and credit of the Government and its people a difference between the belligerents of Europe to which we were and are

[3] Kitchin was the most resolute and unyielding of the Democratic leaders who opposed Wilson.

utter strangers."[4] This was a view many isolationists, North and South, could accept.

Kitchin and the South resented, among other things, Britain's blockade because of its adverse effect on cotton and tobacco growers. Southern resentment was particularly strong in the first two years of the war, for the South suffered more from the blockade than did any other section. In 1914 a war-stimulated crisis demoralized the cotton market and caused prices to drop from eleven to four cents a pound. The South lost about half the value of the 1914 cotton crop. The possibility that the Southerners in Congress might join with German-American and Irish-American elements to force a retaliatory arms embargo against the British for suppression of the cotton trade with Central Europe appeared in 1915 as a grave threat to Anglo-American relations.

"The cotton producers of North Carolina and the entire South are aroused over the action of Great Britain in declaring cotton contraband," Claude Kitchin announced, according to the Greensboro *Daily News* of August 27, 1915, "and they want the Administration to be as emphatic in dealing with England on this score as it has been in dealing with Germany over others." Throughout the South there was a widespread campaign for retaliation against the British government. The pro-British senator from Mississippi, John Sharp Williams, believed at the time that every politician in the South had to be anti-British.

The British, to pacify the South, finally made a secret agreement with the American government to buy enough cotton to stabilize the price at ten cents a pound. But for a time after the British had placed cotton on the absolute contraband list Southerners exerted heavy pressure on the government. British buying, however, soon drove up cotton prices and the crisis passed.

Later, after the United States entered the war, cotton enjoyed a prosperity and an immunity from government control that irked other sections. Under wartime conditions cotton prices zoomed to astonishing heights. To the Western farmer the opportunity for Southern profiteering on cotton seemed the grossest kind of favoritism on the part of an administration dominated mainly by Southerners. "No part of the world is profiting by the war as is the South," declared the Topeka *State Journal* of August 15, 1918.

Economic conditions in the South during the period of American neu-

[4] Believing that Kitchin did not represent the views of most North Carolinians, the Raleigh *News and Observer*, April 6, 1917, disagreed. "In an hour of crisis in our national life," it said, "no man is truly a Representative of the people who interposes his own personal views, his own personal state of mind, between them and the position which they would have their country take."

trality, it seems clear, had driven some of its political leaders to support isolationism; and altered economic conditions after the United States entered the war, ironically, led them in part to support the government's foreign policy. For parts of the South at least, isolationism obviously was not a consistent ideology.

Since the South, heavily engaged in world economics, found itself inevitably drawn into international politics, it long held a reputation for economic internationalism. That reputation held good after the First World War, particularly in matters of trade and tariffs. The South in those years upheld its long tradition of supporting free trade.

The Smoot-Hawley tariff of 1930 restricted American exports by reducing imports and by provoking other nations to raise trade barriers against American goods. The South, still primarily a producer of raw materials and the coarser types of manufactured goods, suffered heavily. It normally exported from 50 to 60 per cent of its cotton and 40 per cent of its tobacco. The South, therefore, supported the Reciprocal Trade Agreements program inaugurated in 1934 under Secretary of State Cordell Hull. In 1938 a Gallup poll suggested that 92 per cent of the people of the South favored the general principles of trade underlying the Hull program, but that half of them had never even heard of Hull's efforts to put them into effect. In Congress 95 per cent of the Southerners voted for the Hull program. That program tended to widen foreign markets for Southern cotton and tobacco, as well as for some other Southern products.

Despite the South's general support of free trade, some Southern industrialists in the twentieth century have always desired protection. After the First World War textile manufacturers expressed doubt as to the virtues of free trade. By 1919 many European cotton mills, stilled by the war, were back in full production, and Japanese textiles, hitherto not serious competitors, made deep inroads on the South's foreign markets. American millowners, many of them from the South or with factories in the South, found themselves with productive equipment too great for the markets they could hold permanently. In the 1930's and 1940's the South, even with the Hull program, was losing part of its export market for cotton primarily because foreigners could produce textiles more cheaply.

But the South as a whole remembered that it had always suffered from high American tariffs which forced its people to buy in a protected domestic market and to sell most of their products in unprotected foreign markets. Thus, in the period before the Second World War, except for special pressure groups like those of the sugar and textile industries, the South still generally opposed protectionism.

When the Second World War broke out the South's cotton industry again suffered a crisis; it lost almost all of its foreign markets. Consequently, the federal government during the war years poured over ten billion dollars into the South for defense plants as planned compensation for its loss of cotton markets, and also tobacco markets, abroad. In those years the new industries may have helped to stunt the growth of isolationism in the South, but after the war they would add strength to the economic isolationists of the section.

During the war period, however, the South proved an indispensable political ally to the government's foreign policy. Southerners, with very little dissent in their ranks on foreign policy, showed a higher cohesion in support of international collaboration than did members of Congress from other sections. The South, in fact, gave President Franklin D. Roosevelt the essential political power he needed to carry out his foreign policy. Since Southerners held about half the Democratic seats in the House of Representatives and slightly less than half of those in the Senate, it is clear that without their votes no legislation on foreign policy could have survived in either house.

Southerners held the key committee chairmanships, and a Southerner, Cordell Hull, was Secretary of State. President Roosevelt relied upon and cultivated Southern support for his foreign policy.[5] Politically, the Solid South prior to the attack on Pearl Harbor could justifiably claim to be the chief sectional bulwark against isolationism.

Isolationist organizations like the America First Committee, even though they tried, could make no headway in the South. Public opinion polls from September 1939 to December 1941 showed the South to be friendlier to the British cause than any other region, and its people, more than than other Americans, favored war in support of Britain. They led others in the fall of 1939 in favoring the repeal of the embargo on the shipment of arms abroad, and more than other Americans they favored peacetime conscription. Before the draft went into effect more Southerners enlisted in the armed forces than did men from any other section. Alabama's congressman Luther Patrick said "they had to start selective service to keep our Southern boys from filling up the army." But the South led all other sections in Congress in support of the Burke-Wadsworth Selective Service Act of September 1940. In the House of Representatives Southerners voted 103 to 3 in favor of the bill and in the Senate they voted 28 to 2 for it. Middle Westerners, however, by large majorities voted against it.

The importance of Southern support of Roosevelt's foreign policy can

[5] One special reason why Roosevelt retained Hull as Secretary of State was Hull's prestige in the Congress, particularly with the Southerners who virtually ran it.

be seen clearly in the congressional vote on the crucial Lend-Lease bill passed in March 1941. In the House 120 Southerners voted for it and only five opposed it. In the Senate twenty-nine Southerners were for it and only one, Senator Robert Reynolds of North Carolina, whose isolationist views at the time appeared unique in the South, voted against it. The Middle West, by large majorities, voted against the bill. Without Southern support the bill would not have become law. Other internationalist bills also became law because of overwhelming Southern support.

A Gallup poll of early October 1941 asked this question: "Which of these two things do you think is the more important, that this country keep out of war, or that Germany be defeated?" Eighty-eight per cent of the Southerners questioned thought defeating Germany was more important, whereas only 63 to 70 per cent of the other Americans questioned thought so. The results of that poll were typical of virtually all regional polls of the period. Southern conservatives, like Carter Glass of Virginia, and Southern liberals, like Claude D. Pepper of Florida, showed a unity in favor of internationalism that they seldom demonstrated on domestic issues.

What explains the South's belligerency and its opposition to isolationism? several writers have asked. Various theories have been advanced as possible answers. Professor Benjamin B. Kendrick, in a presidential address before the Southern Historical Association, pointed to the South's economic serfdom. The South, he said, was an economic colony of Northern finance capitalists. Those capitalists, who exercised greater political power in their "colony" than at home, he explained, were imperialistic, and hence through their influence the South clamored for intervention.

Senator Carter Glass had a simpler explanation. "My notion," he wrote, "is that the attitude of the South is due both to superior character and to exceptional understanding of the problem involved."

Another former president of the Southern Historical Association, Professor Francis B. Simkins, has explained the South's belligerency and internationalism by traditions, saying Southerners inherited pro-British, antiforeign, and military traditions to a greater degree than most Americans. The columnist Dorothy Thompson said it was poverty that offered the key. Since Southerners had less to lose in war than other Americans, they were readier to take a chance. The North Carolina newspaper editor Jonathan Daniels seemed to agree. " 'Have not' people" he said, "are all more inclined to belligerency than 'have' people."

Others have advanced various far-fetched theories and modified versions of those mentioned. They spoke of the "Anglo-Saxon blood and cultural tradition" of the South, the memory of England's sympathy for the Confederacy in the Civil War, the effect of Southern climate, the influence of the Woodrow Wilson tradition, Southern loyalty to the Democratic party and the New Deal, the one-party system of the South, its military tradition and its pantheon of soldier heroes, its lack of a pacifist tradition, its indifference to violence, and its long dependence on British capital and on British mills as a market for its cotton.

The cultural and blood tie to Great Britain, the "Anglo-Saxon blood and cultural tradition" theory, appears to offer one of the most logical explanations for the anti-isolationist attitude of the South, particularly for that of Southern intellectuals and politicians who made up the leadership of the section. From the beginning of the twentieth century through the Second World War, solidarity with England was a basic doctrine of American foreign policy. And the South, proud of its British heritage, cherished and supported that doctrine.

Southerners took pride in asserting that their region was the "most American" section of the nation. That emphasis on "native-born" Americans offers an explanation of its attachment to England and of its anti-isolationist position in the period of the Second World War. Excluding the Negro, the South has been racially and culturally the most homogeneous section of the nation. Its white people were and are almost wholly of British stock; over 90 per cent of them were and are native-born Americans descended from early British settlers. They have not mixed with other national strains to any appreciable degree.

In the twentieth century the South has had a far smaller percentage of foreign-born than any other region. In 1930, for example, only about 500,000 native whites of foreign or mixed parentage and only 200,000 foreign-born whites lived in the eleven Southeastern states. The largest single group of foreign-born whites or those of mixed parentage were Germans, about 180,000 of them. The second largest non-British group was composed of Italians, about 95,000 of them. But most of the Italians were concentrated in the New Orleans area.

Since those foreign groups comprised an insignificant minority in a population of some twenty-eight and a half million, they could do nothing to modify the British cultural and political attitude of the region. To challenge that prevailing attitude in the period of the Second World War, in fact, was dangerous. The Negro, comprising the largest non-British minority in the South, had no political or cultural ties to a mother country. Therefore, the Negro, a member of a large but submerged minority, could not and had no basic reason to challenge the foreign policy attitude of the ruling majority.

The overwhelming British composition and heritage of the South's people, the theory goes, explains both its "Americanism" and its "internationalism." Many Southerners wanted to intervene in the war, according to the theory, because they wanted to help their mother country, Great Britain, in an hour of need.

John Temple Graves has advanced an even more convincing version of this theory. More than the existence of the strong blood and cultural ties to Great Britain, he said, the lack of a German, Irish, or other foreign tradition explains the South's belligerency and immunity from isolationism in the neutrality period of the Second World War. From this flows the logical conclusion that the South's zeal for intervention arose not out of ties with and special concern for Hitler's victims, but out of a lack of ties with any European country other than Great Britain.[6] The South was interventionist and internationalist, then, not because it was less isolated from Europe than, say the Midwest, but because it was more isolated. For despite the South's historic connections and economic ties abroad, the Southerner has not been noted for cultural or political understanding of foreigners or of foreign problems. Of all regions the South has been the most rural and most isolated, and abroad it has been the least understood and the most distrusted. Its attitudes on race, religion, and foreigners have not been conducive to cordial international relations. The South's distrust of strangers and "furrinism" is long-standing. More than other Americans its people have flourished on phobias and have been unilingual and suspicious of foreign talk. Foreign policy issues have usually meant little to the isolated rural white of the South.

It would seem to be a mistake, therefore, to assume on the basis of the experience of the Second World War, or even of the first, that the South was intrinsically less isolationist than other sections of the country. Its people reacted to the issues of the war as did the people of other sections—in accordance with their own interests and their own unique cultural and historic traditions.

Under the special circumstances of the Second World War ethnic, cultural, economic, and political influences relatively unique to the region thrust the South into an anti-isolationist position. When foreign policy issues do not offer special support to Great Britain, aid the South's economy, or appeal to Southerners as a matter of party allegiance, the Southerner does not appear any more internationalist than representatives of any other section, and perhaps less so.

It appears safe to conclude that the South's "internationalism" has meaning only when the historian applies it to specific circumstances and to a specific time, as in the period of neutrality of the Second World

[6] The "Anglo-Saxon blood and cultural tradition" theory, Graves said, perhaps explained the attitude of Southern intellectuals, romanticists, ancestor worshippers, and the historical minded, but not that of the Southern masses.

War. The seeds of isolationism were always embedded in Southern soil. The "new isolationism," new in time and in the circumstances which make it bloom, may be a new growth, but its roots are old.

9. The Colonial South

CLARENCE H. DANHOF

The uneven rate of industrialization and diversification in the various regions of the United States in the nineteenth century fostered the idea that the South and much of the West were economic colonies of the powerful Northeast. The rhetoric of the agrarian revolt and the antitrust movement constantly invoked this theme, and it also found expression in the politics of the progressive era. The notion that the South was being subjected to northern economic control by such means as the protective tariff, discriminatory railroad rates, monopoly, and absentee ownership was countered to some extent by the New South ideology.

The depression of the 1930s and certain New Deal programs stimulated a fresh image of the South's economic subservience. In a survey of the literature since 1920 on various approaches to a more satisfactory southern economy, Clarence H. Danhof, formerly of The Brookings Institution, gives an interesting critique of the "conspiracy theory" as an explanation of the South's colonial status. Whether or not this status was the result of policies determined outside of the region, many Southerners were prepared to believe that this was the case. Challenging the validity of the conspiracy theory, Danhof contends that its consequences were unfortunate and shows how the idea not only influenced economic planning and political action in the South, but also contributed to the making of national policy.

From "Four Decades of Thought on the South's Economic Problems," in Melvin L. Greenhut and W. Tate Whitman (eds.), *Essays in Southern Economic Development* (Chapel Hill, 1964), pp. 30–51. Reprinted by permission of the University of North Carolina Press. The material presented here is only one section of Danhof's lengthy essay. Most of the footnotes in the original paper have been omitted.

. . . IN 1936 HOWARD ODUM, IN THE SOUTHERN REGIONS OF THE United States, after describing the South's resources in an optimistic vein, turned to an appraisal of the technology applied to their development. That technology he found deficient not in what it included but in its incomplete range. He observed, as had many others before, that: "Until recently, the South was a furnisher of raw materials to the manufacturing regions, essentially colonial in its economy." A few years later he removed the qualification. Observing that New York was the economic center of the national economy and that other metropoles, towns, and villages arranged themselves into series ranks, he concluded that "some regions are still in the status of colonial economy. . . . The southern region has traditionally filled this role within the United States, and partly because of that fact, seems destined to continue doing so for some time."

Odum saw the "colonial type" deficiency in applied technology as producing an imbalance. "The South's proportion of national manufacturing . . . is still far below its ratio of people and resources." One of the chief causes for this "uneven technology" was "the South's very contracted access to capital, expressing itself in a differential in rates of interest." That differential required that a Southern capital-using enterprise have a higher return than a similar operation in the North. "Accordingly most sorts of manufacture involving elaborate technologies have avoided the South because, as a rule, the elaborate technology is expressed in expensive and elaborate plants." Odum explained further that, like debtor countries, the South, because of the inequality of incomes, tended to import luxuries which resulted in debt and an inability to "enlarge its capital."

The word "colonial," as Odum used it, was probably intended to convey what Colin Clark defined in the now familiar terms of primary as contrasted with secondary production. In this sense "colonial" merely describes an economy primarily concerned with producing, and preliminary fabrication of, raw materials. The word does carry with it the notion of dependence, although it is a dependency in a specialized structure, all elements of which are more or less equally dependent upon each other. Nor does it necessarily carry with it the idea of lower levels of productivity, although in fact primary economics tend to have lower levels of living than do those engaged in more advanced productive activities. In this usage Odum was correct; the South was, and continues in large measure to be, an economy engaged somewhat more largely in primary production. So used, the term "colonial" has a limited connotation. The word came to have a much stronger significance.

In June, 1938, President Franklin D. Roosevelt called a Conference on Economic Conditions in the South. In his letter to the Conference, the President expressed his conviction that the South presented the nation with its Number-1 economic problem. The report of the Conference was prepared by a staff of Southerners and reviewed by the Conference members, who were also all Southerners. The report appears to have drawn heavily from Odum's work as well as from data gathered by the Temporary National Economic Committee. Although it made no explicit reference to the South as suffering from a colonial status, it made some observations that went well beyond the Odum analysis in suggesting subservience and exploitation. The report stated, for example, that:

Lacking capital of its own, the South has been forced to borrow from outside financiers, who have reaped a rich harvest in the form of interest and dividends. At the same time it has had to hand over the control of much of its business and industry to investors from wealthier sections.

After pointing out the high cost of credit in the South, the report continues:

Faced with these handicaps, the South has had to look beyond its boundaries for the financing of virtually all of its large industries and many of its small ones. This has turned policy-making powers over to outside managements whose other interests often lead them to exercise their authority against the South's best advantage. For example, many such companies buy most of their goods outside of the South, and often their sales policies are dictated in the interest of allied corporations in other sections of the country.

Another result of the South's dependence on outside sources of capital was its effect upon state and local government revenues:

So much of the profit from southern industries goes to outside financiers in the form of dividends and interest, that State income taxes would produce a meager yield in comparison with similar levies elsewhere. State taxation does not reach dividends which flow to corporation stockholders and management in other States; and as a result, these people do not pay their share of the cost of southern schools and other institutions.

The efforts of southern communities to increase their revenues and to spread their tax burden more fairly have been impeded by the vigorous opposition of interests outside the region which control much of the South's wealth. Moreover, tax revision efforts have been hampered in some sections by the fear that their industries would move to neighboring communities which would tax them more lightly—or even grant them tax exemption for long periods.

Turning to natural resources, the report stated that:

Because of the poverty in which the South was left after the War between the States, and because of the high cost of credit since that time, a very large share of the natural resources of the South is owned in other regions. To the extent that this is true, the South is exposed to a double danger. On the one hand, it is possible for a monopolistic corporation in another region of the country to purchase and leave unused resources in the South which otherwise might be developed in competition with the monopoly. On the other hand, the large absentee ownership of the South's natural resources and the South's industry makes it possible for residents elsewhere to influence greatly the manner in which the South is developed and to subordinate that development to other interests outside the South.

After enumerating Southern industries which were wholly or almost completely controlled outside the region (almost all public utilities, all the major railroad systems, the transmission of and distribution of natural gas, the richest deposits of iron ore, coal and limestone, most of the rich deposits of bauxite, zinc ores, sulphur, many of the largest cotton and rayon mills), the survey observes that:

For mining its mineral wealth and shipping it away in a raw or semifinished form, the South frequently receives nothing but the low wages of unskilled and semiskilled labor. The wages for manufacturing this natural wealth into finished products often do not go to southerners, but to workers in other areas; and the profits likewise usually go to financial institutions in other regions. When a southerner buys the finished product, on the other hand, the price he pays includes all the wasteful cross-hauling involved in the present system.

Further handicaps to the South were the freight-rate differentials and the tariff:

The present interterritorial freight rates which apply on movements into other areas of many southern manufactured and semifinished goods, and some agricultural products and raw materials, handicap the development of industry in the South. This disadvantage works a hardship particularly with regard to shipments into the important northeastern territory. This region, containing 51 percent of the Nation's population, is the greatest consuming area. The southeastern manufacturer sending goods across the boundary into this region is at a relative disadvantage of approximately 39 percent in the charges which he has to pay as compared with the rates for similar shipments entirely within the eastern rate territory. The southwestern manufacturer, with a 75 percent relative disadvantage, is even worse off. Such a disadvantage applies to the southern shipper, even when, distance considered, he is entirely justified on economic grounds in competing with producers within the eastern territory. In effect, this difference in freight rates creates a man-made wall to replace the natural barrier long since overcome by modern railroad engineering. . . .

An equally serious deterrent to the South's economic development has been the nation's traditional high tariff policy. The South has been forced for generations to sell its agricultural products in an unprotected world market, and to buy its manufactured goods at prices supported by high tariffs. The South, in fact, has been caught in a vise that has kept it from moving along with the main stream of American economic life. On the one hand, the freight rates have hampered its industry; on the other hand, our high tariff has subsidized industry in other sections of the country at the expense of the South. Penalized for being rural, and handicapped in its efforts to industrialize, the economic life of the South has been squeezed to a point where the purchasing power of the southern people does not provide an adequate market for its own industries nor an attractive market for those of the rest of the country.

Moreover, by curtailing imports, the tariff has reduced the ability of foreign countries to buy American cotton and other agricultural exports. America's trade restrictions, without sufficient expansion of our domestic markets for southern products, have hurt the South more than any other region.

The National Emergency Committee report contained no new information. The issues on which it took positions were matters on which there were wide differences of opinion in the South. The dark picture it presented conformed with the depression-spawned school of realism—in fiction and fact—which at the time dominated the nation in general and the South in particular. The report was, then, a curious episode in the depression-stimulated concern with economic-political-social problems. It aroused resentment in conservative anti-New Deal circles in the South, while Liberals felt it was poorly timed, if at all necessary. The report did lead some liberal Southern groups to call a Conference for Human Welfare to consider what action might be taken, but such groups already existed and were in no particular need of the type of publicity provided by Mr. Mellett's pamphlet.[1] The Southerners who signed their names to the report apparently did not meet again as a group.

In the longer run, two results may be distinguished. One was to stimulate, and to call public attention to, the work under way, which was to include numerous appraisals of the data underlined in the report. The other result was that the report supplied ammunition for an upsurge of sectionalism which was to see some of the South's distinguished liberals allied with some of its most notorious demagogues.

The NEC report suggested strongly that the South was being exploited and extended an implied invitation to seek the use of Federal power to secure remedies. The evidence suggested that the South's ills could be ascribed to discriminatory freight-rates, the tariff, monopoly and

---

[1] Lowell Mellett, executive director of the National Emergency Council, under whose general supervision the report was prepared.

absentee ownership, all imposed upon the South by interests outside her borders. Colonialism was thereby given a political rather than a purely economic content. For those who found useful an explanation of the South's economic problems that was external to herself, colonialism was synonymous with imperialism. The data supplied by Vance, Odum, and others, as supplemented and publicized by the NEC report, provided the opportunity. Odum's pursuit of a constructive regionalism was now converted into a renewed sectionalism of a peculiarly vitriolic character.

• • •

These issues had long been part of the stock-in-trade of Southern demagogues and had received some emphasis from Southern figures who cannot justly be so labeled. Some decades earlier, the railroads had been a central target of the populists in the South as they were also in the North. The tariff issue was, of course, the hardy perennial of disputes between the nation's regions. These, together with attacks on absentee corporations and on monopolies, were favorite campaign material of such demagogues as Jeff Davis of Arkansas, James K. Vardaman and Theodore G. Bilbo of Mississippi, Cole L. Blease of South Carolina, Huey Long of Louisiana, Eugene Talmadge of Georgia, "Alfalfa Bill" Murray of Oklahoma, and similar "panderers to the pride and prejudices of their white constituents." The group of intellectuals who constituted the Southern Agrarians had pointed to these problems in support of the argument that it was necessary for the South to seek to develop a society quite different from that of the North. What was more significant was the fact that men of sounder judgment, strong critics of demagogic politicians, were led to criticize those Southern political figures who had refused to participate in these attacks. Those who exercised such restraint were charged with being "agents of the business interests that had tightened their hold on Southern economic life," and therefore "guaranteeing the protection of Northern imperialist interests in the region." John Nance Garner, Carter Glass, Walter F. George, and James F. Byrnes were among those who were held to "speak for the Northern corporate and industrial wealth which has enslaved their own people." It did not follow that their loyalty to the South was necessarily questioned, however, since their subservience to Northern interests might be explained by the fact that they represented a subordinate part of a great capitalistic country.

The tariff, discriminatory railroad rates, monopoly, and absentee ownership of Southern resources and industrial operations by large corporations were the principal targets. In each case the South was forced to accept policies developed and applied from outside the region. There were differences in emphasis, but each or all these together could be looked upon as tools utilized to prevent the region from reaching its goals of either greater agricultural prosperity or of greater industrialization. Sectional conflict, which some held to be inevitable, resulted in a conspiracy, deliberate or fortuitous, on the part of the North, the large national corporations, or some financial groups, with the help of the federal government, to thwart the South.[2] Exposure of the conspiracy and neutralization of its weapons would permit the region, given the great confidence of the South in its resources, to move along the path it wished to follow.

The tariff was, of course, an old sore. Writing in 1934, Peter Molyneaux reminded the South that the first suggestion by Southerners that "the time had come to calculate the value of the Union" had occurred with the passage of the 1824 tariff. He argued that the poverty of the South was not a product of the tenant and crop lien system but was a result of the fact that the region bought most of its manufactured goods from the North and East, while devoting its own energies to the production of export commodities. It was because the ultimate returns from their products are measured in terms of a domestic price level, maintained by a high tariff system, while the prices of their products are adjusted to a world price level, that the South's poverty has persisted, and it is that poverty in turn which has prevented the checking in any degree of the progressive impoverishment of the mass of cotton farmers. "The outlook for the cotton states," he held, "will be determined very largely by whether the United States follows a policy of international economic cooperation, on the one hand, or a policy of narrow economic nationalism on the other."

Molyneaux demanded that this "ancient wrong" be righted. "To say today that the national welfare requires the maintenance of the high-tariff policy is equivalent to saying that the national welfare requires the irreparable submersion, economically and socially, of the greater part of the population of a whole region of the country. . . . A continuance of the high-tariff policy must henceforth be more injurious to the cotton South than it has ever been in the past." A Southern economist, M. D. Anderson, agreed, asserting that "The high protective tariff on manufactured articles . . . has the double effect of cutting off the South from some certain markets for its cotton, and at the same time raises the price

---

[2] The sophisticated view of the exploitative conspiracy was expressed by Donald Davidson: "I do not argue that it represents some deliberate highly wrought conspiracy against the South but rather that it is in the nature of an urban industrialized society to behave thus towards whatever stands in its path."

the South has to pay for manufactured articles its purchases from the North."

The issue of equitable railroad freight rates was one which perennially attracted attention throughout the nation as well as in the South and was a problem to which Congress had addressed itself frequently. The claim that the South suffered regional discrimination under the existing rate structure arose in 1937 when J. Haden Allredge, an economist for the TVA, completed an elaborate analysis of the territorial rate structure. In transmitting a copy of the report to President Roosevelt, Harcourt Morgan . . . of the TVA, wrote that the existing territorial freight rate structure constituted a barrier which tended "to retard substantially the commercial and economic development of the Tennessee River drainage basin and adjoining areas in the South." That charge became the basis for the agitation over the following two decades over territorial freight rates, a charge that was quickly incorporated in the conspiracy thesis.

Jonathan Daniels, writing in 1938, declared that New England prosperity seems to be based on the freight differential and the tariff: "imperial advantages which New England took as its loot after the Civil War." There was, he continues, "some sort of bargain then, now dimly seen. The Negroes were sold down the river again after emancipation, and the price paid was a fixed economic differentiation, which left the whole South in slavery to New England instead of some of the South in slavery to other Southerners."

Interviewing Southern public officials, Daniels quotes Governor Bibb Graves of Alabama as holding that "the United States is divided into empires on the one hand and satrapies on the other by the freight rate differential." Others, Daniels found, referred to the freight rate differential as if it were the product of an invisible conspiracy. In Daniels' view, there was an historical explanation for the higher rates south of the Ohio, but he suspected that both the Northern and Southern railways were controlled by the same banks. "Was it possible," he asked, "that the great railroad investment north of the wall must be protected at all costs, that the migration of manufacture to the South must be watched lest Northern traffic be threatened?" And must then, the Interstate Commerce Commission, "acting in the public interest, take no action that would threaten this section? Was it, in sum, possible that the course of economic history had made the stability of the American system depend upon that region and simultaneously, was it to the advantage of finance capital that it remain so?" Daniels concludes that it may be "that the cruelest aspects of conquest were not involved in Reconstruction in the South but in the use of national power to entrench sectional advantage elsewhere over the South."

Ellis Arnall, then Governor of Georgia, was a leader active in the campaign for revision of railroad rates. He demanded the "abandonment of a colonial policy toward the Southern and Western States," declaring that this exploitation was "more wasteful than that practiced by the most greedy of European powers in Africa or the Pacific." "Only exploitation," he asserted, "can account for the enormous waste of human and natural resources. Why were not these people engaged in more intelligent farm operations, planting crops that would not loot the earth of the stored richness that they were obligated as men to leave as a legacy to their children's children? Why were not any of them engaged in industrial employments?" Arnall complained further that federal grants-in-aid programs to the aged, to highways, to dependent children, to public health and to vocational rehabilitation were deliberately intended to maintain colonialism, since they were predicated upon an ability to match federal funds with the result that Southern states must levy crippling taxation or provide inadequate services.

Less pugnaciously, Hodding Carter told millions of readers that before the South can conquer its bigotry, its people must be better educated and better paid. A higher income level in the South would eliminate most of the frictional competition among the submarginal whites and Negroes. Before these things can be accomplished, Carter asserted, "the South must be freed from the economic despotism imposed by the North."

Men like Arnall occupied themselves also in seeking to attract new industries, branch plants of large corporations being attractive prospects. But others saw the South's problems epitomized in the absentee ownership that was concomitant. M. D. Anderson felt strongly on the matter. "Another factor to be reckoned," he said, "is the financial control of the national banking mechanism by Northern and Eastern interests. By means of this control, the rich resources of the South, other than cotton (petroleum for instance) are bought at relatively low prices by concerns operating under Northern control and ownership, and the products are sold back to the South and to other regions at a stiff profit, impoverishing the people who might have developed these resources to their own advantage if they had had financial control."

The distinguished Southern historian, Walter Prescott Webb, joined in the attack, declaring that "whereas the South and West have within their boundaries most of the natural wealth of America," the North "has gathered practically all the economic fruits of a nation's industry and labor."[3] This, Webb held, had been accomplished by the two hundred largest Northern corporations supported by the federal government by a variety of devices. Among these were the tariff and the federal patent policy, which operated as a government subsidy to the North. Taking his cue from the widespread interest at the time in the concentration of power in large corporations, Webb urged reforming the structure of the nation's business organization by repealing that part of the 14th Amendment to the federal Constitution which protected the corporation as a legal person.

Assistance came also from an influential Northern source as Thurman Arnold adapted his crusade against monopoly to aid in the exposure of the exploitation conspiracy and at the same time invited Southern support for his efforts. Arnold argued that the relationship between the industrial East and the South and West had developed along colonial lines with the East functioning as the Mother country. The East had garnered to itself the raw materials of the other two regions and exploited them by selling them "manufactured necessities at artificially controlled prices." Since the East was the principal source of both the capital and organization applied in the development of the South, it controlled that development "in the way which would contribute the most to its domination." In the process "the competitive energy of the South and West had been stifled." As a result, local independent capital disappeared and local independent enterprise has constantly been handicapped, with the farmer the chief victim. This was accomplished through the "age-old principle of colonial empires": tightly organized cartels which controlled supply, transportation, and distribution "in such a way as to put new competing enterprise in the colonies under a continuing handicap."

Monopoly was not viewed primarily as a source of injury to the South because of the higher prices that might prevail on Southern purchases. The Justice Department was not accused of dealing with Southern instances of monopoly in any way differently from the manner with which it dealth with monopoly elsewhere; in fact, monopolies would tend to be national in scope and to have nation-wide effects. The problem was the possibility that monopolistic control over South-

[3] Walter P. Webb, *Divided We Stand, the Crisis of a Frontierless Democracy* (New York, 1937). In more recent writings, Webb has abandoned this position and taken a much more conciliatory and optimistic view. See "The South and the Golden Slippers," *Texas Quarterly,* I (1958), 1–13; and "The South's Call to Greatness: Challenge to All Southerners," *Texas Business Review,* October, 1959, p. 1.

The exploitation view, however, has become imbedded in the writings of historians on the South.

ern resources might result in rates of resource utilization lower than would be the case under competitive conditions. There were suspicions and charges that such was the situation in the Birmingham coal and iron industry. That industry had not expanded in accord with the rosy prospect held out when the United States Steel Corporation entered the area.

George Stocking supplied data supporting the view that the Birmingham steel plants enjoyed the lowest costs in the nation's steel industry on some basic products. The growth of the Birmingham industry did not reflect such advantages. The basing point pricing system, Stocking held, placed Southern steel fabricators at a disadvantage in supplying their "natural market" and restricted the size of that market while the United States Steel Corporation "subordinated the management of its southern properties to the combined interests of its national operations."

Meanwhile the nation had entered upon World War II. The changes that might be brought about were not foreseen; instead, the possibility that the South would suffer damage through loss of foreign markets without participating in production of war materiel gave support to the imperialistic thesis. Frank L. Barton, one of the few economists who supported this point of view, pointed out that orders for war production were not going to the Southern states in significant volume, partly because Southern firms were handicapped by high freight rates in bidding on war contracts. Admitting that heavy industrial capacity simply did not exist in the Southeast, that the freight-rate structure alone should not be blamed for the present lack of industrial development in the South and West, and that those residing in the South must shoulder part of the blame, he asserted that "it seems that the freight-rate structure is a manifestation of a fundamental situation in the national economy—a part of the design in the national economic pattern."[4] That design, Barton felt, was well described in Thurman Arnold's exposition.

The South was soon to be assured by the Chairman of the War Production Board that it was the nation's Opportunity No. 1, and the region did participate heavily, though somewhat belatedly, in the war effort. Though that participation had great impact, the imperialistic theme persisted. A Southern historian observed that "it was the task of outside capital to direct Southern manpower and resources toward performing their share in the war effort." Purchases by Northern interests of South-

---

[4] That the South lacked skilled labor and that most defense orders would consequently go elsewhere was recognized in a study of the South's needs for a large quantity of better-balanced industry: Harriet L. Herring, *Southern Industry and Regional Development* (Chapel Hill, 1940), esp. p. 79.

ern-owned textile mills proved that absentee ownership was still much in evidence. A Northern journalist labeled Texas—the Southern state which enjoyed the greatest industrial expansion during the war—"New York's most valuable foreign possession." During the war, it was held, monopoly strengthened its hold everywhere, so that "the South will continue to ship out huge sums in interests and profits."

In 1947 Wendell Berge, then Assistant U. S. Attorney General, assured the Southern Economic Association that: "Absentee ownership and control of Southern industry and economic assets are still very much in the picture. They represent, basically, the major economic problems of the South." Though railroad rates remained a problem, the South, he held, must be especially concerned with monopoly because it "has many new industrial capacities which will be a target for monopolies seeking to extend their control." The total cost of such monopolies, Berge said, is incalculable, "but it has been estimated that the price paid by the South for the existence of just one monopoly, that in commercial fertilizers, was great enough to have provided a college education for every high school graduate of the southern states." He added ominously that "at the present time, such factors as the control of technology, of research, and of 'know-how' are far more likely to be the basis of monopoly power. Where these are not sufficient, the while array of ingenious devices may be employed to substitute monopoly power for the free play of competition in the market."

Acceptance of the exploitation doctrine logically called for compensation of some kind, and the approach of the end of World War II provided the opportunity to make such demands. Adherents of the conspiracy thesis were not the only proponents of federal reconversion policies that would discriminate regionally in the lifting of wartime priorities and in disposal of war plants—but they pressed their proposals most vigorously. Spokesman for such a policy in the U. S. Congress was not a Southerner but Senator Pat McCarran of Nevada. As Chairman of a Special Committee to Investigate Industrial Decentralization, Senator McCarran submitted a report which asserted that "Our major industries have fought a desperate and ruthless battle, subverting our whole transportation system to their purpose, to deny the West and South the industries they can support and to which they have every right." To redress the alleged wrongs, McCarran proposed a program for the South as follows:

1. Immediately the World War ends, production, particularly of chemical products, textiles, clothing, ammunition, and shells should be shifted to this area.

2. Government-owned plants and war surpluses should be so disposed of as to allow maximum encouragement to new industries in this area.

3. Through federal aid, research and technological assistance should be provided so as to encourage more indigenous operation and ownership of local industries. Changes in freight rates must be pressed immediately to make it possible for new industries to meet competitive prices on the Nation's markets. Precautions must be taken not to sacrifice the raw-materials producers in this region, as well as the seventeen Western states, to the policy being pressed in industrial circles to make this Nation primarily an exporter of producer's goods and a large-scale importer of raw materials.

McCarran's efforts aroused little support in the Congress, and with that failure ended significant efforts to carry the conspiracy thesis to its logical conclusion. The thesis nevertheless continued to have adherents. One of the most vigorous and unqualifiedly defiant assertions of this point of view appeared in 1952 and components of the doctrine continue to appear in the literature.

•　•　•

The claim that a conspiracy exists is a common reaction to a difficult and possibly disagreeable problem. This approach is attractive because it absolves of responsibility and offers a solution through identifying the culprits, bringing them to justice, and levying compensation through political or legal action. The alternative of accepting full responsibility for the problem is unpleasant and may appear to impose an impossible burden. As in the present instance, conspiracy explanations typically rest upon assumptions regarding the relative importance of the factors involved in a situation, with emphasis being placed on those which support the charge while others are ignored. A conspiracy thesis also rests typically upon overly simplified concepts of economic, political, and social relationships and upon naive concepts of the constraints which operate upon those who seem to personify power and influence. These are characteristics of the conspiracy approach that render any specific reply difficult, if not futile.

No social scientists undertook a direct critique of the conspiracy thesis. Each of the specific charges was, however, analyzed and evaluated effectively, if somewhat belatedly, over the five years immediately following the war.[5] A comprehensive analysis which represented a broad consensus of most economists on the issues was made by Calvin Hoover

---

[5] It is useful to recall Frederick C. Mills' observation that "one of the serious disabilities from which the social sciences suffer arises from their failure to give prompt and effective quietus to useless, meaningless, even to false theories." In Introduction to Alfred C. Neal, *Industrial Concentration and Price Flexibility* (Washington, 1942), p. vii.

and Benjamin U. Ratchford, another by the Committee on the South-west Economy.[6]

The tariff. The tariff has been the hardy perennial of conflict be-tween the North and South. Southern views, however, had long since become increasingly divided, particularly as industry became important. There were two opposed positions with many variations in between.

One was the traditional position which looked upon the South as an exporter of raw materials to world markets and which objected to any restraint upon its freedom to sell in such markets as well as its freedom to buy manufactured goods. Free trade in world markets guaranteed protection against Eastern monopolies. This point of view was based on a commitment to an agrarian society and made no pro-vision for the South's industrial development.

A second position not only made no objection to tariffs but favored them as a source of protection of established interests or as a method for promoting more rapid industrialization. William Hicks as early as the 1870's argued that through protectionism the South could achieve equality with New England.

William J. Robertson in more recent years held a similar position, suggesting that "the South demand a protective tariff that would be designed to benefit the nation as a whole." An increasing number of textile manufacturers took positions favorable to the tariff as the in-dustry encountered stronger competition from world producers. Sugar and cattle interests also tended to be pro-tariff.

Whatever the effect of the tariff on the South's historic economic position, in the 1930's the region was far from united on the issue. The world situation had, moreover, become exceedingly complex, with tariffs merely one of a wide variety of interferences with world trade. In Cordell Hull, the South had a strong advocate of its traditional point of view in a position of high responsibility. By that date it was clear that the tariff was a national question that reflected differences in industry groupings rather than sectional interests. In the 1940's, the South's dependence on foreign trade in agricultural products declined further while the operation of agricultural price support programs operated very much to the region's advantage, since her farm products were sold in world markets at prices that represented a substantial subsidy. Meanwhile, the region's interest in foreign markets for manu-

---

[6] Hoover and Ratchford, *Economic Resources;* "The Southwest" (Report of the Committee on the Southwest Economy to the President's Council of Eco-nomic Advisors, Washington, 1952). "The Southwest" includes an analysis and the critical appraisal of the notion of colonialism as applied to the region. (Chap. IX, pp. 6–8.)

factured products continued to increase while Southern manufacturers were increasingly concerned with competition from abroad. The tariff argument as used by the conspiracy school was then obsolescent, and the fact that it was employed is open to the interpretation that it was conceived of not so much as an economic issue as an identification with internationalism which "served to set limits to the South's integration into American culture."

Railroad rates. Although the charges of railroad-rate discrimination suggest that there had been a long neglect of harmful abuses, such was not the case. The Southern rate structure had developed out of the needs of the shippers in the region and, like rate structures elsewhere, was under more or less continuous review either by shipper negotiation with the railroads or by action of the Interstate Commerce Commission. No charges of discrimination were made regarding the commodity rates under which much the larger volume of traffic moved. The charges were made by public officials rather than by shippers and were directed towards class rates which accounted for a minor part of freight movement. With regard to these rates, the Interstate Commerce Commission found that inter-territorial inequities did exist. Appropriate changes were ordered in an action which was upheld by the Supreme Court.

The significance of this adjustment as it related to Southern economic development was probably slight. Reviewing the evidence as presented in the Southern Governors' and related cases, Hoover and Ratchford conclude that "high freight rates are not now, and never were, a major barrier to the economic development of the South." "The difference in rates has not been presented in its true perspective and its importance has been greatly exaggerated since most traffic moved by commodity rates while the charges were directed at class rates." Furthermore, as Milton Heath pointed out, some of the differentials that existed might have been advantageous to Southern producers, a fact that explained why Southern shippers did not give significant support to the Southern Governors.

Monopoly. The sweeping charges made regarding the effects of monopoly on the South found few adherents. Albert S. Keister denied Arnold's charges that the Northern monopolies were throttling the South. He pointed to the acceleration of industrialization, which was "proceeding much more rapidly during the past generation than that of the country at large," and added, "Nor is local independent capital disappearing in the South, if one may judge by bank deposits. . . . These evidences of capital increased between 1930 and 1940 more rapidly in the South than in the nation at large."

More specific was the question of monopoly as presented by the steel industry. The basing point system of pricing in that industry was under critical attack for reasons much broader than the South's interest. With the abolition of that pricing system by the Federal Trade Commission, there were expectations that activity in the iron and steel industries in the Birmingham area would be stimulated. That no appreciable gain followed stimulated another study of the Southern iron and steel industry. That study observes that while "policies have not always been those that would stimulate the greatest development," the "slow development of metal-using industries and the markets for steel in the South cannot be charged too heavily to the policies of the big iron and steel companies." "It must be emphasized that substantial progress has been made in the Southern industry and that the United States Steel Corporation and other steel makers have had an important place in that record of progress."[7]

Absentee Ownership. The South's concern with the organization and practices of business, specifically with monopoly and absentee ownership, was a facet of a larger group of dissatisfactions with big business which were widely expressed throughout the Nation. The basic source of concern was the fact that the emergence of very large business corporations appeared to have changed the structure of the American economic order, which no longer conformed to the abstract ideal of an economy of small owner-managed firms operating competitively. The depression had exposed the system as very vulnerable to financial difficulties and to instability in employment. Serious doubts were being cast upon the basic justification for very large firms—their superior efficiency. Moreover, the apparent ability of the very large firms to escape the pressure of competition raised problems with regard to the responsibility with which their great power was exercised, problems accentuated by the separation of ownership from management. To the South, the facts of very large size and the consequent concentration of power seemed, or were suspected of being, particularly serious since the region was dependent upon decisions made outside the region.

There could be no denial that there was much absentee ownership of Southern resources, that much of such ownership had been welcomed, and that many agencies were seeking to increase it. It has been the South's experience that its business adventures outside of agriculture and commerce tended to fall under the control of firms headquartered outside the region. After the Civil War, the region's railroads were partially rebuilt by local interests with local and governmental funds, but the task of ex-

---

[7] H. H. Chapman and others, *The Iron and Steel Industries of the South* (University, Alabama, 1953), p. 389.

tending the lines and consolidating them into systems was assumed by railroad interests from outside the region. The South's early industrialization—the cotton mill movement of the 1880's—originated in local enterprise applying local risk capital. It too, though in lesser degree, came under the control of Northern companies. Much the same has been true in such developments as in the iron and steel, furniture, rayon and synthetic fibers, petroleum and other industries. Instances of Southern industrialists controlling firms which have achieved national dominance of their industries exist but have been limited, cigarettes and soft drinks being the major examples. Even such Southern contributions to technological advance as the production of pulpwood from Southern pine were not applied until Northern sources of capital and management undertook to do so.

Given the great gap which was a result of the South's persistent agrarianism, the region had developed only a relatively small group of men who were cognizant of modern technologies, alert to markets and marketing institutions, possessed of managerial competencies, and with access to capital resources. Though Southerners frequently did assume the initiative, what the South had to offer in raw material, untrained labor, and modest markets it could not supplement with adequate managerial and financial resources. Though other methods of solving its problems were not ruled out, the South chose to emphasize the one most readily available to it: the acceleration of industrialization by importing the wherewithal to bring it about.

John B. McFerrin provided an appraisal of the net effects on the South of this process. He argued that Southern corporations did and should continue to go outside the region for their capital requirements. The complaint that they thereby lost some control and that income was drained out of the region by payment of interest and dividends, he dismissed by pointing out that "the income would not be there . . . if the original capital had not been imported." The suggestion, implicit in the objections to absentee ownership, that, if the South had been able to generate more capital, as out of retained profits, it would have prospered more rapidly is exceedingly dubious. Given a national market, capital will flow where the opportunities are most attractive.

The fact is that the Southerners most directly involved operated from the assumption that what chance the South had of accelerating its growth rested on its ability to attract capital to provide the foundations of a more productive economy. The problem was not only that the region lacked capital but also and perhaps principally that the region lacked men with the ability to command the capital available in the nation. To obtain the employment it desired, the South, historically and contemporaneously, had to join the rest of the nation in accepting corporate organization, absentee ownership, and, what was perhaps a more immediate source of annoyance, outside management of its plants. The attacks on monopoly and on absentee ownership were then, in part, an expression of values held by some Southerners in conflict with those held elsewhere in the nation. In the words of one of the Agrarians, the South wanted an economy with a wide distribution of tangible capital properties—a kind of economy which the region could understand. Many non-agrarians appeared to agree.

Their view implied a preference for the local employer, possibly paternalistic, as in the textile towns—though that relationship found its fair share of critics in the South itself. It was also naive in that it failed to recognize that, in the American experience, industry tended to become large scale, and large-scale industry over time typically and inevitably became an absentee-owned operation. That separation posed issues of policy, but they were national problems and did not explain the difference between the South's economic development and that of the rest of the nation.

If large corporate organizations presented problems, they also presented opportunities that escaped the nostalgia of the Agrarians, critics of industrialism such as Webb, and others. Milton Heath called attention to such opportunities when he wrote: "I do not fear for the future of free productive enterprise within the corporate structure. But there is need for a new doctrine of liberalism which comprehends the greatly expanded potential of the corporate organization for both production and consumption and which integrates the aims and possibilities of free activity in both spheres."

The colonial-imperialistic thesis of conspiracy must be considered an unfortunate episode—a resurgence of a crude sectionalism—that diverted the attention of some of the South's ablest men from constructive approaches to the region's problems. It was attractive to some who held the liberal belief that a more nearly perfect mobility of factors would solve the South's difficulties. It was also attractive to some who found in it an escape from the burdens they carried. The conspiracy thesis shifted those burdens to others, and carried with it claims for compensation to be secured from the federal government.

That the thesis dealt with significant matters is obvious, but they were national problems and their relationship to the South's economic retardation highly doubtful. While the South's legitimate claims were recognized, as in the rate cases, there is no evidence that such changes were of any significance to its growth. Though it did not always eschew the charges and demands of the exploitation school, the main stream of thought and action continued to press for solutions along the well-established lines of promoting new industry and approving out-migration. . . .

10. Regionalism and the Southern Literary Renascence

LOUIS D. RUBIN, JR.

In the field of literature the South has certainly not been a colony of the North. The region's best claim to national preeminence is based on the brilliant literary renascence which exploded among southern writers in the 1920s and had been accepted as an American phenomenon by the time of World War II.

Professor of English at Hollins College, the author of the following essay has produced such major works in the field of American literature as *Southern Renascence: The Literature of the Modern South* (with Robert D. Jacobs, 1953), and *The Faraway Country: Writers of the Modern South* (1963).

Here he attempts to place the Southern Renascence in historical perspective. The southern literary ferment of the 1920s is seen as the product of a changing South, of a region undergoing an important transition in its social and economic life. The major contributors to the Southern Renascence were deeply rooted in the culture of their native section, although in some measure they were also alienated from it and thus partially able to get outside of it. Influenced by their experiences in northern cities and in Europe, southern writers mirrored in their novels and poems the conflict between progress, associated with the North, and the traditions of the old regional order. Yet if their rebellion against the old order was stimulated by outside forces, they were frequently disturbed by the South's abandoning "cherished ways of faith and life" in faddish imitation of northern "progress."

Rubin's essay focuses on the interplay between past and present in the

Originally published as "Southern Literature: The Historical Image," in Rubin and Robert D. Jacobs (eds.), *South: Modern Southern Literature in its Cultural Setting* (Garden City, 1961), pp. 29–47. Reprinted by permission of the author.

South, but it also points to the role of the North and the outside world in precipitating regional change. In essence the ambivalence reflected in the works of southern authors reflects the clash between southern particularism and the nationalizing forces in modern America.

TOWARD THE END OF HIS LONG LIFE, THE CONFEDERATE GENERAL James Longstreet is supposed to have visited the town of Oxford, Mississippi, where his sister lived and where his uncle, the Judge Longstreet of the *Georgia Scenes,* had once resided. It was after Longstreet's extended dispute with other former Confederate leaders over the responsibility for the Southern defeat at Gettysburg, and so when a small boy came up to the old man and asked him, "General, what happened to you at Gettysburg?" Longstreet almost suffered a stroke then and there. The name of the small boy, the story goes, was William Faulkner.

The episode almost certainly never took place. Longstreet's biographer places it in 1898, when Faulkner was one year old, and not even William Faulkner would have displayed such precocity as that. It probably happened in Chicago, not Oxford, and if anyone asked such a question of Longstreet, it was Faulkner's long-time friend Phil Stone.

The point is, however, that it does not *seem* an implausible story. It *might* have happened; indeed, one could even maintain that it *should* have happened. For given Faulkner, given the South, given the fact of Southern history, what would seem more normal than that story?

The anecdote recalls a passage from Faulkner's *Intruder in the Dust.* Lawyer Gavin Stevens is talking to his young nephew, Chick Mallison:

"It's all *now* you see. Yesterday wont be over until tomorrow and tomorrow began ten thousand years ago. For every Southern boy fourteen years old, not once but whenever he wants it, there is the instant when it's still not yet two o'clock on that July afternoon in 1863, the brigades are in position behind the rail fence, the guns are laid and ready in the woods and the furled flags are already loosened to break out and Pickett himself with his long oiled ringlets and his hat in one hand probably and his sword in the other looking up the hill waiting for Longstreet to give the word and it's all in the balance, it hasn't happened yet, it hasn't even begun yet, it not only hasn't begun yet but there is still time for it not to begin against that position and those circumstances which made more men than Garnett and Kemper and Armstead and Wilcox look grave yet it's going to begin, we all know that, we have come too far with too much at stake and that moment doesn't even need a fourteen-year-old boy to think *This time. Maybe this time* with all this much to lose and all this much to gain: Pennsylvania, Maryland, the world, the golden dome of Washington itself to crown with desperate and unbelievable victory the desperate gamble, the cast made two years ago; or to anyone who ever sailed even a skiff under a quilt sail, the moment in 1492 when somebody thought *This is it:* the absolute edge of no return, to turn back now and make home or sail irrevocably on and either find land or plunge over the world's roaring rim."

As Chick Mallison recalls those words of his uncle, he faces the decision of what to do about Lucas Beauchamp, the Negro who faces a lynch mob. At this critical juncture, he thinks instinctively in historical terms of the problem that confronts him. That Faulkner has him do this is of far more importance than whether, when a boy, he actually went up to General Longstreet and asked about Gettysburg; it was of this historical moment of transcendent Southern ambition and destiny that Faulkner thought when he set about to describe a young Mississippi boy at the point of decision.

When in the course of twenty-five or thirty years a distinct geographical and historical region, noted for its artistic barrenness, produces a veritable galaxy of important novelists and poets, then naturally we look at the time and the place in order to see what might have caused so spectacular a literary explosion. And when that sudden outburst of distinguished literature is filled with historical images, crowded with the events and the attitudes of the region's history, we think at once to examine that history to determine what its relation to the literature might be.

Most of the Southern writers whose stories and poems attained prominence during the 1920s were born in the two decades immediately preceding and following the close of the nineteenth century. William Faulkner was born in 1897. John Crowe Ransom was born in 1888, Donald Davidson and Erskine Caldwell in 1893. Katherine Anne Porter was born in 1894, Caroline Gordon in 1895, Allen Tate in 1899, Thomas Wolfe in 1900, and Robert Penn Warren in 1905.

All of these writers, whose literary excellence has caused their time to be known as the period of the Southern Literary Renascence, grew up in a period when the Southern states were just emerging from a condition of shock. The South had engaged in a war. It had been beaten, and for fifteen years occupied by its conqueror. When, by the 1870s, the occupation forces were withdrawn and the carpetbag governments ousted, what remained was an exhausted land. For the succeeding generations, poverty was the rule. Southerners saw the American Union growing stronger and greater all around them. The great railroad trunk lines drew the West and the Pacific Coast toward the industrial East, and the nation became richer —while they remained where they were, sweating to gain a living from the soil, without capital goods, with little power in the national government, a colonial people. The New South of Henry W. Grady came, without making very many inroads upon the region's precarious farming economy. The Gradys, Walter Hines Pages, John Spencer Bassetts, and Francis Warrington Dawsons might preach the gospel of industrialization. Maurice Thompson might compose poems like the following:

> *The South whose gaze is cast*
> *No more upon the past*
> *But whose bright eyes the skies of promise sweep*
> *Whose feet in paths of progress swiftly leap*
> *And whose fresh thoughts like cheerful rivers run*
> *Through odorous ways to meet the morning sun.*

Yet the facts were otherwise. The chief occupation was still the land. The prosperity of the semicolonial South depended upon farm prices. The farmer was the backbone of the South—and a mighty droopy one much of the time. The new century was well under way before the South really began to come back into the American Union, to regain its place in the sun. Not until after 1900 did industrialization become much more than a slogan for most of the South.

For many years after Appomattox, then, the South struggled to make a bare living. It was left to itself, to think about the past, to brood over the price of union. Almost every Southern family had felt the war, shared in the defeat. The specter of the Lost Cause was there to contemplate. The war, memories of the war, results of the war, dominated life in the South for four decades or more. Walter Hines Page declared that he

. . . sometimes thought that many of the men who survived that unnatural war unwittingly did us a greater hurt than the war itself. It gave every one of them the intensest experience of his life and ever afterward he referred every other experience to this. Thus it stopped the thought of most of them as an earthquake stops a clock. The fierce blows of battle paralyzed the mind. Their speech was a vocabulary of war, their loyalties were loyalties, not to living ideas or duties, but to old commanders and to distorted traditions. They were dead men, most of them, moving among the living as ghosts; and yet, as ghosts in a play, they held the stage (Burton J. Hendrick, *The Life and Letters of Walter Hines Page,* 1922–1925, I, 90–91).

Richard M. Weaver has remarked that "for thirty years the atmosphere was so suffused with the sense of tragedy and frustration that it was almost impossible for a Southern man to take a 'normal' view of anything" ("Agrarianism in Exile," *Sewanee Review,* LVIII [1950], 587). On every street corner Confederate veterans were to be found. Not to have served in the war was almost to be disqualified from a political career. In most Southern houses gilded frames enclosed lithographs of Lee and Jackson. As Douglas Freeman expressed it, "The Confederate tradition was for fifty years the strongest influence, political and social, in the South" (*Lee's Lieutenants,* 1942–1944, III, 587).

History—defeat, the war, the past; in the South these were not abstractions. To a child growing up in the South, they were very real. Southerners knew that history was not merely something in books. In his *Origins of the New South,* C. Vann Woodward quotes a passage from Arnold Toynbee:

I remember watching the Diamond Jubilee procession myself as a small boy. I remember the atmosphere. It was: Well, here we are on the top of the world, and we have arrived at this peak to stay there—forever! There is, of course, a thing called history, but history is something unpleasant that happens to other people. We are comfortably outside all that. I am sure, if I had been a small boy in New York in 1897, I should have felt the same. Of course, if I had been a small boy in 1897 in the Southern part of the United States, I should not have felt the same; I should then have known from my parents that history had happened to my people in my part of the world (Woodward, *Origins of the New South, 1877–1913,* 1951, viii).

It was this kind of atmosphere, charged with the image of the war and the past, into which most of the writers of the Southern Renascence were born.

Then, as the twentieth century got under way, the South gradually began to change. The old veterans were dying off; the old loyalties were adjusted to conform to new conditions. "By far the greater portion of the generation which had listened with awe while the guns boomed in Virginia and the ships of war steamed on the Mississippi," the historian Paul H. Buck has written of the South after 1900, "slept in silent graves in which the issues for which they had contended were buried with them. The old had given way to the new. Around the lingering survivors pressed eager youth. Slowly the bent figures of the past took their leave" (*The Road to Reunion, 1865–1900,* 1937, 304–5). In the "formative years" of Faulkner, Wolfe, Tate, Davidson, Ransom, and the others, the industrial New South which had been so much talked about and, save in some few cities such as Richmond, Birmingham, and Atlanta, so little evident, finally began to make its impact on the region. Various writers have described the expanding development of the business and commercial South in the new century. "Looms and furnaces, factories and stores, railroads and water power," Edwin Mims remarked of the twentieth-century South, "have led to the prosperity of the few and the well-being of the many" (*The Advancing South,* 1926, 112). Such journals as John Spencer Bassett's *South Atlantic Quarterly* and the older *Sewanee Review,* which William Peterfield Trent had founded in 1892, spoke the new note for literature and culture no less than the *Manufacturers' Record* of Baltimore proclaimed it for business and industry.

With the First World War, the South was back in the Union again. Thousands of young Southerners went into training camps all over the North and West. Many more thousands of persons from other parts of the Union came to live in the South. Even before that, the South had been getting set for the change. Chambers of commerce made their appearance. Upon a basically agrarian, ingrown, easygoing, impecunious society, industrial America moved in.

Change—this was the keynote of Southern life during the years when the writers of the Southern Renascence were growing to manhood. Here is how Thomas Wolfe chose to describe life in Libya Hill just before young George Webber was born:

> The railroad was then being built and would soon be finished. And only a year or two before, George Willetts, the great Northern millionaire, had purchased thousands of acres of the mountain wilderness and had come down with his architects to project the creation of a great country estate that would have no equal in America. New people were coming to town all the time, new faces were being seen upon the streets. There was quite a general feeling in the air that great events were just around the corner, and that a bright destiny was in store for Libya Hill.
>
> It was the time when they were just hatching from the shell, when the place was changing from a little isolated mountain village, lost to the world, with its few thousand native population, to a briskly-moving modern town, with railway connections to all parts, and with a growing population of wealthy people who had heard about the beauties of the setting and were coming there to live (*The Web and the Rock*).

In Asheville, in Nashville, in cities and towns all over the South, things were going on. What the parents of the future writers of the Southern Literary Renascence had known as certainty seemed to their children to be less and less sure. New ways, new beliefs, new interests were making themselves felt. The three specters of Walter Page's South—"the Ghost of the Confederate dead, the Ghost of religious orthodoxy, the Ghost of Negro domination"—began to relinquish their hold over the Southern mind.

"Progress" came increasingly to be the favorite slogan. Every Southern town and city had its booster club, its chamber of commerce. As Donald Davidson remembered it:

> In those years industrial commercialism was rampant. In no section were its activities more blatant than in the South, where old and historic communities were crawling on their bellies to persuade some petty manufacturer of pants or socks to take up his tax-exempt residence in their midst. This

industrial invasion was the more disturbing because it was proceeding with an entire lack of consideration for its results on Southern life. The rural population, which included at least two-thirds of the total Southern population, was being allowed to drift into poverty and was being viewed with social disdain. Southern opinion, so far as it was articulate, paid little serious attention to such matters. The older liberals of the Walter Hines Page school still believed in the easy humanitarianism of pre-World-War days. The younger liberals were damning the Fundamentalists, and rejoicing in the efforts of the sociological missionaries who were arriving almost daily from the slum-laboratories of Chicago and New York. The business interests were taking full advantage of the general dallying with superficial issues (" 'I'll Take My Stand': A History," *American Review,* V [1935], 304–5).

There was the moral impact of the First World War itself, with its sudden and awful impression of death, bestiality, waste. Donald Davidson and John Ransom served as army officers overseas; William Faulkner trained in the Royal Air Corps. And for all the others, as well, there was the sudden letdown of idealism, the swift transition from Woodrow Wilson to Teapot Dome. Thomas Wolfe describes it vividly in the opening pages of *Of Time and the River.* Marcus Cunliffe, in his history of American literature, has remarked that the young Americans were in the World War for only a comparatively short time and yet, paradoxically, the war's impact upon their idealism seems to have been extraordinarily strongly pronounced. Donald Mahon, in Faulkner's *Soldiers' Pay,* comes home, the mutilated hulk of what once was a young man. Young Bayard Sartoris, his brother dead in France, arrives home, in the novel *Sartoris,* to race his automobile along country roads and finally to die in a plane wreck, deliberately courting death to avoid the everyday tedium. The army veteran of Donald Davidson's *The Tall Men* applies for a job:

> *'Well, what are your*
> *Qualifications?' I said 'Qualifications?*
> *In the army I learned the Impossibles.'*
> *He said, 'We'll file your application.' I said,*
> *'Thank you, sir,' and walked out buttoning tarnished*
> *Buttons and swinging O.D. sleeves with a yellow V,*
> *Meaning fodder for moths and spider-webs.*

The Southern Literary Renascence occurred in a period of transition for the South. Certain young writers, reared in one kind of world, saw that world changing into another kind. They were themselves *of* that new, changed world, and yet apart from it and conscious of the difference. In Allen Tate's words: "After the war the South again knew the world, but it had a memory of another war; with us, entering the world once more meant not the obliteration of the past but a heightened consciousness of it; so that we had, at any rate in Nashville, a double focus, a looking two ways, which gave a special dimension to the writings of our school—not necessarily a superior quality—which American writing as a whole seemed to lack" ("The Fugitive, 1922–1925," *Princeton University Library Chronicle*, III [1942], 83). Tate sensed that the unique quality which seemed to give force and range to the work of himself and his contemporaries was a kind of historical vision. "With the war of 1914–1918," he has elsewhere written, "the South re-entered the world, but gave a backward glance as it stepped over the border: that backward glance gave us the Southern renascence, a literature conscious of the past in the present" ("The New Provincialism," *On the Limits of Poetry*, 1948, 292).

The writers of the Southern Renascence were able to recreate the life around them, about which they were writing, not simply because they were blessed with somewhat superior powers of description, but as if they had been gifted with a kind of historical perspective, which translated what they saw in terms of what *had been* as well as what now *was*. They were able to observe the South and its people *in time,* as they were in the present and as they used to be in the past. They could understand the older South as well as their own South. They could see a Thomas Sutpen, a Bayard Sartoris, a George Posey, a Percy Munn, not only as moderns saw figures remote in time, but as these men were seen in their own right, by their own contemporaries. The present was focused into perspective by the image of the past lying behind it.

The two-way vision was possible to the Southern writers of Tate's generation not only because of their ability to believe in the value and meaningfulness of their people's past but also *because they could disbelieve.* Being of that first twentieth-century generation of Southerners, they had been strongly reared in the ways of an older South, vividly taught the beliefs and loyalties of the nineteenth century as the South knew them. But they were of the twentieth century, not the nineteenth. They understood equally well the attraction of the new ways, as the writers of the previous generation could not have done. A mutation was demanded of them: a qualitative change in values and outlook. And being artists, gifted with the perception of artists, they sensed only too clearly the meaning of what was happening. They could believe in the old Army of Northern Virginia kind of belief, and yet share the self-consciousness and skepticism of postwar America and the world.

In *The Web and the Rock,* Thomas Wolfe uses the figure of an old house set back from the highway to illustrate what happened to the South. After the war and the troops, he says, an old man went back into the house and did not emerge again. The grass and weeds grew, obliterating the path to the house, and the house stayed on.

It shone faintly through that tangled growth like its own ruined spectre, its doors and windows black as eyeless sockets. That was the South. That was the South for thirty years or more.

That was the South, not of George Webber's life, nor of the lives of his contemporaries—that was the South they did not know but that all of them somehow remembered. It came to them from God knows where, upon the rustling of a leaf at night, in quiet voices on a Southern porch, in a screen door slam and sudden silence, a whistle wailing down the midnight valleys to the East and the enchanted cities of the North, and Aunt Maw's droning voice and the memory of unheard voices, in the memory of the dark, ruined Helen in their blood, in something stricken, lost, and far, and long ago. They did not see it, the people of George's age and time, but they remembered it.

They had come out—another image now—into a kind of sunlight of another century. They had come out upon the road again. The road was being paved. More people came now. They cut a pathway to the door again. Some of the weeds were clear. Another house was built. They heard wheels coming and the world was *in,* yet they were not yet wholly of that world.

Of the New South, and yet not of it, seeing the life of the 1920s against the image of an earlier period, the young Southerners began to write their novels and stories and poems and plays and essays. In Nashville, they started a magazine, *The Fugitive.* In the first number it was announced that the contributing poets were fleeing most of all from "the high-caste Brahmins of the Old South." By that they meant the sentimentalists, the mint julep South of Thomas Nelson Page and a host of lesser local colorists. They wanted no truck with local color, with the pleasant provinciality of iron grillwork, magnolia, and the resident poetry society. Instead they proposed a hard, meaningful, disciplined art of full engagement and intellectual judgment. They were poets, they believed in poetry, and they were not going to stand for any nonsense from ladies' clubs and poetesses laureate of the United Daughters of the Confederacy.

At this time, in the early 1920s, the Fugitives rather thought of themselves as representatives, on the literary plane, of the idea of the new, modern, progressive South. It was in this light too that exponents of the New South saw *The Fugitive,* welcoming it as evidence that Southern literature was, along with Southern culture, Southern education, and Southern business, throwing off the blinders of the South's past. As the Nashville *Tennessean* remarked: "For one thing, *The Fugitive* is an advertising instrument for this city and this state, which reaches a public that could be reached in no other way and by no other means. There are a good many people in different parts of the world, who, a year ago, if the word 'Nashville' had been mentioned would have had a vague idea of a city somewhere or other in the South, but who, today, at the mention of the name would say, 'Oh, yes; Nashville. That's the city in Tennessee where *The Fugitive* is published' " (May 27, 1923).

In *The Advancing South* (198–201), Edwin Mims saw the work of his younger literary colleagues and students at Vanderbilt as representing "a critical intelligence, a sense of literary values, and a reaction against sentimentalism and romance which has not been hitherto regarded as characteristic of Southern writing." Of one of the Vanderbilt poets, John Crowe Ransom, Mims declared that "He, like the other poets of the group, has little or no local colour, and is not consciously Southern except in an indirect protest against a sentimentalized South and commercialized South."

Yet before long it began to be evident to the leading Fugitive poets—Tate, Ransom, Davidson, Warren—that the chief opposition would not come from sentimentalists about the Old South. Even when presented in so polished a form as the romances of Du Bose Heyward and other local-color novelists and poets, Southern ancestor worship did not constitute much of a threat. Instead the menace was something quite different. Soon the leading Fugitives were taking their stand as Agrarians and were pounding away at it.

What was wrong was just what Maurice Thompson had hailed some decades before: "The South whose gaze is cast/No more upon the past." All around them the young Southern writers saw a country doing its best to become "modern," "progressive," "up-to-date," and, as they viewed it, achieving only faddishness, unbelief, and a tawdry commercialism. In the South's eager race to emulate the rest of the country, all the things that they had been taught were good were being cast aside. Business was in the saddle; the chamber of commerce reigned. Intellectually, culturally, economically, the South was courting modernity. What was most frothy, most rootless, most amoral about the 1920s, they felt, was being held up to the South as the model it should follow. In its eagerness to become progressive, to throw off the taint of provincialism, to "belong" to the age, the South was callously throwing off cherished ways of faith and life.

Others, not so socially and politically articulate as the Nashville group, nevertheless shared the basic artistic impulses that underlay the attitudes in *I'll Take My Stand*. Like the young men of letters who produced the Agrarian symposium, Faulkner, Wolfe, and the other Southern novelists and poets felt the spiritual unrest, the dissatisfaction with the modern mode, the distrust of conventional standards and values that characterized American and European literature during the years between the two world wars. It was not, for example, in the poetasters of the pre-World War I

South that the Fugitives found their poetic confreres; rather, they looked toward Eliot, Pound, Yeats, Mann, Hart Crane, Robert Graves, Wallace Stevens. It was not Southern local color that Wolfe and Faulkner studied; it was Sherwood Anderson, Sinclair Lewis, Dreiser—above all, Joyce. They were part of a world literary movement, a worldwide artistic questioning of their time and place.

Yet they were Southern, and their modernity was spoken with the Southern accent. The artistic achievement of their response, the quality and quantity of their novels, stories, and poems inevitably directs our attention to their time, their region, their particular history and tradition. It was not an abstract "tradition" that confronted them, both as it hung on and as it gave way before the new. It was the Southern tradition, a particular set of attitudes and values produced by a particular history in a specific and bounded American region.

Again and again, throughout the work of the writers of the Southern Renascence, we find pictured the debasement of Southern tradition. In all of Thomas Wolfe's fiction, there is no more moving episode than that in which Eliza Gant rents out her home as a boardinghouse and begins speculating in real estate. To her family, it constitutes a betrayal of her feminity. Donald Davidson's epic poem *The Tall Men* is about many things, and especially it is a lament for the vanishing image of the Tennessee frontiersman and his old virtues, before the cheap lures of modernity.

> *The Fire! What fire? Why God has come alive*
> *To damn you all, or else the smoke and soot*
> *Have turned back to live coals again for shame*
> *On this gray city, blinded, spoiled, and kicked*
> *By fat blind fools. The city's burning up?*
> *Why, good! Then let her burn!*

What is Temple Drake's own particular corruption in Faulkner's *Sanctuary* but Southern womanhood defiled and mocked, the flower of her tradition who goes to school mostly to extend her sexual range and who, imprisoned in a Memphis bawdy house, neither seeks to flee nor complains, because it is what she really wants? Equally ineffective if only somewhat less corrupted is Gowan Stevens, young Southern gentleman, University of Virginia graduate, who can neither hold his liquor nor protect his lady.

From this judgment of the present by standards of an impossible past, Faulkner's whole Yoknapatawpha saga takes much of its theme and tone. Sartorises and Compsons, sons of the older families, lose their strength and their belief. As they become increasingly incapable of handling the modern world, up from the South's thickets and gully lands rise the swarming hordes of Snopeses, lacking principle or code, rapacious, sterile, evil, to take over the ravaged land. "I've seed de first en de last," the Negro cook Dilsey says in *The Sound and the Fury*. "I seed de beginnin, en now I sees de endin." Of all the members of the once-proud Compson family that she had served, only the gelded idiot Benjy and the sordid Jason survive, and Jason has ceased to be a Compson and has become a Snopes in all but the name.

The image of the heroic past renders the distraught present doubly distasteful, just as it is the guilt and falseness of this same heroic past that has caused the present. This they saw too. This is the burden of the South: the impossible load of the past that kills Quentin Compson in *The Sound and the Fury*, the heroic and immense figures of Sutpens and Compsons, the terrifying impact of their characters, against whose history a Quentin Compson cannot hope to measure himself with pride. In their rooms at a New England college, Quentin tells the Canadian Shreve Mc-Cannon the tragic history of Thomas Sutpen that constitutes the story of *Absalom, Absalom!* Mirrored in it is the story of the South, and the nation as well. To the Canadian it is a fascinating tale.

"Jesus, if I was going to have to spend nine months in this climate, I would sure hate to have come from the South. Maybe I wouldn't come from the South anyway, even if I could stay there. Wait. Listen. I'm not trying to be funny, smart. I just want to understand it if I can and I don't know how to say it better. Because it's something my people haven't got. Or if we have got it, it all happened long ago across the water and so now there aint anything to look at every day to remind us of it. We dont live among defeated grandfathers and freed slaves (or have I got it backward and was it your folks that are free and the niggers that lost?) and bullets in the dining room and such, to be always reminding us to never forget. What is it? something you live and breathe in like air? a kind of vacuum filled with wraithlike and indomitable anger and pride anger and pride and glory at and in happenings that occurred and ceased fifty years ago? a kind of entailed birthright father and son and father and son of never forgiving General Sherman, so that forevermore as long as your children's children produce children you wont be anything but a descendant of a long line of colonels killed in Pickett's charge at Manassas?"

"Gettysburg," Quentin said. "You cant understand it. You would have to be born there."

Quentin tells his story in 1910, at Harvard, but though the events he describes occurred for the most part many years ago, they are not over. The entire time structure of *Absalom, Absalom!* is interwoven, working back on itself. Thomas Sutpen's past causes his present and future, and the lives of all with whom he comes into contact are changed because of that past. Gavin Stevens' remark in *Requiem for a Nun* that "the past is never dead, it's not even past," is descriptive of *Absalom, Absalom!*—for in the consciousness of Quentin Compson as he pieces out the events in Sutpen's saga, yesterday and today are inextricably intertwined. "The South," Shreve McCannon says after the story is concluded, "the South. Jesus. No wonder you folks all outlive yourselves by years and years and years." Surely this is so for Quentin. "I am older at twenty than a lot of people who have died," he tells Shreve. And in *The Sound and the Fury* he finds time so inescapable, so remorseless in its progress, that he smashes his watch and drowns himself to get outside of his time.

The interplay of past and present, of the historical and the contemporaneous, causes all the modern Southern writers to be unusually sensitive to the nature and workings of time. Allen Tate's *Ode to the Confederate Dead* closes with one certainty—the omnipresence of time:

> *Leave now*
> *The shut gate and the decomposing wall:*
> *The gentle serpent, green in the mulberry bush,*
> *Riots with his tongue through the hush—*
> *Sentinel of the grave who counts us all!*

The ancient symbol of time, the serpent, stays on, while the modern watcher at the gate no more than the buried Rebels may live and die.

Thomas Wolfe's time consciousness is not merely sensitivity, but close to preoccupation. Everything in the Wolfe novel is cast against a backdrop of time. At all points along the way, one is forcibly reminded of that added dimension. Allen Tate has written that it is the awareness of time that marks the difference between the true regional writer and the provincial local-color artist. Regionalism, he says, is "that consciousness or that habit of men in a given locality which influences them to certain patterns of thought and conduct handed to them by their ancestors. Regionalism is thus limited in space but not in time." Upon the historical sense to which he falls heir, the regional artist draws in order to see persons historically and to make them think and act along lines of history. In contrast to this, Mr. Tate continues, is the provincial attitude, which

. . . is limited in time but not in space. When the regional man, in his ignorance, often as extensive and creative ignorance, of the world, extends his own immediate necessities into the world, and assumes that the present moment is unique, he becomes the provincial man. He cuts himself off from the past, and without benefit of the fund of traditional wisdom approaches the simplest problems of life as if nobody had ever heard of them before ("The New Provincialism," 286).

Thus a Howard Fast, let us say, or a Joseph Hergesheimer or a Kathleen Winsor, can read up on the events of the history of a previous era, concoct a plot or a message, decorate it with the historical paraphernalia, in order to give it "color" and "atmosphere," and produce a best seller. Yet an historical sense of time and place and region is hardly involved. To decorate one's own thoughts and problems in antique garb is not to understand the past. Howard Fast's characters live in bygone times, but they are not people of bygone times; they are purely and markedly modern, created to pursue modern goals and make contemporary political points, and only in their artifical historical trappings do they bear any resemblance to the people of the age in which their author has placed them. The genuine historical consciousness, rather, is to be seen in *Absalom, Absalom!*, in *World Enough and Time,* in *The Long Night.* In such novels as these the true and deepest understanding of an earlier time and earlier men is possessed by the author and transmitted to the reader, not on modern terms alone, but independently and for the sake of the historical moment itself. It is then that the universal elements of time and character, present both then and now, are best revealed, because it is in the particulars, the day-by-day issues and habits and beliefs, that the true universals are embodied—not in the false draping of moderns in historical clothes to provide "atmosphere." Living in his time, Thomas Sutpen is a nineteenth-century Southerner. His concerns are of the day, and his values, passions, and actions are directly attuned to the events of his time. Faulkner makes no point, tells no story that would not be true and suitable for Sutpen's time. Yet in the very particularity, in the fidelity to historical time, the universal pity and terror and love and honor stand out. Sutpen, riding into the town of Jefferson, is not merely a particular individual coming into a Mississippi town to seek his fortune. He is the Man on Horseback, the stranger, coming from nowhere into somewhere. He is the Myth, cast up against a background of past, present, and future, assuming his depth in perspective. We see him *then,* not as a mere reflection of now, but *then* in his own right; and he looms large, for Faulkner saw him that way.

The historical perspective works both ways. We remember that the image of the Confederates facing the unknown at Gettysburg illuminates Chick Mallison's hour in *Intruder in the Dust.* Thomas Wolfe expresses the same notion in *The Web and the Rock.* George Webber and his friends from North Carolina visit Richmond for a football game, and walk in the streets of the former capital of the Confederacy:

They felt in touch with wonder and with life, they felt in touch with magic and with history. They saw the state house and they heard the guns. They knew that Grant was pounding at the gates of Richmond. They knew that Lee was digging in some twenty miles away at Petersburg. They knew that Lincoln had come down from Washington and was waiting for the news at City Point. They knew that Jubal Early was swinging in his saddle at the suburbs of Washington. They felt, they knew, they had their living hands and hearts upon the living presence of these things, and upon a thousand other things as well. They knew that they were at the very gateways of the fabulous and unknown North, that great trains were here to do their bidding, that they could rocket in an hour or two into the citadels of gigantic cities. They felt the pulse of sleep, the heartbeats of the sleeping men, the drowsy somnolence and the silken stir of luxury and wealth of lovely women. They felt the power, the presence, and the immanence of all holy and enchanted things, of all joy, all loveliness, and all the beauty and the wonder that the world could offer. They knew, somehow, they had their hands upon it. The triumph of some impending and glorious fulfillment, some impossible possession, some incredible achievement was thrillingly imminent. They knew that it was going to happen—soon. And yet they could not say how or why they knew it.

Not only do George Webber and Thomas Wolfe remember the historical past; they identify themselves with it. It is their past. They are part of the history. Now is then, and then is now; they walk the streets of the capital of the Confederacy in the 1900s, and in the year 1864. They are in Richmond, they face northward, and the enemy is there.

But they *did* go north; that is the point. Almost all the young Southern writers at one time or another packed their suitcases and headed for the cities of the Northeast, toward the center of modernity, toward the new. Some turned around and came back to stay; others remained. No matter; the North, the new, the modern world had come to the South too, and come to stay. All their lives they had been feeling its impact. The trunkline railroads daily brought a steady stream of newcomers into the South, and an equally steady stream of young Southerners northward to the schools and commercial opportunities in the metropolitan centers of the Northeast. Freight trains rumbled into town with the mass-produced goods of industrial America, the mail cars laden with bundles of the magazines and newspapers published in New York and Philadelphia. Along the right of way the telegraph lines hummed with news. In Richmond, in Charleston, Atlanta, New Orleans, Memphis, Savannah, Nashville, the modern world was received and transmitted to the rural South.

Desirable or undesirable, what happened to the South in the twentieth century now seems inevitable. And the very inevitability has been instrumental in producing the tensions, the dramatic contrasts that helped nourish the amazing outburst of Southern writing in our own times. The history of the twentieth-century South is one of continuity and change, with all the cross-purposes involved therein. It was this interaction that provided the images that so vividly figure in the work of the modern

Southern writers. One cannot pick up a novel by a modern Southern writer, or a volume of poetry, without constantly encountering the image of change. Southern literature is dominated by time, the awareness of it, its consequences. Molded by the past, tempered by the present, the litera-ture of the modern South is truly an historical literature. The attitude of the writers who created it was historical, and both the way they saw their task and the way they approached it are deeply grounded in Southern history.

"Real historical understanding," Herbert Butterfield has written, "is not achieved by the subordination of the past to the present, but rather by our making the past our present and attempting to see life with the eyes of another century than our own" (*The Whig Interpretation of History*, 1951, 16). Born as they were into one kind of world, and growing up as that world was swiftly changing into another, the Southern writers of the twentieth century were gifted with the perspective to achieve just such an understanding. What they did with it is a matter of record. That the history of the South gave it to them seems clear.

---

11. *The Changing Mind of the South*

LESLIE W. DUNBAR

A perceptive student of southern history and politics, the author of the next essay taught political science at Mount Holyoke College and Emory University and served as executive director of the Southern Regional Council before assuming his present position as an officer of the Field Foundation, Inc.

In this provocative paper Dunbar asserts that the mind of the white South is changing "through the action of the black South." Today, he points out, "the Negro grip on the levers of social change is secure." Examining the

Originally published as "The Changing Mind of the South: The Exposed Nerve," in *The Journal of Politics*, XXVI (February, 1964), 3–18. Reprinted by permission of the Southern Political Science Association and the author. A portion of the original article and most of the footnotes have been omitted.

meaning of community from the perspective of the "direct-action" movement of the 1960s, this paper throws light on a wide range of intangibles associated with the mind and culture of the South, including the makeup of the "essential Southerner," the ambivalence of the southern liberal, and the Southernism of the region's Negroes. Although he emphasizes the Negro's new self-knowledge, Dunbar tries to suggest what it was like to be a Negro Southerner for a century after the Emancipation Proclamation.

These matters are discussed within a national rather than a purely regional context. Indeed, the author contends that in such areas as race relations the South is "America's exposed nerve," that the region's ancient calling has been to "deflect pain and guilt from the rest of the nation."

I

I PREMISE THAT THERE HAS BEEN SUCH A THING AS A SOUTHERN FOLK, clearly if not definably more a single people than any other Americans, composed of two grades of persons, both of whom have been truly part of the same folk, and yet one of whom, the Negro Southerners, because they were ruled by the other did not sense and hallow as did the whites their folk integrity and their distinctness from the rest of the nation. And because white Southerners have consciously known that they were set apart, they have struggled to define themselves, have striven for self-identity, and with every Cash or Percy—or Faulkner—asking "Who am I?" have moved nearer the point which comes in every self-examination, where discovery means either release or reunion.

Who is there who is not tired of this search, who would not rather give it up before he has to choose between release and rejection, or recoil into the mind of the South, who would rather not stop short in self-discovery and become what history makes of him? And indeed, there has been a re-directing of the South's self-study. The intellectual and artistic concern is changing, has changed, from a deep, self-combative hoeing and chopping of souls and history and eternity, and toward commitment to the active issues of the day. The dark, Faulknerian, problems recede.

The classic interpreters of the South began with the conviction that there was a "South" and a "Southerner," and they hunted for definitions. Because the interpreters were themselves Southerners, dredging their prey up through their memories and revealing it as a Protean substance, their definitions were never abstract, and they never tired of examining countless aspects. Nor did they, however, ever yield the belief that something constant and essential lay under the aspects. The

Only the public figures of the South defined themselves in activity, and the interpreters tended to be less interested in them than in regarding the South's election of them as another aspect of the essential being which needed to be pondered. The essential Southerner acted occasionally, savagely and without premeditation, and this proclivity of his was another aspect to be explained. But except for this, the Southerner "was"; he did not, since the Civil War, "do."

Our preoccupation today is with how Southerners do and will act. For this is a time of testing. We are re-learning an old truth, which historians have nearly always known and social scientists have frequently forgotten, that men reveal themselves more accurately through their action than through their established feelings, opinions, and beliefs.

Another change has occurred as well. Cash, writing as late as 1941, was not really much attentive to Negro Southerners, and Percy, writing also in 1941, could say that he was "usually in a condition of amazed exultation over the excellent state of race relations in the South." James Agee, almost the quintessential New Dealer, took only an occasional and not seriously interested glance at the Negro neighbors of his white Alabama sharecroppers. Of the classic writers, only Lillian Smith had the greatness to wrestle with what the others saw, but passed by, and that was the centrality of race to the southern self-consciousness.[1]

In fact, not until the sit-in movement began in Greensboro in 1960 did the "mind" of Negroes become of conscious interest to white Southerners, in the sense that an active awareness began that the southern consensus had to include Negro values and desires. Even in the titanic controversies after 1954, the actors—those who were conspicuously making history—were almost always white: Senator Byrd, Governor Faubus, and the other captains of massive resistance. Negroes appeared only as a shadowy mass, from whom now and then emerged an impersonal lawyer or a poker-faced schoolchild walking through white faces lit with expression. The state of North Carolina might well put one of its historical markers at that dime store in Greensboro: here is where, after more than three centuries, the white and the Negro South were finally met.

In result, they have learned to know each other better. One Negro civil rights leader remarked to me that southern racial relations in the past had been like an unfaithful marriage, which could be preserved only by the two parties not speaking the truth to each other. Negro

[1] W. J. Cash, *The Mind of the South* (New York, 1941). W. A. Percy, *Lanterns on the Levee* (New York, 1941); the quotation is from p. 286 of the 1959 reprinting. James Agree, *Let Us Now Praise Famous Men* (New York, 1960); the book was written in the late 1930's. Lillian Smith, *Killers of the Dream* (New York, 1949, revised edition 1961).

Southerners are today speaking the truth to their white neighbors. If white Southerners can learn to live with this truth, the marriage can be continued, and may even become a fruitful one. Still today, no Southerners are more bred to the essence of the region's distinctive history, manners, and outlook than are the Negroes. If Dixie is not yet ready for its epitaph, it will be only because Negroes, freed of illegitimacy, may give it new life.

For earlier white Southerners, even for those as late as Cash, a decision about racial policies was not socially crucial. Men had different opinions and beliefs, but these were like other personal preferences, or even convictions, that were tolerable by the folk. Southern racial relations were like Hinduism, able to absorb and contain many changes and interests and ideas. The advent of industrialization, the steady immigration of non-Southerners, the growth of learning, the magnification of cities—all had come and had modified the old patterns and would surely in time overthrow them. But the endurance—what a Southerner might call the "cussedness"—of the old ways was remarkable.

But now this changes, and I know no better way to illustrate the change at its profoundest—though infrequently perceived—level than by contrasting Faulkner with that present-day southern writer who, in surface aspects, is most like him. The genius of Faulkner was such that he was able to suffuse his characters in life and individuality even though, in fact, they were little more than marionette's. They were held in the hand of God, but that hand which controlled them kept them in ceaseless confrontation with their home, i.e., with southern history, and in it they defined themselves. Miss Flannery O'Connor's characters are also marionettes and also in the grasp of God. They are Southerners too, but this is only an artist's detail. They could be anyone, they are caught directly, as simple individuals, in the human predicament, and they act directly to meet it, not, as Faulkner's characters always did, as Southerners, but as mere people.

Fundamentally, this is where Southerners find themselves today, forced to act directly without validating their acts against their history, much of which is sinking fast underneath them. Another southern writer, Allen Tate, in his novel *The Fathers,* depicts the deep psychological hurt felt by conservative Virginians in 1860–1861 when pressures from the cotton states and from the North were mysteriously pushing Virginia into severance from the government in Washington, of which over the years since 1787 they had come to feel as proprietors. Something similar is happening today over the South, as men see institutions which they had thought were theirs (e.g., the churches, the town school), relationships which they had thought secure (e.g., mistress and maid), begin to take on new shape and purpose.

All this has meant that, for today's white Southerner, an explicit rationalizing of his views about race has become the most urgent of his intellectual and spiritual tasks, and that he has had to achieve it on his own, or with new referents. He has had to attune himself, harmoniously or discordantly, to the authoritative words and practices of institutions from outside his region, such as the federal government, national church bodies, national media, and even—in fact—Wall Street. Perhaps still a man living in a remote Black Belt county untouched as yet by racial controversy may be as unengaged as nearly all of us were but a few years past. But I suspect that no white man living now in a Danville or an Albany or a Birmingham can support himself either by mores or by Faulknerian brooding. For the strong segregationist, the mores will appear too mild when the protest comes; for nearly all men, the brooding will seem irrelevant.

It is astonishing how often a southern white liberal can date his acceptance of racial equality at some specific episode in his life, much as did the ex-Communists in *The God That Failed* tend to date their break with Communism with a decisive, illuminating event. It is even more notable that almost every liberal can (and often does) recount the history of his changing attitudes. This sort of keen self-awareness occurs only with those life problems deeply and genuinely felt. Nevertheless, in accepting racial equality, the southern liberal does not typically reject the South. In Turgenev's *Fathers and Sons,* when Bazarov's tolerance of an older conservative is asked—"you must take into account his upbringing as well as the times in which he lived the best part of his life"—, Barzarov exclaims: "His upbringing: Every man should educate himself. . . . As to the times, why should I depend upon them: Much better they should depend on me. No, brother, all that is just loose thinking, there's nothing solid behind it!" To a Southerner, if to no one else, this is questionable doctrine, because inadequate tolerance; and rightly or wrongly, the key word of southern liberalism has been "tolerance."

Southern liberalism deserves more serious study than it has had. What, in this context, is worth remarking is the long sustained refusal of southern liberals to repudiate the South, and this is one side of the tolerance which they have elevated above all other social virtues. Few liberals have acted out their beliefs. They do not try to enter their children in Negro schools, do not usually refuse to eat in segregated restaurants or worship in segregated churches, do not spontaneously and widely mingle socially with their Negro peers. This is not well described as either hypocrisy or timidity. It is something a good bit more basic. The general conformity of the liberal to social practices which he opposes is a mark of his dogged refusal to alienate himself from southern society. He has counted himself a Southerner, with an obligation to respect the community and, so far as possible, to keep it whole. He often will, in fact, contend (and not only from polemical motives) that he—and not the defenders of segregation—represents the core of southern traditions, and he will sometimes appeal to other values acknowledged to be "southern," such as "courage" or "manners" or "individuality," against the less venerable practice of segregation. The tenacity with which liberals hold to southern culture, while endeavoring to reform it, is a quality which cannot be measured, but it would seem at least as intense as the somewhat comparable spirit of the Benthamites and later Labourites in England; they too insisted on behaving as Englishmen as they went about changing the country.

On the whole, this attitude of respect toward the community is not alien to a great many of the Negro leaders. And on the whole, this shared attitude presents the only real possibility, for those of us who want one, of preserving the South as a cultural organism, and not merely as a cultivated, but mummified, memory, analogous to New England. It is not a very strong possibility, though the relative poverty of the region may help along its chances: poverty is a strong folk-tie. I may be wrong and shortly proved so, but I see the white South today, outside the Black Belt but even there in some measure, as disposed, though often reluctantly, to accept more and more racial integration, but wanting also to keep the community much as it has been. I see Negro Southerners wanting equality desperately and angrily, but disposed to keep the community much as it has been, if they are admitted to it.

The South that Cash sought to track down was the white South, and, assuming that Cash found what he sought, it was unprepared for 1954. That South is still here. But because, being what it was and is, it stayed distant from the black South, called itself and itself only "the South," it has become an inert thing, a mere environment. Within this environment and against it, the southern leaders of today—the Negroes— act. It is the antithesis of motion against matter, and unless it can be cured there is not even a meager chance that the South will persevere. The white South is become an object, and only subjects can, even in a Faulknerian sense, endure.

II

Myrdal remarked that, "The intellectual energy spent on the Negro problem in America should, if concentrated in a single direction, have moved mountains." In truth, almost the profoundest thing one can say about southern race relations is that it *is* an old problem, toughened and complicated and made wondrously intricate by age, which has confused its diagnosis, rendered uncertain its treatment, and obscures its prognosis. Ancient as it is, it has had changing definitions, and these have, in the past, been determined by the interests and policies of white people. As Myrdal put it,

It is thus the white majority group that naturally determines the Negro's 'place.' All our attempts to reach scientific explanations of why the Negroes are what they are and why they live as they do have regularly led to determinants on the white side of the race line. In the practical and political struggles of effecting changes, the views and attitudes of the white Americans are likewise strategic. The Negro's entire life, and, consequently, also his opinions on the Negro problem, are, in the main, to be considered as secondary reactions to more primary pressures from the side of the dominant white majority.

This analysis was undeniably correct as an interpretation of the pre-1945 period; it is no longer so. Beginning about the close of World War II, the power to determine the Negro's "place" began to shade off from white control. Today, the Negro grip on the levers of social change is secure, and much more firm than the remnants of white direction.

The race relations policy of the southern white leadership from 1619 until Reconstruction, and from about 1890 until the 1940's, was governed by the objective, *How to get the maximum satisfaction from the Negro population.* The policy was pursued in economic, political, and social relationships, frequently with unsuccess. This fairly unanimously held single policy has, in the years since the 40's, been both losing adherents and singleness of application; the growth of Negro votes combined with pressures from Washington are forcing on our public life policies markedly more progressive than those which still dominate our churches and other more or less privately determined activities. Perhaps only in Mississippi today is there near unanimity about racial policy. But it is not the old policy of maximum satisfaction. Instead, it is, *How to maintain white control of the institutions of society.* At least, Negroes are not regarded as instruments and tools, but as antagonists. That, in itself, is a higher status.

If initiative has passed from the white majority to the Negro minority, the principal cause has been the success of Negroes in achieving a new and more stable self-knowledge. The dilemma—intellectual, emotional, political—of the Negro, especially the Negro male, has always been the problem of identity. A man's valuation of himself is derived and sustained by his reading of other people's assessment of him, and at all times in a person's life there are some "other people" whom he regards as the most authoritative assessors. Because of history and color,

Negroes for centuries got maddeningly confusing reports whenever they inquired of their society, "Who am I?"

With some notable variations, they adopted the social values and standards of the dominant white society. For generations, Negro Southerners had no sustained insight into white society beyond their own neighborhood, and they consequently shaped their self-portrait through the terms of local opinion. The past three or four decades have been a time, even for rural Negroes, of awareness of a larger universe of values and authoritative opinions, and increasingly they have tended to disregard local definitions in preference for more favorable nation-wide and world-wide judgments of their worth. But even in the old days, the answer to their question, "Who am I?", was far from clear. The Christianity they had been taught affirmed some things so surely that not even the utmost ingenuity of white pastoral apologists could altogether obscure them. The grand generalities of American democracy seeped into their consciousness. Their white neighbors behaved toward them with contradictory manners, producing what was (and, to a large extent, still is) surely one of the most weirdly implausible patterns of human relations ever observed. And always, Negroes were accompanied by a few stereotypes which sprang easily into the minds of white persons, even those a Negro might regard as friends, and displaced the actual Negro person they knew—or thought they knew.

The stereotypes were and are the damning judgments of white society on Negro identity. What is happening today is that Negroes are disowning the stereotypes, the white man's creations, are refusing any longer to acknowledge themselves to *be* what the white man said they were. White Southerners are confronted with a blunt demand from the Negro that he be accepted on his terms: *and this is the crucial problem of race relations today*. For years, whites have decreed that Negroes must think of themselves as the whites thought of them. Negroes now are insisting that the white majority revise its opinion of them in accord with their own, newly fashioned self-conception.

Negroes found that in the same European-American culture which had relegated them to inferiority, white supremacy had become a strand of that culture which "tends to wear away protective strata, to break down its own defenses, to disperse the garrisons of its entrenchment." The words are Schumpeter's,[2] and taken from a context which, though not analogous, is suggestive. Some other words of his are exactly applicable

[2] J. A. Schumpeter, *Capitalism, Socialism, and Democracy*, 3rd edition (New York, 1950), p. 143. Schumpeter's brilliant analysis (pp. 121–164) around the theme of capitalism's "crumbling walls" illuminates racial unrest throughout the world. As capitalism sponsored its own intellectual and emotional opposition, so European-American culture has sown the denials of its own privileges.

to contemporary Negro agitation: "Secular improvement that is taken for granted and coupled with individual insecurity that is acutely resented is of course the best recipe for breeding social unrest." A concatenation of economic and educational factors, supported haphazardly and minimally by politics, produced the secular improvement; another array of political, emotional, and social circumstances caused and kept strong the individual insecurity. The social unrest is a direct outcome of the combination, and is given its specific form and intensity through the re-infusion of ideas and values into American culture by a constantly growing number of educated Negroes who have derived these ideas and values from the cultural property of western white peoples, the terms of whose inheritance require them to admit nonwhites with whom they come into regular communication to equal shares in the property.

III

Lincoln began his Gettysburg Address by recalling that "fourscore and seven years ago" there had been brought forth "a new nation conceived in liberty and dedicated to the proposition that all men are created equal." If, in this centennial year of the Emancipation Proclamation, of Gettysburg and Vicksburg, we look back four score and seven years, we confront a less happy and auspicious event: 1876, the year when Hayes defeated Tilden, or Tilden defeated Hayes, whichever it was. Hayes became President through the Compromise of 1877, and for the next 70 years or so the white South was left alone by the nation in its policies and in its relationships toward Negro citizens.

The Civil War had freed the slaves and preserved the union. It had, besides, put on two Amendments to the Constitution—the 14th and 15th —which in the years after 1876 would be, as to Negroes, well nigh meaningless: four generations of Negro and white Southerners would come and go and live without acknowledging that Negroes could and should vote, or that laws should give them equal protection. The Civil War, moreover, left all these people in a ravished region, where men would get used to desperate poverty. The War and its aftermath made the South feel its spiritual and cultural separation from the rest of the nation more keenly even than before.

Then, earlier, and now, we have defined "the South" by its differences from the rest.

Southerners and non-Southerners have been, in fact, much alike. White men everywhere ruled, and Negroes were subservient, and treated as inferiors. Society belonged—and still largely does—to the white man.

Protestants ruled, dominating the economic and cultural and political life of the nation. Society placed a high sentimental value on farm or small-town culture and people, and long after the bulk of our population moved into cities the rural districts kept political power. And North and South, East and West, we all believed that *any* man who worked hard could get ahead.

These common qualities of American life, native both to the South and the non-South, are dissolving. And the present crisis in the South, which became acute in 1954, does not result from traditional differences from the nation; it results instead from the dissolution of things which have in the past united us.

Six landmark dates conveniently illustrate the changes. Although they affect the whole nation they are a special challenge to the South. Somebody—Arthur Koestler, I think—once spoke of the Jews as humanity's exposed nerve, feeling first and most sharply all the troubles and pains. Sometimes one feels that the South is America's exposed nerve, and that issues which are national in scope are most intense, or at least most apparent, here.

There was 1944, and *Smith v. Allwright,* and the ensuing erosion of the white monopoly of power to make political decisions. There was 1954, and *Brown v. Topeka,* which in its deeper import signified that the civic institutions of American society could no longer be operated as if they were the property of one race, and which, in its application since the New Rochelle case, has upset the North as well as the South. There was 1960, and confirmation that non-Protestants have a share in the power to make the country's highest decisions. There was 1962, and *Baker v. Carr,* and the consequent remarkably fast crumbling of the rural fortress of political power.

There was 1940, the last year before our entry into World War II, the last year of a peace-time economy. After seven years of prodigious effort by the New Deal, unemployment in the United States was 14.6% of the working force. We went into the war and unemployment virtually ceased. We came out of the war and unemployment stayed low while the country was busily engaged in converting to peace-time needs. We had a recession in 1948, and the next year unemployment shot up to 5.9%. We went into the Korean fighting, and again unemployment declined. We had another recession in 1954, and unemployment was up again. We had yet another recession in 1958, and this time unemployment really rose—to 6.8% of the working force of this country. After each recession, recovery was slower. There has been little improvement since, and President Kennedy in March 1963, called unemployment our "number 1 economic problem," and reported that it was still about 6%; the rate for

August 1963 was a seasonal 5.5%. Many economists believe that the government's way of computing unemployment seriously minimizes its extent.

Neither the policies of Republican nor Democratic administrations have, as yet, been able to lick this problem. Unemployment is high despite the boosting of the economy with huge expenditures for armaments and for space exploration; without those would we be back to the 14.6% unemployed of 1940?

Here we meet a tragic irony; as has happened in the past Negroes seem to be the victims not only of discrimination, but of impersonal history. After the first World War the country severely restricted the flow of immigrants from abroad. Up to then, American industry had grown by drawing on a boundless labor supply of European immigrants. With immigration drastically cut, industry met its need for new labor by drawing from the farms of America, including those of the South. Beyond this last large supply of white manpower, waited in economic succession the Negro. The tragic irony is that when his turn is come, the job market is declining. This is occurring in manufacturing and mining, chiefly, and these are fields which have been a gateway for new entrants into the free competition for economic advancement. No one seriously can continue to believe that America is for everyone now a land of opportunity where *any* man, unaided, can get ahead by dint of his own hard work. Some five to seven per cent or more of those people who want to work, find that there are no jobs, even though there is general prosperity in the country, and for the Negro the unemployment rate is about double that for whites.

And, finally, there was 1947, when Mr. Truman appointed the President's Committee on Civil Rights, and later espoused its recommendations, even at the cost of a party split at the Democratic convention of 1948. No political act since the Compromise of 1877 has so profoundly influenced race relations; in a sense, it was the repeal of 1877. Among the consequences were (a) a shift of emphasis from Negro "uplift"—essentially a paternalistic approach—to civil rights, i.e., the achievement of more than nominal citizenship; (b) a renewal of the fateful rupture between South and non-South; and (c) the ensuing complications for economic and social reform by statute, so that, since 1948, law-making for domestic problems has fallen into desuetude.

These six landmarks suggest, if I am not mistaken, that we shall have much more democracy in the United States. The price of that will be the ending of certain old ways and traditions. Groups who have led and controlled the country from its earliest days will have to accept a lessening of their influence. And if the South had trouble joining the old union—which, like it, was white, Protestant, and rural in its outlook and leadership—can it join this new union? The South was separated from the basically similar non-South of yesterday by a sharp enough cleavage; the new division would be a gulf.

To put it differently, the policies which Mississippi represents would not merely perpetuate North-South differences. The longer these policies are pursued, the greater becomes the alienation of Mississippi and the Black Belt generally from the American consensus. Just by standing pat, residents of these places will become strangers in their own land, because the nation as a whole is moving farther and farther from them.

IV

Over the years, Negro Southerners tried various methods of effecting change. They occasionally resorted to violence in the slave revolts of the ante-bellum period. During Reconstruction they sought the power of office. In Populist days they experimented—to their sorrow—with an electoral alliance with small farmers and mechanics. They tried the Booker T. Washington regimen of self-improvement, in the expectation that they would be accepted when their uplift was completed. They left the South, for the uncertain and often unrewarding North and West.

Finally—and with really their only success—they converted the political issue of equality into the Constitutional issue of equal rights. The "direct-action" movement has been a new force, and one of tremendous effect. It has produced results and it has unleashed and directed energies. Yet even its appeal has been to values thought to be in or implied by the Constitution, and the safety and success of the movement have been protected throughout by the procedural guarantees of the Constitution. The reform of the Negro question in the United States has been a striking instance of the effect of a constitution upon the life and events of a society. The constitution, created by the society, becomes a force which changes society.

The Constitution becomes a revolutionary instrument, for Negroes, being political outcasts, have had to combat the government, and not merely the government of the day. Nowhere yet in the old Confederacy does a politically representative body debate and settle on policy, except in two circumstances: to shore up the legal defenses of segregation; or to circumscribe as closely as possible the scope of a judicial decree when defiance is considered inexpedient. Nowhere has a deliberative body accepted the premise that social change is necessary or inevitable, and that action to guide that change is its responsibility.

None has done so, because southern political theory has been incapacitating. Although formal democracy has been in short supply in the

South, the tone and practice of southern politics has been democratic almost to an extreme—among the whites. Probably nowhere else in the country have there been closer personal relationships between voters and representatives, at all levels of government. But a democracy which is short on formal controls and efficient methods of obtaining popular consensus, and which puts a high value on informal means of effecting accountability, is going to be a conservative society. And when not all the inhabitants are constituents, the conservatism will be, in fact defensiveness. Thus both the democratic and the conservative spirits of the South combined to defend the folk, its monopoly of power and its cultural integrity. There is nothing to deliberate about, and to do so is betrayal. There is no relief from this paralysis except through an enlarged Negro vote, and a few municipalities of the South are already tasting this emancipation.

We may well ask again whether, when a conflict runs deep, democratic politics and its institutions can solve it. If the southern conflict is being resolved, it is because it was possible to appeal it to a constitution, whose first principle is that it itself is enforceable law. There is still some life left in the old maxim that democracy requires agreement on fundamentals, although it may more accurately be this: that democratic politics cannot be counted on to bridge deep chasms of opinions and values unless undergirded by a fundamental authority (e.g., a self-enforcing constitution) which is independent of parties and legislatures.

Impersonal causes—the boll weevil, farm technology and chemicals, faster-paced industrialization, communications media, and still others—re-arranged the roots of southern life after World War I. But human action did not, until the last decade.

Now Southerners are not only being moved by their environment, but are revising themselves and their manners of living with and getting along with each other. Events and change are pell-mell, and unpredictable. Whatever we say, we must say most tentatively. I note, therefore, that the case has often, even usually, been that white Southerners can and do change their racial mores when inescapably confronted by a community-wracking situation to which they must respond in one way or another. But I note further that this has not been invariably so; witness, e.g., Albany (Ga.). Those places, however, which have refused to yield to the Negro demands, modest as they often have been in the South, have been able to do so only through techniques of suppression which tear at precepts of the Constitution. They have maltreated the right of assembly, denigrated the supremacy of federal law, whored the police powers of the states.

The Negro demands have been within the Constitution. The Negro methods have been within the liberties and privileges of the Constitution; only occasionally have they violated the rules of the game. Southern communities have been tested, therefore, not only in their customs and morality, but in their understanding of and affection for the Constitution. Those many which have accommodated, and have stepped into the currents of change, have shown to us that the feelings men have do not necessarily determine their actions or reactions; that when confronted with practical choices, men discover themselves more accurately than they had before. I have to leave to others the scientific analysis, but I believe we can see the mind of the white South changing through the action of the black South and the accommodating reaction of the white South, and that a new South is shaping itself through history-making, and not through history-consciousness. . . .

12. The Search for Southern Identity

C. VANN WOODWARD

With books such as *Tom Watson: Agrarian Rebel* (1938), *Origins of the New South, 1877–1913* (1951), *The Strange Career of Jim Crow* (1955), and *The Burden of Southern History* (1960) C. Vann Woodward, Sterling Professor of History at Yale, has contributed more than any other modern historian to the prevailing interpretation of the South since Reconstruction. In this essay he poses the question whether the South can long survive the impact of change as anything more than a geographical expression.

Writing in 1958, Professor Woodward suggested some of the attributes of Southernism that may continue to identify the region after the bulldozer has completed its revolution. He conceded that virtually all of the South's peculiar institutions—even in race relations—have disappeared or seem to be in the process of being obliterated. While much of this change may be all to the good, Woodward injects a note of caution. There is some danger, he says, that illusions of sectionalism may be replaced by myths of American

From The *Virginia Quarterly* Review, XXXIX (Summer, 1958), 321–338. Reprinted by permission of the author and the publisher.

nationalism, and he warns of the "disintegrating effect of nationalism and the pressure for conformity." He points to southern history—the collective experience of the southern people—as the one aspect of Southernism not likely to disappear. The southern heritage of poverty, failure, guilt, and tragedy contributes something unique in American history, and, ironically, this heritage could help all Americans understand the human condition in much of the world today. In a more recent article, "From the First Reconstruction to the Second" (*Harper's Magazine, CCXXX,* April, 1965, 127–133), Woodward places less stress on the theme of tragedy in the southern experience and seems to have greater faith in the progressive tradition.

THE TIME IS COMING, IF INDEED IT HAS NOT ALREADY ARRIVED, when the Southerner will begin to ask himself whether there is really any longer very much point in calling himself a Southerner. Of if he does, he might well wonder occasionally whether it is worth while insisting upon the point. So long as he remains at home where everybody knows him the matter hardly becomes an issue. But when he ventures among strangers, particularly up North, how often does he yield to the impulse to suppress the identifying idiom, to avoid the awkward subject, and to blend inconspicuously into the national pattern, to act the rôle of the standard American? Has the Southern heritage become an old hunting jacket that one slips on comfortably while at home but discards when he ventures abroad in favor of some more conventional or modish garb? Or perhaps an attic full of ancestral wardrobes useful only in connection with costume balls and play acting—staged primarily in Washington, D. C.

Asking himself some similar questions about the New England heritage, Professor George W. Pierson of Yale has come forth with some disturbing concessions about the integrity of his own region. Instead of an old hunting jacket, he suggests that we call New England "an old kitchen floor, now spatter-painted with many colors." He points out that roughly six out of every ten Connecticut "Yankees" are either foreign-born or born of foreign or mixed parentage, while only three have native forebears going as far back as two generations, and they are not necessarily New England forebears at that. "Like it or not," writes Pierson, "and no matter how you measure it—graphically, economically, racially, or religiously, there is no New England Region today." It has become instead, he says, "an optical illusion and a land of violent contrast and change." And yet in spite of the wholesale and damaging concessions of his essay, which he calls "A Study in Denudation," he concludes that, "as a region of the heart and mind, New England is still very much alive."

One wonders if the Southerner for his part can make as many damaging admissions of social change and cultural erosion as our New England friend has made and come out with as firm a conclusion about the vitality of his own regional heritage. More doubt than assurance probably comes to mind at first. The South is still in the midst of an economic and social revolution that has by no means run its course, and it will not be possible to measure its results for a long time to come. This revolution has already leveled many of the old monuments of regional distinctiveness and may end eventually by erasing the very consciousness of a distinctive tradition along with the will to sustain it. The sustaining will and consciousness are also under the additional strain of a moral indictment against a discredited part of the tradition, an indictment more uncompromising than any since abolitionist times.

The Southerner may not have been very happy about many of those old monuments of regional distinctiveness that are now disappearing. He may, in fact, have deplored the existence of some—the one-horse farmer, one-crop agriculture, one-party politics, the sharecropper, the poll tax, the white primary, the Jim Crow car, the lynching bee. It would take a blind sentimentalist to mourn their passing. But until the day before yesterday there they stood, indisputable proof that the South was different. Now that they are vanished or on their way toward vanishing, we are suddenly aware of the vacant place they have left in the landscape and of our habit of depending upon them in final resort as landmarks of regional identification. To establish identity by reference to our faults was always simplest, for whatever their reservations about our virtues, our critics were never reluctant to concede us our vices and faults.

It is not that the present South has any conspicuous lack of faults, but that its faults are growing less conspicuous and therefore less useful for purposes of regional identification. They are increasingly the faults of other parts of the country, standard American faults, shall we say? Many of them have only recently been acquired, could, in fact, only recently be afforded. For the great changes that are altering the cultural landscape of the South almost beyond recognition are not simply negative changes, the disappearance of the familiar. There are also positive changes, the appearance of the strikingly new.

The symbol of innovation is inescapable. The roar and groan and dust of it greet one on the outskirts of every Southern city. That symbol is the bulldozer, and for lack of a better name this might be called the Bulldozer Revolution. The great machine with the lowered blade symbolizes the revolution in several respects: in its favorite area of operation for one, the area where city meets country; in its relentless speed for another; in its supreme disregard for obstacles, its heedless methods; in what it demolishes and in what it builds. It is the advance agent of the metropolis. It encroaches upon rural life to expand urban life. It demolishes the old to make way for the new.

It is not the amount of change that is impressive about the Bulldozer Revolution so much as the speed and concentration with which it has come, and with which it continues. In the decade of the forties, when urbanization was growing at a swift pace in the country as a whole, the cities of the South's fifty-three metropolitan areas grew more than three times as fast as comparable cities in the rest of the country, at a rate of 33.1 per cent as compared with 10.3 per cent elsewhere. For every three city dwellers in the South at the beginning of that decade there were four at the end and for every five farm residents there were only four. An overwhelmingly rural South in 1930 had 5.5 millions employed in agriculture; by 1950 only 3.2 millions.

According to nearly all of the indices, so the economists find, the economic growth of the South in recent years greatly exceeds the rate maintained in the North and East. The fact is that the South is going through economic expansion and reorganization that the North and East completed a generation or more ago. But the process is taking place far more rapidly in the South than it did in the North. Among all the many periods of change in the history of the South, it is impossible to find one of such concentration and such substantive impact. The period of Reconstruction might appear a likely rival for this distinction, but that revolution was largely limited to changes in legal status and the ownership of property. The people remained pretty much where they were and continued to make their living in much the same way. All indications are that the bulldozer will leave a deeper mark upon the land than did the carpetbagger.

It is the conclusion of two Southern sociologists that the South's present drive toward uniformity "with national demographic, economic, and cultural norms might well hasten the day when the South, once perhaps the most distinctively 'different' American region, will have become in most such matters virtually indistinguishable from the other urban-industrial areas of the nation."

The threat of becoming "indistinguishable," of being submerged under a national steamroller, has haunted the mind of the South for a long time. Some have seen it as a menace to regional identity and the survival of a Southern heritage. Premonitions of the present revolution appeared during the industrial boom that followed the First World War. Toward the end of the twenties two distinctive attempts were made by Southerners to dig in and define a perimeter of defense against further encroachment.

One of these entrenchments was that of the Twelve Southerners who wrote "I'll Take My Stand." They sought to define what they called "a Southern way of life against what may be called the American or prevailing way," and they agreed "that the best terms in which to represent the distinction are contained in the phrase, Agrarian *versus* Industrial." Agrarianism and its values were the essence of the Southern tradition and the test of Southern loyalty. Their credo held that "the whole way in which we live, act, think, and feel," the humanist culture, "was rooted in the agrarian way of life of the older South." They called for "anti-industrial measures" which "might promise to stop the advances of industrialism, or even undo some of them. . . ."

Even in 1930 the agrarians were prepared to admit "the melancholy fact that the South itself has wavered a little and shown signs of wanting to join up behind the common or American industrial ideal." They admonished waverers among the younger generation that the brave new South they contemplated would "be only an undistinguished replica of the usual industrial community."

A quarter of a century later the slight "wavering" in the Southern ranks that disturbed the agrarians in 1930 would seem to have become a pell mell rout. Defections came by the battalion. Whole regiments and armies deserted "to join up behind the common or American industrial ideal." In its pursuit of the American Way and the American Standard of Living the South was apparently doing all in its power to become what the Agrarians had deplored as "only an undistinguished replica of the usual industrial community." The voice of the South in the 1950's had become the voice of the chamber of commerce, and Southerners appeared to be about as much absorbed in the acquirement of creature comforts and adult playthings as any other Americans. The twelve Southerners who took their stand in 1930 on the proposition that the Southern way stands or falls with the agrarian way would seem to have been championing a second lost cause. If they were right, then our questions would have already been answered, for the Southerner as a distinctive species of American would have been doomed, his tradition bereft of root and soil. The agrarian way contains no promise of continuity and endurance for the Southern tradition.

Two years before the agrarian pronouncement appeared, another attempt was made to define the essence of the Southern tradition and prescribe the test of Southern loyalty. The author of this effort was the distinguished historian, Professor Ulrich B. Phillips. His definition had no reference to economic institutions but was confined to a preoccupation with race consciousness. The essential theme of continuity and unity in the Southern heritage, wrote Professor Phillips, was "a common resolve indomitably maintained" that the South "shall be and remain a white man's country." This indomitable conviction could be "expressed with the frenzy of a demagogue or maintained with a patrician's quietude," but it was and had been from the beginning "the cardinal test of a Southerner and the central theme of Southern history."

Professor Phillips' criterion of Southernism has proved somewhat more durable and widespread in appeal than that of the agrarians. It is not tied so firmly to an ephemeral economic order as was theirs. Nor does it demand—of the dominant whites, at least—any Spartan rejection of the flesh pots of the American Living Standard. Its adherents are able to enjoy the blessings of economic change and remain traditionalists at the same time. There are still other advantages in the Phillipsian doctrine. The traditionalist who has watched the Bulldozer Revolution plow under cherished old values of individualism, localism, family, clan, and rural folk culture has felt helpless and frustrated against the mighty and imponderable agents of change. Industrialism, urbanism, unionism, and big government conferred or promised too many coveted benefits. They divided the people and won support so that it was impossible to rally unified opposition to them.

The race issue was different. Advocates and agents of change could be denounced as outsiders, intruders, meddlers. Historic memories of resistance and cherished constitutional principles could be invoked. Racial prejudices, aggressions, and jealousies could be stirred to rally massive popular support. And with this dearly bought unity, which he could not rally on other issues, the frustrated traditionalist might at last take his stand for the defense of all the defiled, traduced, and neglected values of the traditional order. What then is the prospect of the Phillipsian "cardinal test" as a bulwark against change? Will it hold fast where other defenses have failed?

Recent history furnishes some of the answers. Since the last World War old racial attitudes that appeared more venerable and immovable than any other have exhibited a flexibility that no one would have predicted a dozen years ago. One by one, in astonishingly rapid succession, many landmarks of racial discrimination and segregation have disappeared and old barriers have been breached. Many remain, of course —perhaps more than have been breached—and distinctively Southern racial attitudes will linger for a long time. Increasingly the South is aware of its isolation in these attitudes, however, and in defense of the institutions that embody them. They have fallen into discredit and under condemnation from the rest of the country and the rest of the world.

Once more the South finds itself with a morally discredited Peculiar Institution on its hands. The last time this happened, about a century ago, the South's defensive reaction was to identify its whole cause with the one institution that was most vulnerable and to make loyalty to an ephemeral aspect which it had once led in condemning the cardinal test of loyalty to the whole tradition. Southerners who rejected the test were therefore forced to reject the whole heritage. In many cass, if they were vocal in their rejection, they were compelled to leave the South entirely and return only at their peril. Unity was thus temporarily achieved, but with the collapse of the Peculiar Institution the whole tradition was jeopardized and discredited for having been so completely identified with the part abandoned.

Historical experience with the first Peculiar Institution strongly discourages comparable experiments with the second. If Southernism is allowed to become identified with a last ditch defense of segregation, it will increasingly lose it appeal among the younger generation. Many will be tempted to reject their entire regional identification, even the name "Southern," in order to dissociate themselves from the one discredited aspect. If agrarianism has proved to be a second lost cause, segregation is a likely prospect for a third.

With the crumbling of so many defenses in the present, the South has tended to substitute myths about the past. Every self-conscious group of any size fabricates myths about its past: about its origins, its mission, its righteousness, its benevolence, its general superiority. But few groups in the New World have had their myths subjected to such destructive analysis as those of the South have undergone in recent years. Southern historians themselves have been the leading iconoclasts and their attacks have spared few of the South's cherished myths.

The Cavalier Legend as the myth of origin was one of the earlier victims. The Plantation Legend of ante-bellum grace and elegance has not been left wholly intact. The pleasant image of a benevolent and paternalistic slavery system as a school for civilizing savages has suffered damage that is probably beyond repair. Even the consoling security of Reconstruction as the common historic grievance, the infallible mystique of unity has been rendered somewhat less secure by detached investigation. And finally, rude hands have been laid upon the hallowed memory of the Redeemers who did in the Carpetbaggers, and doubt has been cast upon the antiquity of segregation folk ways. These faded historical myths are weak material for buttressing Southern defenses, for time has dealt as roughly with them as with agrarianism and racism.

Would a hard won immunity from the myths and illusions of Southern sectionalism provide some immunity to the illusions and myths of American nationalism? Or would the hasty divestment merely make the myth-denuded Southerner hasten to wrap himself in the garments of nationalism? The danger in the wholesale rejection of the South by the modern Southerner bent on reaffirming his Americanism is the danger of affirming more than he bargains for.

While the myths of Southern distinctiveness have been waning, national myths have been waxing in power and appeal. National myths, American myths have proved far more sacrosanct and inviolate than Southern myths. Millions of European people of diverse cultural backgrounds have sought and found identity in them. The powerful urge among minority groups to abandon or disguise their distinguishing cultural traits and conform as quickly as possible to some national norm is one of the most familiar features in the sociology of American nationalism. European ethnic and national groups with traditions far more ancient and distinctive than those of the South have eagerly divested themselves of their cultural heritage in order to conform.

The conformist is not required or expected to abandon his distinctive religion. But whether he remains a Protestant, a Catholic, or a Jew, his religion typically becomes subordinate or secondary to a national faith. Foreign observers have remarked that the different religions in America resemble each other more than they do their European counterparts. "By every realistic criterion," writes Will Herberg in his study of American religious sociology, "the American Way of Life is the operative faith of the American people." And where the mandates of the American Way of Life conflict with others they take undisputed sway over the masses of all religions. Herberg describes it as "a faith that his its symbols and its rituals, its holidays and its liturgy, its saints and its sancta," and it is common to all Americans. "Sociologically, anthropologically, if one pleases," he writes, the American Way of Life "is the characteristic American religion, undergirding American life and overarching American society despite all indubitable differences of region, section, culture, and class." Differences such as those of region and section, "indubitable" though he admits them to be, he characterizes as "peripheral and obsolescent."

If the American Way of Life has become a religion, any deviation from it has become a sort of heresy. Regionalism in the typical American view is rather like the Turnerian frontier, a section on the move—or at least one that should keep moving, and moving in a course that converges at not too remote a point with the American Way. It is a season's halt of the American caravan, a temporary encampment of an advancing society, eternally on the move toward some undefined goal of progress.

The same urge to conformity that operates upon ethnic or national minorities to persuade them to reject identification with their native heritage or that of their forebears operates to a degree upon the Southerner as well. Since the cultural landscape of his native region is being altered almost beyond recognition by a cyclone of social change, the Southerner may come to feel as uprooted as the immigrant. Bereft of his myths, his peculiar institutions, even his familiar regional vices, he may well reject or forget his regional identification as completely as the immigrant.

Is there nothing about the South that is immune from the disintegrating effect of nationalism and the pressure for conformity? Is there not something that has not changed? There is only one thing that I can think of, and that is its history. By that I do not mean a Southern brand of Shintoism, the worship of ancestors. Nor do I mean written history and its interpretation, popular and mythical, or professional and scholarly, which has changed often and will change again. I mean rather the collective experience of the Southern people. It is in just this respect that the South remains the most distinctive region of the country. In their unique historic experience as Americans the Southerners should not only be able to find the basis for continuity of their heritage, but also make contributions that balance and complement the experience of the rest of the nation.

At this point the risks of our enterprise multiply. They are the risks of spawning new myths in place of the old. Awareness of them demands that we redouble precautions and look more cautiously than ever at generalizations.

To start with a safe one, it can be assumed that one of the most conspicuous traits of American life has been its economic abundance. From early colonial days the fabulous riches of America have been compared with the scarcity and want of less favored lands. Immense differentials in economic welfare and living standards between the United States and other countries still prevail. In an illuminating book called "People of Plenty," David Potter persuasively advances the thesis that the most distinguishing traits of national character have been fundamentally shaped by the abundance of the American living standard. He marshals evidence of the effect that plenty has had upon such decisive phases of life as the nursing and training of babies, opportunities for education and jobs, ages of marriage and childbearing. He shows how abundance has determined characteristic national attitudes between parents and children, husband and wife, superior and subordinate, between one class and another, and how it has moulded our mass culture and our consumer oriented society. American national character would indeed appear inconceivable without this unique experience of abundance.

The South has at times shared this national experience, and in very recent years has enjoyed more than a taste of it. But the history of the South includes a long and quite un-American experience with poverty.

As recently as 1938, in fact, the South was characterized by the President as "The Nation's Economic Problem No. 1." And the problem was poverty, not plenty. It was a poverty emphasized by wide regional discrepancies in living standards, per capita wealth, per capita income, and the good things that money buys, such as education, health, protection, and the many luxuries that go to make up the celebrated American Standard of Living. This striking differential was no temporary misfortune of the great depression but a continuous and conspicuous feature of Southern experience since the early years of the Civil War. During the last half of the nineteenth and the first half of the twentieth centuries, when technology was multiplying American abundance with unprecedented rapidity, the South lagged far behind. In 1880 the per capita wealth of the South, based on estimated true valuation of property, was $376 as compared with $1,186 per capita in the states outside the South. In the same year the per capita wealth of the South was 27 per cent of that of the Northeastern states. That was just about the same ratio contemporaneously existing between the per capita wealth of Russia and that of Germany.

Generations of scarcity and want constitute one of the distinctive historical experiences of the Southern people, an experience too deeply embedded in their memory to be wiped out by a business boom and too deep not to admit of some uneasiness at being characterized historically as a "People of Plenty." That they should have been for so long a time a "People of Poverty" in a land of plenty is one mark of enduring cultural distinctiveness. In a nation known around the world for the hedonistic ethic of the American Standard of Living, the Southern heritage of scarcity is distinctive.

A closely related corollary of the uniquely American experience of abundance is the equally unique American experience of success. Some years ago Arthur M. Schlesinger made an interesting attempt to define the national character which he brought to a close with the conclusion that the American character "is bottomed upon the profound conviction that nothing in the world is beyond its powers to accomplish." In this he gave expression to one of the great American legends, the legend of success and invincibility. It is a legend with a firm foundation in fact, for much can be adduced from the American record to support it and explain why it has flourished. If the history of the United States is lacking in some of the elements of variety and contrast demanded of any good story, it is in part because of the very monotonous repetition of successes. Almost every major collective effort, even those thwarted temporarily, succeeded in the end. American history *is* a success story. Why should such a nation not have a "profound conviction that nothing in the world is beyond its power to accomplish"? Even the hazards of war—including the prospect of war against an unknown enemy with untried weapons—proves no exception to the rule. For these people have never known the chastening experience of being on the losing side of a war. They have solved every major problem they have confronted—or had it solved for them by a smiling fortune. Success and victory are national habits of mind.

This is but one among several American legends in which the South can participate only vicariously or in part. Again the Southern heritage is distinctive. For Southern history, unlike American, includes large components of frustration, failure, and defeat. It includes not only an overwhelming military defeat but long decades of defeat in the provinces of economic, social, and political life. Such a heritage affords the Southern people no basis for the delusion that there is nothing whatever that is beyond their power to accomplish. They have had it forcibly and repeatedly borne in upon them that this is not the case. Since their experience in this respect is more common among the general run of mankind that that of their fellow Americans, it would seem to be a part of their heritage worth cherishing.

American opulence and American success have combined to foster and encourage another legend of early origin, the legend of American innocence. According to this legend Americans achieved a sort of regeneration of sinful man by coming out of the wicked Old World and removing to an untarnished new one. By doing so they shook off the wretched evils of feudalism and broke free from tyranny, monarchism, aristocracy, and privilege—all those institutions which, in the hopeful philosophy of the Enlightenment, accounted for all, or nearly all, the evil in the world. The absence of these Old World ills in America as well as the freedom from much of the injustice and oppression associated with them, encouraged a singular moral complacency in the American mind. The self-image implanted in Americans was one of innocence as compared with less fortunate people of the Old World. They were a chosen people and their land a Utopia on the make. De Tocqueville's patience was tried by this complacency of the American. "If I applaud the freedom which its inhabitants enjoy, he answers, 'Freedom is a fine thing, but few nations are worthy to enjoy it.' If I remark on the purity of morals which distinguishes the United States," complained Tocqueville, " 'I can imagine,' says he, 'that a stranger, who has been struck by corruption of all other nations, is astonished at the difference.' "

How much room was there in the tortured conscience of the South for this national self-image of innocence and moral complacency? Southerners have repeated the American rhetoric of self admiration and sung the perfection of American institutions ever since the Declaration of Independence. But for half that time they lived intimately with a great social evil and the other half with its aftermath. It was an evil that was even condemned and abandoned by the Old World, to which America's moral superiority was an article of faith. Much of the South's intellectual energy went into a desperate effort to convince the world that its peculiar evil was actually a "positive good," but it failed even to convince itself. It writhed in the torments of its own conscience until it plunged into catastrophe to escape. The South's preoccupation was with guilt, not with innocence, with the reality of evil, not with the dream of perfection. Its experience in this respect was on the whole a thoroughly un-American one.

An age-long experience with human bondage and its evils and later with emancipation and its shortcomings did not dispose the South very favorably toward such popular American ideas as the doctrine of human perfectibility, the belief that every evil has a cure, and the notion that every human problem has a solution. For these reasons the utopian schemes and the gospel of progress that flourished above the Mason and Dixon Line never found very wide acceptance below the Potomac during the nineteenth century. In that most optimistic of centuries in the most optimistic part of the world, the South remained basically pessimistic in its social outlook and its moral philosophy. The experience of evil and the experience of tragedy are parts of the Southern heritage that are as difficult to reconcile with the American legend of innocence and social felicity as the experience of poverty and defeat with the legends of abundance and success.

One of the simplest but most consequential generalizations ever made about national character was Tocqueville's, that America was "born free." In many ways that is the basic distinction between the history of the United States and the history of other great nations. We skipped the feudal stage, just as Russia skipped the liberal stage. Louis Hartz has pointed up the infinitely complex consequences for the history of American political thought. To be a conservative and a traditionalist in America was a contradiction in terms, for the American Burke was forever conserving John Locke's liberalism, his only real native tradition. Even the South in its great period of reaction against Jefferson was never able fully to shake off the grip of Locke and its early self-image of liberalism. That is why its most original period of theoretical inspiration, the "Reactionary Enlightenment," came such a complete cropper and left almost no influence upon American thought.

There is still a contribution to be derived from the South's un-American adventure in feudal fantasy. The South was born Lockeian, but, as Hartz admits, it was long "an alien child in a liberal family, tortured and confused, driven to a fantasy life." There *are* Americans, after all, who were not "born free." They are also Southerners. They have yet to achieve articulate expression of their uniquely un-American experience. This is not surprising, since white Southerners have only recently found expression of the tragic potentials of their past in literature. The Negro has yet to do that. His first step will be an acknowledgment that he is also a Southerner as well as an American.

One final example of a definition of national character to which the South proves an exception is an interesting one by Thornton Wilder. "Americans," says Mr. Wilder, "are abstract. They are disconnected. They have a relation, but it is to everywhere, to everybody, and to always." This quality of abstraction he finds expressed in numerous ways, in the physical mobility of Americans, in their indifference or, as he might suggest, their superiority to place, to locality, to environment. "For us," he writes, "it is not *where* genius lived that is important. If Mount Vernon and Monticello were not so beautiful in themselves and relatively accessible, would so many of us visit them?" he asks. It is not the concrete but the abstract that captures the imagination of the American and gives him identity, not the here-and-now but the future. " 'I am I,' he says, 'because my plans characterize me.' Abstract! Abstract!" Mr. Wilder's stress upon abstraction as an American characteristic recalls what Robert Penn Warren in a different connection once described as "the fear of abstraction" in the South, "the instinctive fear, on the part of black or white, that the massiveness of experience, the concreteness of life, will be violated; the fear of abstraction."

According to Mr. Wilder, "Americans can find in environment no confirmation of their identity, try as they may." And again, "Americans are disconnected. They are exposed to all place and all time. No place nor group nor movement can say to them: we are waiting for you; it is right for you to be here." The insignificance of place, locality, community for Thornton Wilder contrasts strikingly with the experience of Eudora Welty of Mississippi. "Like a good many other [regional] writers," she says, "I am myself touched off by place. The place where I am and the place I know, and other places that familiarity with and love for my own make strange and lovely and enlightening to look into, are what set me to writing my stories." To her "place opens a door in the mind," and she speaks of "the blessing of being located—contained."

To do Mr. Wilder justice, he is aware that the Southern states constitute an exception to his national character of abstraction, "enclaves or residual areas of European feeling," he calls them. "They were cut off, or resolutely cut themselves off, from the advancing tide of the country's modes of consciouness. Place, environment, relations, repetitions are the breath of their being."

The most reassuring prospect for the survival of the South's distinctive heritage is the magnificent body of literature produced by its writers in the last three decades—the very years when the outward traits of regional distinctiveness were crumbling. The Southern literary renaissance has placed its writers in the vanguard of national letters and assured that their works will be read as long as American literature is remembered. The distinguishing feature of the Southern school, according to Allen Tate, is "the peculiar historical consciousness of the Southern writer." He defines the literary renaissance as "a literature conscious of the past in the present." The themes that have inspired the major writers have not been the flattering myths nor the romantic dreams of the South's past. Disdaining the polemics of defense and justification, they have turned instead to the somber realities of hardship and defeat and evil and "the problems of the human heart in conflict with itself." In so doing they have brought to realization for the first time the powerful literary potentials of the South's tragic experience and heritage. Such comfort as they offer lies, in the words of William Faulkner, in reminding us of "the courage and honor and hope and pride and compassion and pity and sacrifice" with which man has endured.

After Faulkner and Wolfe and Warren and Welty no literate Southerner could remain unaware of his heritage or doubt its enduring value. After this outpouring it would seem more difficult than ever to deny a Southern indentity, to be "merely American." To deny it would be to deny our history. And it would also be to deny to America participation in a heritage and a dimension of historical experience that America very much needs, a heritage that is far more closely in line with the common lot of mankind than the national legends of opulence and success and innocence. The South once thought of itself as a "peculiar people," set apart by its eccentricities, but in many ways modern America better deserves that description.

The South was American a long time before it was Southern in any self-conscious or distinctive way. It remains more American by far than anything else and has all along. After all, it fell to the lot of one Southerner to define America. The definition that he wrote voiced aspirations that were deeply rooted in his native region before the nation was born. The modern Southerner should be secure enough in his national identity to escape the compulsion of less secure minorities to embrace uncritically all the myths of nationalism. He should be secure enough also not to deny a regional heritage because it is at variance with national myth. It is a heritage that should prove of enduring worth to him as well as to his country.

SELECTIVE
BIBLIOGRAPHY

Useful surveys of southern history since 1865 are provided by John Samuel Ezell, *The South Since 1865* (1963); William B. Hesseltine and David L. Smiley, *The South in American History,* 2nd ed. (1960); and Francis Butler Simkins, *A History of the South,* 3rd ed. (1963). For the period of Reconstruction see James G. Randall and David Donald, *The Civil War and Reconstruction,* 2nd ed. (1961), a comprehensive treatment, and Kenneth M. Stampp, *The Era of Reconstruction, 1865–1877* (1965), a synthesis of revisionist scholarship. New light is thrown on the sectional compromise of 1876–1877 by C. Vann Woodward's *Reunion and Reaction: The Compromise of 1877 and the End of Reconstruction* (1951; paperback*), while the theme of sectional reconciliation is well treated in Paul H. Buck's *The Road to Reunion, 1865–1900* (1937; paperback). On southern Republicanism and northern attitudes in the post-Reconstruction era, see Vincent P. De Santis, *Republicans Face the Southern Question*

---

* The word "paperback" indicates that the work is now available in paperback. If only the word "paperback" appears after the work cited, its original publication was in paper.

—*The New Departure Years, 1877–1897* (1959), and Stanley P. Hirshson, *Farewell to the Bloody Shirt: Northern Republicans & the Southern Negro, 1877–1893* (1962). C. Vann Woodward, *Origins of the New South, 1877–1913* (1951; paperback), is not only a general history of an era but also a perceptive interpretation of southern ideas and institutions; chapter XI is a cogent interpretation of the colonial character of the New South economy. Thomas D. Clark, *The Emerging South* (1961), is an informative work on social and economic changes since 1920.

Wilbur J. Cash's *The Mind of the South* (1941; paperback) is a brilliant probing of the southern mystique. Interpretative studies illuminating the divided mind of the New South are C. Vann Woodward, *The Burden of Southern History* (1960; paperback); Charles Grier Sellers, Jr. (ed.), *The Southerner as American* (1960; paperback); and Frank E. Vandiver (ed.), *The Idea of the South: Pursuit of a Central Theme* (1964). Twelve Southerners, *I'll Take My Stand: The South and the Agrarian Tradition* (1930; paperback) is sharply critical of the New South ideology. Sectional implications of a cultural character are revealed in Kenneth K. Bailey, *Southern White Protestantism in the Twentieth Century* (1964); Charles C. Alexander, *The Ku Klux Klan in the Southwest* (1965); and Louis D. Rubin, Jr., and Robert D. Jacobs (eds.), *Southern Renascence: The Literature of the Modern South* (1953). Rupert B. Vance and Nicholas J. Demerath (eds.), *The Urban South* (1954), explores the impact of urbanization on the region.

In studying the racial theme a good place to begin is John Hope Franklin, *From Slavery to Freedom: A History of American Negroes,* rev. ed. (1956). C. Vann Woodward's *The Strange Career of Jim Crow,* rev. ed. (1966; paperback) is an illuminating interpretation of the origins and evolution of segregation in the South. Rayford W. Logan, *The Negro in American Life and Thought: The Nadir, 1877–1901* (1954; paperback), is valuable for northern attitudes and national policies. August Meier, *Negro Thought in America, 1880–1915: Racial Ideologies in the Age of Booker T. Washington* (1963), and I. A. Newby, *Jim Crow's Defense: Anti-Negro Thought in America, 1900–1930* (1965), are useful and complementary studies. Specialized works of great merit are Samuel R. Spencer, *Booker T. Washington and the Negro's Place in American Life* (1955; paperback); Vernon Lane Wharton, *The Negro in Mississippi, 1865–1890* (1947; paperback); George B. Tindall, *South Carolina Negroes, 1877–1900* (1952; paperback); Charles E. Wynes, *Race Relations in Virginia, 1870–1902* (1961); Paul Lewinson, *Race, Class & Party: A*

History of Negro Suffrage and White Politics in the South (1932; paperback); Horace Mann Bond, *Negro Education in Alabama: A Study in Cotton and Steel* (1939); and Louis R. Harlan, *Separate and Unequal: Public School Campaigns and Racism in the Southern Seaboard States, 1901–1915* (1958). An older, sympathetic discussion of the work of the Southern Education Board, written by a participant in the educational crusade, is Charles William Dabney, *The Southern Education Movement* (1936). Wilma Dykeman and James Stokely, *Seeds of Southern Change: The Life of Will Alexander* (1962), contains information on the activities of the Commission on Interracial Cooperation in the South. John P. Dollard, *Caste and Class in a Southern Town* (1937; paperback), and Hylan Lewis, *Blackways of Kent* (1955; paperback), are examples of anthropological studies.

Outstanding volumes on the civil rights movement, school desegregation, and the Negro's growing political influence are Howard Zinn, *The Southern Mystique* (1964); James W. Silver, *Mississippi: The Closed Society,* rev. ed. (1966; paperback); Benjamin Muse, *Ten Years of Prelude: The Story of Integration Since the Supreme Court's 1954 Decision* (1964); Hugh Douglas Price, *The Negro and Southern Politics: A Chapter of Florida History* (1957); Jack Walter Peltason, *Fifty-Eight Lonely Men: Southern Federal Judges and School Desegregation* (1961); Louis E. Lomax, *The Negro Revolt* (1962; paperback); Howard Zinn, *SNCC: The New Abolitionists* (1964; paperback); and Charles E. Silberman, *Crisis in Black and White* (1964; paperback).

The classic study of modern southern politics is V. O. Key, Jr.'s *Southern Politics in State and Nation* (1949; paperback), a penetrating analysis of power structures and the political process. T. Harry Williams, *Romance and Realism in Southern Politics* (1961; paperback), and Dewey W. Grantham, Jr., *The Democratic South* (1963; paperback), are brief interpretations. For southern Republicans, see Alexander Heard, *A Two-Party South?* (1952), and Donald S. Strong, *Urban Republicanism in the South* (1960). Recent political developments are discussed in Allan P. Sindler (ed.), *Change in the Contemporary South* (1963), and Avery Leiserson (ed.), *The American South in the 1960's* (paperback).

Among the best state studies are Roger W. Shugg, *Origins of Class Struggle in Louisiana: A Social History of White Farmers and Laborers during Slavery and After, 1840–1875* (1939); Allan P. Sindler, *Huey Long's Louisiana: State Politics, 1920–1952* (1956); Albert D. Kirwan, *Revolt of the Rednecks, Mississippi Politics: 1876–1925* (1951; paperback); Elmer L. Puryear, *Democratic Party Dissension in North Carolina, 1928–1936* (1962; paperback); William C. Havard and Loren P. Beth, *The Politics of Mis-Representation: Rural-Urban Conflict in the Florida Legislature* (1962); and James R. Soukup *et al., Party and Factional Division in Texas* (1964).

Examples of political biographies are C. Vann Woodward, *Tom Watson: Agrarian Rebel* (1938; paperback); Francis Butler Simkins, *Pitchfork Ben Tillman: South Carolinian* (1944); Robert C. Cotner, *James Stephen Hogg: A Biography* (1959); Oliver H. Orr, Jr., *Charles Brantley Aycock* (1961); and Virginius Dabney, *Dry Messiah: The Life of Bishop Cannon* (1949).

For manifestations of southern sectionalism in Congress, see Theodore Saloutos, *Farmer Movements in the South, 1865–1933* (1960; paperback); Frank Freidel, *F.D.R. and the South* (1965); and David Eugene Conrad, *The Forgotten Farmers: The Story of Sharecroppers in the New Deal* (1965). The role of the modern South in foreign affairs is analyzed in Charles O. Lerche, Jr., *The Uncertain South: Its Changing Patterns of Politics in Foreign Policy* (1964), and Alfred O. Hero, Jr., *The Southerner and World Affairs* (1965).

Several important books throw light on the colonial economy of the South. They include John F. Stover, *The Railroads of the South, 1865–1900: A Study in Finance and Control* (1955); Walter Prescott Webb, *Divided We Stand: The Crisis of a Frontierless Democracy* (1937); William H. Joubert, *Southern Freight Rates in Transition* (1949); and George W. Stocking, *Basing Point Pricing and Regional Development: A Case Study of the Iron and Steel Industry* (1954). For a recent review of the regional economy, see Melvin L. Greenhut and W. Tate Whitman (eds.), *Essays in Southern Economic Development* (1964). For an example of southern political action directed at an alleged obstacle to regional development, see Robert A. Lively, *The South in Action: A Sectional Crusade Against Freight Rate Discrimination* (1949; paperback). William H. Nicholls, *Southern Tradition and Regional Progress* (1960), emphasizes the restraining influence of regional traditions. The impact of mechanization and industrialization on southern agriculture is assessed in James H. Street's *The New Revolution in the Cotton Economy: Mechanization and Its Consequences* (1957), and Anthony M. Tang's *Economic Development in the Southern Piedmont, 1860–1950: Its Impact on Agriculture* (1958).

Personal accounts of distinction include Jonathan Daniels, *A Southerner*

Discovers the South (1938); William Alexander Percy, *Lanterns on the Levee: Recollections of a Planter's Son* (1941); Ben Robertson, *Red Hills and Cotton: An Upcountry Memory* (1942); Katharine Du Pre Lumpkin, *The Making of a Southerner* (1947); David L. Cohn, *Where I Was Born and Raised* (1948); Hodding Carter, *Where Main Street Meets the River* (1953); Ralph McGill, *The South and the Southerner* (1963; paperback); and Frank E. Smith, *Congressman from Mississippi* (1964). For broader regional portrayal see: David E. Lilienthal, *TVA: Democracy on the March,* rev. ed. (1953; paperback); Lillian Smith, *Killers of the Dream* (1949; paperback); Carl T. Rowan, *South of Freedom* (1952); Wilma Dykeman and James Stokely, *Neither Black Nor White* (1957); Harry S. Ashmore, *An Epitaph for Dixie* (1958); James McBride Dabbs, *The Southern Heritage* (1958) and *Who Speaks for the South?* (1964); Henry Savage, Jr., *Seeds of Time: The Background of Southern Thinking* (1959); William Peters, *The Southern Temper* (1959); Harry M. Caudill, *Night Comes to the Cumberlands: A Biography of a Depressed Area* (1963; paperback); and Willie Morris (ed.), *The South Today, 100 Years After Appomattox* (1965; paperback).

A comprehensive guide to recent southern historical literature is contained in Arthur S. Link and Rembert W. Patrick (eds.), *Writing Southern History: Essays in Historiography in Honor of Fletcher M. Green* (1965).